Blood and Oil in the Orient

Lev Nussimbaum, "Essad Bey", circa 1913

Essad Bey

Blood and Oil
in the Orient

My childhood in Baku and my hair-
raising escape through the Caucasus

Translated from the German by
ELSA TALMEY

With an Afterword
by TOM REISS

BRIDGES
PUBLISHING

First published 1931
by *Grayson & Grayson, London*

Second Edition 2008

Afterword "The Orient of the Imagination"
Copyright 2008 by Tom Reiss.
All rights reserved.

Book cover: Rosi Weiss, Freiburg/Germany
Layout and typesetting: Hans-Jürgen Maurer, Freiburg/Germany

All rights of this edition reserved by the publisher.

This book is published by:
Bridges Publishing
Verlag Hans-Jürgen Maurer
P.O. Box 207
79002 Freiburg
Germany

www.bridges-publishing.de

ISBN 978-3-929345-36-0

CONTENTS

PART THREE
The Flight

PART I

IN THE LAND OF THE ETERNAL FIRE

CHAPTER 1

MY ANTECEDENTS

Forty years ago Baku was a desert city; in many respects it has remained so until today. In the earlier time, however, there was not a single street that might be considered European. Not a single tree sheltered the inhabitants from the burning heat. The whole city consisted only of clay huts and a few barbaric palaces, which were built on the desert sand and surrounded by a single wall; the thick walls of the palaces afforded but slight shelter from the sun. There was no water in the city; there were no rippling fountains such as every other house in the Orient possesses; water had to be brought in sacks from a distance and hardly sufficed for drinking and washing. When the heat became unbearable, the wealthy people left their houses and went to the seashore, where they could pretend or imagine that it was cooler.

Today there are gardens laid out along the shore, with theatres, coffee-houses, bath-houses, promenades, and sporting clubs; then there was nothing of the sort. The shore was desolate, stony, and unsheltered; deposited far and wide the oil dregs and rubbish of the city covered it. It smelled of salt and decay. Only a single building stood on this shore—a stately prison, in which countless prisoners were abandoned to the heat, the odour of decay, and the prison guard. And in front of this prison, on the shore, the aristocratic people strolled—the oil-kings, the Beys, and the Khans, who sought protection from the sun behind the thick prison walls. Then, with all their money—they were on the average the richest oil-magnates in the world—they had not yet learned to make gardens and fountains spring from the earth.

One day a young man promenaded in front of this prison, an oriental sheepskin cap on his head and in his hand a rosary of amber, without which no one can get along in Baku. He had the facial expression, imperturbable, weary, and yet eager for activity, of an Oriental who has transferred the old traditions of command to the social life of the young oil-city. The summer afternoon was very hot. Trying to enjoy the shade, he walked as close to the building as possible. The barred windows of the cells were vacant; prisoners were forbidden to stand at the windows during the day, as the sight of them might be unpleasant to the elegant gentlemen who strolled up and down in front of the prison. But one inquisitive head down in the basement dared to approach the barred window; it was that of a young girl who looked out curiously through the bars upon the promenaders. The man, however, did not notice her; he watched the sea, apparently absorbed in thought. Behind him strode two armed, wild-looking fellows, who did not take their eyes from him and his surroundings for one moment; they formed the body-guard which every owner of oil-fields in Baku—if he valued his life at all—was compelled to have. One of the men caught sight of the girl and looked worried.

Allah knew what the girl had in mind! Perhaps an attempt on the life of his master, and then . . . perhaps not. It is hard to serve in the body-guard. One must think, consider! But only the master can do that. At last he made his decision, approached his master, cleared his throat, and told what was worrying him.

A prisoner, in spite of the restrictions, was looking at the gentleman for quite a while. Did the gentleman want to tolerate that?

The young man turned round, saw the girl and smiled. A very young girl with dark eyes ... Why should she plan evil? He approached the barred window, looked at the girl more carefully, and asked in Azerbaijanian: "Why did they lock you up?"

The girl was silent; evidently she did not understand the language.

"How long have you been here?" the man then asked in Russian.

"Three months," the girl answered, and smiled sadly.

"And how much longer must you stay?"

The girl had no chance to answer. An officer of the watch approached the cell, drew a revolver from his pocket and roared: "Back, or I'll shoot!" The head disappeared. The officer greeted the young man. "I am sorry that a prisoner annoyed you with silly pleas," he said. "One cannot be severe enough with these people."

The young man nodded understandingly and asked what was the number of the girl's cell. Then he bowed again, but, instead of continuing his walk, turned about and, followed by his body-guard, passed through the broad prison gates. There he asked for the warden, and inquired of him why the prisoner in cell No. - had been arrested.

"She is a dangerous criminal," answered the warden. "Prison is much too lenient a punishment for her."

"Why, what crime did she commit?"

"She is a member of the Bolshevist party of Russia, and came to Baku on behalf of the party, to stir up discontent among the honest and dutiful workers. She was to organize a strike, but her criminal purposes were unmasked, and she was arrested, thanks to the efficiency of the police."

The young man knew nothing about the Bolshevist party of Russia; on his oil-fields there had never yet been a strike. He could not even imagine that such a thing was possible.

"Look here," he said to the prison inspector, "I shouldn't object if you let the girl go."

The man smiled. No, that couldn't be done, not with the best will. A thief or something like that, gladly; but a political prisoner could not be released.

The face of the young man darkened; he put his amber rosary in his pocket and drew out his money-bag.

"If you don't let the girl out," he said, "I'll get her for myself. My guard is more numerous than your prison rats."

The official thought it over; after all, the gentleman was right. What chance had he and his people against an oil-magnate's fierce troops? His express instructions were to keep on a good footing with the oil and landowners. And besides, wasn't there the money-bag, too?

Nevertheless he asked as a matter of form: "What the devil do you want a Russian political prisoner for?"

The one who was questioned knitted his brow, considered for a few moments, and then replied in a calm, matter-of-course tone: "To marry!"

The girl was released and moved into a small house in the city near the large one in which her liberator lived. He did not live alone; wives and children, slaves and eunuchs, servants and dependants were there—all that belongs to an Oriental household. Now the wives and children had to leave. The Russian girl was to rule the house. Advocates with long beards and sly eyes obeyed orders, drew up deeds and documents. The women and children moved away to the country, to the villages which the young man gave to them. The girl from the prison cell moved into the big house, where the wedding took place on the same day.

That young gentleman was my father, and the girl my mother.

CHAPTER 2

THE OIL-FIELDS

The oil-derricks which rise in hundreds near Baku form a fantastic picture, never to be forgotten. Steeped with oil, their wooden walls—only in the more recent times are the derricks built of alabaster—cover the deep bore-holes, from which the oil is drawn incessantly day and night. The derricks must not rest, nor may the workers who starve beside them. The neighbouring earth is pily, black, and liable to catch fire, just like the Caspian Sea, where it borders immediately on the oil-land. There, if one throws a burning match into the water, the sea begins to burn and flames for ten or fifteen minutes, a sight which is shown to every stranger, for nowhere else in the world can such a phenomenon be seen.

For the inhabitants of Baku this sea is a torment, particularly in the summer; those who bathe in it emerge from the water black; the whole body is covered with a thin layer of oil, and an ordinary bath in filtered water must be taken immediately, for which suitable provision is made on the shore.

The oil-fields on the Caspian Sea form a state in themselves, which is subject to separate laws and has a special conception of justice. The laws of the oil-fields are unwritten, but are more respected than the written laws of the government. Highest in command of the derricks is the engineer, who has the power of life and death over his subordinates. But few can become engineers in the oil-fields; one must be born to that. No knowledge and no study will train the man properly, if he has not the innate disposition to be an autocratic ruler who must at times be executioner, too. He must not only know how to extract the oil and guard it from conflagration, but also how to stick a lead funnel into the mouth of any suspected incendiary—whose guilt need not be proved—and pour the raw oil or petroleum into his gullet until the faces of all present turn grey with fright. This, however, is one of his simplest tasks.

It is much more difficult, for example, to recognize, or fail to recognize a corpse, such as is often enough fetched out of the oil-wells, according to the desire of the owner of the well.

Several times during the day one of the workers, sitting in an ordinary pail, would have to dive down into the bore-hole, a procedure which meant death nine times out of ten. Often the pail was pulled up without the workman, who, suffocated by gases, had sunk into the oil. His corpse would not be found for weeks, and often not at all. The bandits of the country could unobtrusively throw anyone into the shaft and if they were on good terms with the engineer, escape all suspicion. But to be on good terms with the engineer was in general possible only for the owner of the oil-field, his master.

The owner always lived in the city, some distance from the wells, visiting them only two or three times a month, always escorted by a large guard, since the way was often very dangerous. For the journey he equipped himself as for war, for his way led through the desert, where enterprising bands would lie in wait for an unarmed traveller. The few who felt safe were those who had grown up among the derricks, for whom there were no secrets, who might proudly number themselves among the founders of the oil industry, because they were the first who caused the derricks to rise from the sandy ground. Among these was my father, to whom a number of oil-fields in Azerbaijan owe their discovery. He was not yet seventeen years old when he travelled through regions which were still quite wild at that time. With a keen perception—which even formerly few oil-owners possessed, but now is not found at all—he was able to smell out the sections in the desert which waited to be exploited. A few lots of sandy land which he then bought for barely seventy-five dollars, later reached the value of many millions. Even he had not expected such an increase, for he sold a great part of the newly discovered land for almost nothing. Nevertheless, he was considered one of the finest judges of the Azerbaijanian oil. He was one of the few who felt at home among the wild labourers and among the engineers who were scarcely less wild. For him an expedition to the derricks entailed no danger, so that he did not even hesitate to take me with him.

I was six years old when my oil-baptism, which others did not dare to undergo until they were twenty, took place. The baptism with oil, which was, so to speak, the introduction into the ruling class, was carried out for every new owner and his grown children. It consisted of sprinkling, by means of a tube equipped with a sprayer, great quantities of oil on the new magnate before the assembled workers and officials. This lasted a few minutes, and was called the "Golden Rain". Sometimes during the extraction of oil, a fine oil-mist came from the derricks. Everyone was glad if the mist fell on his clothes, for the "Golden Rain" was considered lucky, and the spots which it caused were never wiped away.

Derricks constitute the most beautiful industrial landscape in the world—without vapours, without the tainted air inseparable from factory and mine. Hundreds of slender towers standing close together remind one of a fantastic fairy-tale forest. In Azerbaijan they maintain that the oil-fields and the air of the oil-land are particularly suited to the healing of lung trouble. An altruistic oil-owner even wanted to erect close to his derricks a sanatorium for consumptives. I do not know whether the air is actually so health-giving, but the odour of raw oil, as distinguished from petroleum, benzene, and machine oil, is really noticeably refreshing. The workmen at the wells knew this, and made us of the oil in a curious way. They collected the heavy, saturated loam, found in masses along the canals through which the oil was conveyed, and with it washed their hands and body. It took the place of soap, too, which was entirely unknown to the workers.

The workmen came from Azerbaijan, Daghestan, Persia, and Russia. The Russians were not fitted for the hardest labour and formed the most disturbing element. The best were the Orientals, who alone possessed the diffident fatalism required for work at the oil-wells. The difference between these two types was very striking. The Russian, all his life, was just a workman, who hated the oil-derricks and their owners most bitterly and opposed them whenever possible. The Oriental, on the other hand, who came direct from the country, felt himself to be a man of high position on the oil-fields; to work there meant his first contact with European civilization, and he was very proud of this. Besides, he did not let himself be permanently bound; when he had enjoyed European culture sufficiently, he moved back to his village where he was regarded as an experienced man-of-the-world. The Daghestanians, for example, came to Baku mainly to learn the Azerbaijanian language. In Daghestan, as far as the language is concerned, total anarchy rules; practically every village speaks a language—not a dialect—of its own, which is understood by no outsider. For this reason the simple and easily acquired Azerbaijanian language was raised to the dignity of an international medium of communication. To be esteemed at home as cultured people, the Daghestanians went to Baku for a few years, worked on the oil-fields, and then returned to their mountains.

The Persians and Azerbaijanians worked in order to marry well, that is, to buy themselves pretty brides at home with the money they saved. They never called for their wages, preferring to let the money remain in the office, and when they withdrew it later, they would ask whom they must pay for having taken care of it. As regular, experienced workmen, only the Russians came into consideration. As half-Europeans, however, they could never become accustomed to the Oriental conditions. They despised the native workmen, demanded double wages for half the work, and constantly threatened to strike. It must be admitted that the living conditions on the oil-fields of Baku were not to be compared with anything else in the world. Today these conditions are long past, but one is still horrified, remembering these earlier days. The thousands and thousands of workmen lived in damp, unlighted, dark, dirty barracks, where three slept together on a small, uncovered wooden cot. There was no other furniture, and the cots were placed so close together—to save space—that sometimes there was not enough room left for aisles. Water was very scarce, and was solely for drinking; all washing—without soap—had to be done in the oil-dregs. Pains were taken not to pay the Russian workmen in cash, but in produce; they were provided with water and bread, and that was counted as full wages. This procedure was justified with the assertion that cash lessened the Russian labourers' capacity for work. The work at the oil-wells under the burning sun was hardly easier than toiling in coalmines. The working day lasted for sixteen hours without interruption; even that seemed too short to some of the owners.

This system was, in truth, a penitentiary regime, for most of the owners were perfectly aware of the feelings they aroused among the Christian group of labourers, and therefore had them watched by a private force of Mohammedans who were armed to the teeth. The Orientals, strange to say, were completely satisfied with the conditions. Soap they did not miss, since they had none at home. A cot was surely better than the clay floors in their native huts, and they were already accustomed to the sun. Besides, the native workmen felt more at home on the fields than the Russians, for whom the whole occupation was merely a refined sort of prison: to leave the oil district, to visit the proud city of palaces, was forbidden even on holidays. The owners did not consider it necessary for the workmen to cross the boundary of the city. A well-trained guard took care that the men did not show themselves in the city. But when they were discharged they had to disappear from the oil district with their wives and their children, and find refuge in some dilapidated settlement in the neighbourhood of the city, where usually there was nothing to prevent them from starving to death. The only difference between a penitentiary and an oil-field was that in the penitentiary the food was more palatable.

Once when the workers complained about insufficient food, an owner—who is now comfortably walking up and down the Kurfürstendamm in Berlin as I am—coined the following astounding sentence: "Only when you lie flat on your backs and are convulsed with hunger will you understand what real work means." This he said to the Russians. In Azerbaijanian he added: "You Mohammedans ought to know that I am your true Father, whose heart bleeds daily on your account, just as the. heart of the Prophet for the holy Hussein of Kerbela."

17

No wonder that the Russian workmen, in contrast to the Moham-medans—who, moreover, were quite satisfied with their food—had rather peculiar feelings for their "true" Father.

Between the oil-fields and the city small, scattered settlements were inhabited by thieves, lepers, vagabonds, and other people hard to clas-sify. What occurred in these settlements did not seem to interest any-one; no one guessed that amid the damp, sticky ruins unknown per-sons had established a printing-office. There every night a newspaper was printed, which was often better informed about the conditions on the fields, about the situation in Georgia, Daghestan, Persia, and Russia, than the large newspapers in the city. In a tiny hole—one could call the dwelling nothing else—next to the printing-office, lived the editor of this paper, who also received his assistants there. The assistants, as well as the editor, were but slightly different from the vagabonds. For the most part they were real wanderers, who brought the necessary news from all regions of the East. With each one the editor spoke in his—the assistant's—native tongue, immediately knew the ins and outs of every-thing, and was particularly pleased when long cipher-letters, delivered by vagrants, came from Russia.

The newspaper was called "The Workman of Baku", and its editor was a Georgian, the son of a shoemaker from Tiflis, a former divinity student, who then had just escaped from a Siberian penitentiary, he had a low forehead, a crooked nose, and small, evil eyes which had seen much murder and much blood. He was Joseph Dzshugashvili, the famous terrorist, who now calls himself Stalin.

Very seldom did a strike break out on the oil-fields among the Russ-ian workmen, but when it came they did it thoroughly. Most of the time, however, they lacked the courage to strike, perhaps because they hoped for outside help.

In one of these strikes, strangely enough, I became entangled. It was the only time in my life that I openly took a stand against the class of oil-owners, consequently against myself; but my age—barely ten years—partly excused my activity in the eyes of the members of my class. One day my father issued the order that all the married workmen should be discharged, since the women and children constituted a danger for the oil-wells; also, from that time on, the single workmen should be forbidden to marry, the argument being that their income certainly did not enable them to support a family. Through this edict, then, the owner was looking out for the welfare of his poor children. It was only by chance that I heard of it, as, at the age of ten, I naturally took little interest in the social-political questions. My coachman, however, who took me out driving every afternoon when the weather was fine, was very interested. Since there was no more room in the house, my carriage and pair of horses stood in a little coach-house near the factory where he lived; he was a Russian from the Volga, and therefore the friend of all the Russian workmen.

One day when we were riding on the shore-promenade, he began to lament his sad fate—in Russian, so that the Azerbaijanian footman who accompanied us could not understand. He told me that this was probably the last time he would take me driving, because he, like most of the Russian employees, would be discharged. When I asked in amazement why this was happening, he answered: "Your father does not want to have any more married workmen, and, since we cannot kill our wives and children, we must starve." This sentence, which was only partly true, for my coachman, as a man of higher position, would not have been discharged, aroused my indignation; I could not understand that people should be driven away just because they wanted to have a family. "Turn about," I said to the driver, "we'll ride to the office to see my father." I went into my father's room and asked whether it was true that he was discharging all the married people.

"Only if they are ordinary workmen," he answered.

"Well, why?" I asked.

My father thought it over and then delivered a speech, from which I gathered that the workmen were being discharged for three reasons. First, because the children might set fire to the oil-fields; second, because they could support no one on their wages; and third, because it was in any case desirable to drive away the married Russians.

But I would take no dismissal. "Every man is married," I said. "I, too, will marry soon, because the Koran demands it. How can you forbid the workmen to marry?"

"I don't forbid it at all," answered my father. "Only that I don't want them on the fields. Otherwise they can go right ahead and marry." He turned and went into the next room.

However, I would not give up; I climbed again into my carriage, and commanded the coachman to drive to the Governor-General of the oil district, who I had heard was the mightiest man in the world. The Governor-General lived in a gigantic building and had a very profitable task in supporting the oil-princes in their wise decisions. I did not know that, and entered the pompous waiting-room in full confidence of finding justice. The servant looked me up and down curiously. Never yet had so young an owner of oil come to see the Governor. "The Governor is probably busy," he tried to object. I went to the window and called my armed servant who stood in the street. He entered the room and looked so threateningly at the servant that he immediately announced me.

The Governor, however, seemed really to be busy. From his room came an attaché and inquired on what business I wished to speak to His Excellency. I was not inclined to make explanations. My servant shoved the man aside, and I, angry and excited, pushed my way into the Governor's room.

The old general, with a beard such as Kaiser Franz Joseph wore, was sitting at a desk and conversing with a colleague of my father. Both must have been surprised by my appearance, but made the best of it, as though it were the most ordinary thing in the world. But when I presented my request to the Governor and asked for help, he sympathetically explained to me that he understood me well, but that I was judging the matter wrongly. My father's order was an act of kindness to the unemployed single men, who could now get work. About the fate of those who were discharged I need not worry, as that was the task of the local government. If one considered how many poor people would find work through my father's decision, one really ought to feel proud to be his son.

All this the governor said in dead earnest, and with constant allusion to my great mental talents, which would certainly enable me to comprehend the truth of his arguments, "Visit me more often," said the Governor in parting, "and above all, don't forget to give your father my regards."

Somewhat confused, I left his house, and for a while drove about in the hope that I should think of something on the way. Inwardly I already feared that the Governor might be right.

When I conveyed my doubts to the coachman, he swore to me that the Governor was a beast of prey, even worse than the owners of the oil-wells. That sounded convincing. Suddenly, very suddenly; I had the first real idea of my life, not knowing that it had come to others before me. "Just stop working! But don't let the unmarried workmen get to work either!" I said, without suspecting that I was suggesting a strike.

"That will be hard," the coachman thought. "Your father will send the body-guard, who will shoot us all."

Then I became indignant. "If the guards shoot you, I'll set fire to all the oil-fields myself," I shouted, and with that I was ripe for a lifetime in the penitentiary—the customary punishment for attempts such as I had in mind.

The coachman, however, seemed to have repeated my words to the workmen, for the same evening they spoke at the derricks of great conflicts among the owners, which would shatter the "unified front" against the workmen.

The next day a general strike began, which this time turned out somewhat unfavourably for the owners. Before the guards could surround the workmen as usual, these had occupied the places most liable to catch fire, and demanded the fulfilment of their conditions. My father would not consent, and decided to cut off the supply of food in his district. After a long debate the men proposed to the owners that they should name an impartial arbiter, and set the condition that whoever was selected must not be materially concerned with the oil-fields. The other condition, after all easily understood, was that no matter what the decision, no workman should be taken to court because of threats of incendiarism. The owners agreed, and chose as arbiter the German, Baron von Taube, who then was held in high esteem by the Czar, and from whom a decent attitude of mind (in the sense of the owners) might be anticipated.

The Baron came to Azerbaijan. It was probably the first time in his life that he had visited such settlements. He spoke to the men with the assistance of several interpreters and finally called a secret meeting of the owners, at which it was hoped that he would suggest practical methods of fighting the criminal opposition. The Baron appeared at the meeting in gala attire, decorated with orders; and his speech began with the following sentence: "Gentlemen, I am surprised that the workmen have not yet torn you to pieces; you have richly deserved it!"

The next day his decision was announced; it contained, above all, recognition of the workers' right to marry, and a series of further concessions which were most disconcerting to the owners, who then sent a telegraphic message pleading to be guarded from "the Baron, the public menace". But they received the answer that His Majesty had full faith in the Baron.

After this, respect for the German nobility diminished extraordinarily in all Azerbaijan.

Soon after the strike my father called me to him. "Tell me," he asked, "how did you get the idea of defending the workmen?"

"By myself," said I.

"And the idea of going to the Governor, you got that by yourself, too, I suppose?"

"Certainly."

"Good; but the thought of recommending a strike you could not have conceived by yourself. You never heard anything about strikes."

"I thought of it myself," I answered proudly.

My father looked at me sympathetically, raised his hands in the air and sighed, exclaiming: "What it means if one's mother is a Bolshevist!" What a Bolshevist was he did not explain to me till many years later.

It should be added that my father was considered the most liberal man of his class both by the workmen and the owners. The others were much worse.

CHAPTER 3

ZARATHUSTRA'S LAST TEMPLE

The oil district of Azerbaijan is the most advanced region of the entire East. It presents all the features of a large European industry; Diesel motors, electic light, motor-cars, countless machines, and—the labour question. Here, in the centre of this ultra-modern world, among oil-tanks and oil-derricks, the most notable symbol of old Azerbaijan has survived, the mysterious temple of Zarathustra, which the oil-owners, otherwise quite unsentimental, spared in the richest oil district of Baku, Surachany.

The temple of Zarathustra at Surachany was spared not only by the oil-owners: thousands of years ago the world-conqueror, Genghis-Khan, commanded that it should not be destroyed because his famous predecessor, Haroun al-Raschid, had done the same. Somewhat earlier the Roman, Pompey, and then Antiochus, visited it, each moved by an impulse of vanity, imitating the great Macedonian who was the only outsider allowed to offer sacrifice to the eternal flames of the temple. For this small square temple with a dome in one corner, which appears so small and insignificant in comparison with the oil-derricks, was once the centre of the first great religion of mankind, that of fire-worship, which Zarathurstra, the Azerbaijanian, proclaimed.

In remote antiquity, Azerbaijan was the holy land of the eternal fire-worship, and the rich oil-coast near Baku became the place of pilgrimage for millions of believers. Mighty priests ruled the land; they prayed to the bright god, Ahura-mazda, protected the believers from the evil god, Angro-marya, and alone could decide who was to be emperor from Byzantium to Bucharia. The god, Ahura-mazda, was the fire—the eternal fire, that streamed from the earth in gases, and above which the domes of the temple were erected. Even today this fire is unextinguished; even today oil-gases stream from the holy earth, gases which will burn under the old dome until the last drop of oil is wrung from the earth. It is a curious trick of nature, this eternal flame which has been burning for thousands of years, and at which strangers who visit the temple light their cigarettes, if they do not happen to be fire-worshippers.

In the times of the fire-worship only the rulers of the country and the priests might pray to the fire; the believers contented themselves with kneeling before the dome which covers the flame. The Emperor of Persia, who had conquered Rome more than once, came to Azerbaijan, kissed the dust from the feet of the priests, and washed himself with cows' urine, which was considered especially pious. Sometimes he was deposed by the priests—when he had been conquered by the Romans. A new Emperor of Iran, king of kings, was named to protect the holy fire and fight against the Romans. Thus it continued for centuries, until the Arabs came, killed the last emperor of the fire, Jezdegerd the Unfortunate, drove away the priests, and degraded the great god to an interesting natural phenomenon. With this the dignity of the holy land and the generation of the emperors ended; among them were Cyrus, Kambyses, Darius, and Artaxerxes, of whom the first three are known through school books, and Herodotus, the last from the Bible.

The fire-worshippers were destroyed, were converted to Islam, and soon forgot the meaning of the name Azerbaijan: "The holy land of the eternal fire." The last of the Zarathustra followers fled to India and to Jazd in Persia, where they still live today. Their last temple became a saloon, where under cover of night the poets gathered to enjoy the alcohol which was otherwise under the Islamic prohibition law. Later, when the prohibition was no longer heeded, the temple also was forgotten by the poets. A hundred years ago the two last priests who vegetated there were exiled from the land by a wise khan for drunkenness and idolatry.

The Indian fire-worshippers, however, did not forget their temple. Every few years strange delegates come to Azerbaijan, known at the doors of all the government houses, and beg for permission to perform their religious services before the eternal fire. These Indian and Persian fire-worshippers, who today number 110,000, have queer rites, which, when carried out in the centre of the industrial district, call forth great resentment among the Mohammedans. This indignation has but slight foundation, for there is hardly anything more innocent than the customs of these Parsees. The Parsees live in constant fear of defiling themselves. When they eat, the food may not touch their lips; otherwise they become unclean. For this reason, neither forks nor knives are used; they throw the finely cut food into their widely open mouths with their hands. In drinking, various feats are performed to prevent the liquid from coming in contact with the lips.

Every morning they wash their hands and feet in cow-urine, murmur prayers thousands of years old, and stroke the holy cord which hangs on their turbans. When they die their corpses may not be burned, buried, or sunk, for then fire, earth, and water would become unclean for ever. Therefore the corpses of the Parsees are carried to the Tower of Silence—the best known is in India—and there exposed to the vultures. In addition to the religious precept, this is, in the opinion of the Parsees, a demand of hygiene. These strange fire-worshippers, however, founders of the oldest religion of mankind, are no barbaric nomads or savage mountain tribes. The Indian Parsees—by far the greatest number of the Parsees live in India—are modern bankers, captains of industry, or stock gamblers, to whom India of today owes her economic development. The largest industrial districts of India belong to the Parsees, who appreciate every possibility of gain, with the exception of the Azerbaijan petroleum. For this oil is holy and, together with the cow-urine, belongs to the cultural treasure of their religion. Rightfully the Parsees are called the Jews of India. The Persian Parsees, on the other hand, have not yet developed their commercial ability to the fullest extent. They are known as the most honest subjects of the Shah, and enjoy the great honour of acting as gardeners in his harem.

In Azerbaijan, their holy territory, they do not dwell, but they have erected a poor-house there, and are, as everywhere, known as benefactors. Therefore it happened from time to time that the Indian Parsees also were given the privilege of the religious service among the oil-derricks. But, as I have said, this happens seldom, and in most recent times not at all. The last temple of the eternal fire has been so completely forgotten by mankind, that the members of an expedition of scientists who travelled through Azerbaijan thought in all seriousness that they had rediscovered it, and sent a sensational report about it to Europe. In this report it was stated that, in spite of the diligent search, the discovery, priceless to archaeology, was due to a happy accident.

The temple is in the midst of the oil industry, and is a popular excursion place for the inhabitants of the city. The scientists were just slightly distracted and too eager for discoveries.

The temple, then, is practically forgotten by mankind; and yet nothing in the world is more lasting than the place where a deity was once honoured. Again and again man returns to it; again and again new sancturaries of culture rise upon the old ruins. Whoever is acquainted with the forgotten parts of Asia Minor, knows that the mosques of the small villages are usually built where the Christian churches stood. Excavations show that the churches also rose upon the ruins of the Greek-Roman temples, and that these again have an old temple of some Babylonian deity as foundation. But that does not end the series of religions following one another, for it is known that the Babylonians used to build their temples on the sites of the mysterious sancturaries of the Sumerian cult. There are places where dozens of deities have been honoured one after another. Now the mosques are disappearing, and in their place factories have risen which serve the most modern of all deities.

Around the temple of Zarathustra also the temples of industry came into being. But that was no legitimate succession. It was worthy of another, better deity. Connected with the temple, a new religion developed in Azerbaijan a few years ago—a sect such as often comes into being in the Orient, spreads quickly and just as quickly seems to disappear. Only seems; deep in the soul of the people all deities which have ever ruled the land continue to live, from Astarte and Ahura-mazda to Mohammed and Christ. A faith only appears to die; from time to time it rises again, as recently about the temple of Zarathustra in Azerbaijan.

This remarkable sect is deserving of mention.

One day the police of the oil district reported to the government that at night queer things were happening near the temple of Zarathustra. Sounds were heard; torches burned. Voices were raised; unintelligible murmurs became audible. So there was reason enough to suspect a secret printing-press, or at least a bandits' hiding-place. As bandits and secret printing establishments are highly undesirable in the oil district, the prefect of police decided to surround the temple with a cordon of his men—who, as a matter of fact, could hardly be distinguished from the supposed bandits—and to search it. During the night, when the dangerous symptoms again became evident, the police forced their way into the temple, and thus performed a valuable service to science, for they discovered a new religion, which, until then, had probably not been listed in the annals of religious history.

In the court of the temple, in front of the eternal fire, they found a number of men seated, gazing at a nude woman who stood before the flame. One of the men stood next to the woman and was reverently kissing her breasts; in the meantime the others prayed and waited for their turn. About the walls of the temple were idols and statues of saints of every religion in the world, lighted by torches. The holy Nicholas of Basi was discovered next to the loam figure of the faun, who is a holy symbol of the Anatolian devil-worshippers, and the clay figure of a gigantic phallus stood next to the cheap oil-print of the Shah of Persia, who was also worshipped as a deity.

The members of this sect were arrested and proved to be simple, illiterate peasants from the villages near Baku. For reasons which they would not disclose, they had decided to found a new religion, and chose the age-old temple as its seat. Everyone taking part had to bring along a holy symbol, be it a phallus or a picture of the Shah of Persia. He was then allowed to crouch in front of the holy fire and murmur the prayers which he considered suitable. The only ceremony was the kissing of the naked woman's breasts, and that was to symbolize the love for Mother Earth. To honour all the gods who were brought along by the brothers in the faith was also essential.

In spite of all their endeavours, the police were not able to discover anything more. In the official report this negative result was explained by the low intelligence of the peasants. Since the peasants had not conducted a secret press, and besides had proved their decent character by the exhibition of the picture of the Shah, they were again set at liberty. The practice of their rites within the temple was forbidden them in the oil-section, because of "disturbing of public peace and danger of fire". Thus the last temple of Zarathustra was robbed of these modest followers also.

CHAPTER 4

OIL-GRAFTERS AND OIL-LORDS

A mong the Russian merchants there is a proverb: "Whoever has lived a year among the oil-owners of Baku can never again become a decent person!" Thus spoke the honourable merchants from Petersburg, who made their wills when they had to journey to Azerbaijan. Less honest ones maintained, on the other hand: "Only in Baku are true grafters still trained," and they looked with envy upon these belonging to the guild of the oil-city, who permitted no addition to their circle. These phrases were but slightly exaggerated, for it was impossible for a stranger to undertake anything in Baku. The oil-guild was a closed society, which gladly made difficulties for any stranger. Eastern and Western methods of cheating were combined into a shrewd system of commercial tactics. Nothing was shunned; it was not necessary to fear anyone or anything; one was in the Orient, where right and wrong have ever been elastic terms. Among themselves, too, fairness was not considered suitable. The conception "fair" did not exist at all, unless perhaps among the greatest, who permitted themselves even this caprice at times. Among the two hundred owners of oil-fields there were at most ten whom one avoided cheating, because they were powerful enough to punish the deception with death; and they themselves did not need to cheat anyone.

Among these ten were eight Mohammedans, one Armenian, and one Swede, who had the famous name Nobel. Nobel was the only one in Baku who despised the Oriental methods of fighting and maintained, with justice, that the European method was more successful. According to European views the majority of the oil-princes were ripe for the penitentiary. But those are conditions which rule wherever a brief period of exertion makes it possible to gain quick riches. On the oil-fields of Mexico, of Venezuela, in the gold-mines of Alaska and the Klondike, and among the diamond-prospectors of South Africa the same conditions reigned—the same brutality, deception, and wiles, by means of which a handful of adventurers were able to guard their newly seized fortune.

The first generation is usually thus: in Baku it was perhaps even better than in other places, because, after all, a number of the owners sprang from the old nobility of the country and brought a certain culture into the oil trade. The past of most of my father's colleagues was dark; some had formerly been vagabonds, others smugglers. Some could even tell of Siberian prisons, smirking gaily and cunningly.

Mohammedans, Armenians, Russians, Poles, Georgians, Swedes, formed a caste here which knew no difference of class; its members spoke unwillingly of their past except among themselves, and they numbered, besides smugglers, genuine grand dukes and prices.

A barbaric attitude to life was characteristic of most of them, the incapacity to do anything with their money, and, as soon became evident, the complete decline of the second generation, which grew up under the golden weight. Illiterate, excessively wealthy fathers, who were kind barbarians on the whole, had sons who in the cradle were already tired of life. And these sons nursed thoughts of suicide, and tried to perform misdeeds which would overstep any possible restriction. But what could be forbidden to an oil-prince in Baku? That was the revenge of fate. Only the children of those owners who already had at their command a certain culture—Eastern or Western—escaped this rapid degeneration. Between the single families constant warfare raged which often involved others. Then blood flowed on the streets, people disappeared without trace, and the bands which were always at one's service received double pay. Besides its attraction as the seat of a society of adventurers, Baku still retained all the peculiarities of an Oriental capital. Several owners were not only industrial leaders, but rulers as well; they exercised sovereign power of life and death over their subjects somewhere in the interior, and were constantly drilling troops in their villages. These were the Mohammedans and partly also Armenians, who together formed the majority of the owners and fought against each other bitterly. A few stories about oil-graft and oil-princes may be of interest.

After the extraction, the raw oil is preserved in huge reservoirs, built along the seashore near the refinery; the derricks where the oil is extracted are some fifteen miles away from them. Between the oil-wells and the refinery pipe-lines conveyed the oil of the various owners into a common reservoir. Each company possessed its own pipe-lines from its fields to the tanks, where the amount of oil flowing in was indicated by a meter. The pipe-lines and reservoirs belonged to a firm which preserved the raw oil, later conveyed it to the refineries, and did good business in this way. Since there were more than two hundred owners, the corresponding number oil-pipes were laid across the desert close together; each firm had its own, so that the amount of the oil which it entrusted to the company could be determined exactly when it was received and there was no danger of crediting it to another. The company vouched only for the oil that arrived in the reservoirs, but not for the oil that was conveyed to them. Sometimes the pipes burst or were leaky, so that the amount of oil flowing out and that flowing in did not correspond; for this reason the oil had to be measured after its passage through the desert upon its arrival in the reservoir. Whether this system was good or bad is open to doubt. Hundreds of pipes, however, lay in the desert in disorder and presented a confusing aspect.

One of these lines belonged to the well-known captain of industry, Riza, a worthy gentleman who sought culture most assiduously, travelled abroad every year, and was considered the upholder of the European civilization. The one next to his belonged to a large firm and was in use day and night, for the firm had a million-dollar fountain and did not know what to do with all the oil. One day, however, representatives of the firm noticed that much less oil ran into the reservoirs at the seashore than was extracted, according to an approximate estimate: apparently it disappeared on the way. Riders were sent into the desert to inspect the pipes, but nothing suspicious was noticed; the pipes were intact. Nevertheless the oil continued to vanish. The entire stretch was watched day and night, but in vain. The whole affair was so incomprehensible that the firm might have been suspected of making a fuss about its well purposely in order to reassure its creditors. This lasted for months; but soon it became evident that other firms, too, were being robbed in a similar mysterious manner, and the matter became serious. Those who were robbed gathered their employees, and during the night quietly had all the pipes near their own relaid in the hope of determining the cause of the loss. And then something unheard-of came to light. Riza's pipe-line was found to be connected with the neighbouring ones by a subterranean pipe, so that their oil simply flowed into his line, to be booked as a product of his oil-derricks when it entered the reservoir. Riza, the upholder of culture, had thus discovered a simple method of increasing his gains immeasurably. The oil-owners set an example: Riza was put into prison and his derricks were shut down. The whole oil-caste was indignant, threatened capital punishment and dispossession. But it did not come to that. Riza shot himself in prison and was ceremoniously buried by his inconsolable sons in the presence of all the owners. The proceedings against him were discontinued.

A Riza steals. But should he really have to die for that? Suicide and ceremonious burial do not necessarily mean death. Ten years later, in a cafe in Paris, I saw a dignified old gentleman studying the stock-market quotations. It was Riza, the poor suicide. When he noticed that he had been recognized, he smiled faintly and said: "One does not die so easily." Then he told me how, in prison, he had changed clothes with a corpse, had shot it through the head, and, for not too high a price, had made the governor of the prison understand his longing for freedom. He left his business to his children and considered it better to withdraw modestly to Paris, where he lived on his private income, and, to the authorities, posed as a political emigrant of high position. "Life is too beautiful for one to kill oneself on account of a small joke with oil," he said in conclusion, affectionately gripping my hand and assuring me of his goodwill. He lives in Paris even today. But I no longer know much that is certain about his business. Perhaps for the sake of variety, he has installed a secret pneumatic tube between the Banque de France and his private residence. In any case he is getting on well; life is beautiful. Riza's secret and ingenious plan soon found its imitators. Many small owners installed hidden connections between their pipes and those of their neighbours after that. The bigger ones learned to overlook this, for, after all, they couldn't lock up everyone.

Another representative of the oil industry, Musa Jakub, was cleverer and occoupied himself privately with smuggling weapons into Persia. He really had no need to, for his business was flourishing. Nevertheless, he liked smuggling for its own sake. "My grandfather was a smuggler, my father was a smuggler, I also want to be one," he used to say in his circle of friends. The smuggling of weapons also attracted him because it was dangerous; a world without danger was too monotonous. This Jakub, who is now in Berlin smuggling Russian caviar, is a peculiar personality, characteristic of the East. Image a squat figure with an unfriendly face, small, evil eyes, bow legs, and large, greedy hands. This man speaks exclusively of the dishonesty of mankind, of the sad life which it leads, and of the rough manner in which his nobler feelings are treated by wicked people.

In his youth Mr. Jakub was leader of a band of robbers in Persia; he once carried off a considerable sum, denounced his helpers to the police, and peacefully moved to Baku, where he anticipated better business. In Baku he became rich and miserly, but remained as before, a bandit pure and simple, the difference being that he now preferred to wear a dress coat and gave thousands to charity every year. Incidentally, he never paid. In company he liked jests. For example, he would stealthily take the money-bag from the pocket of one of his table companions and usually forget to return it; or he would loudly ask the host, across the table, whether it was true that he had assaulted a Russian girl the night before at such and such a place. Usually the suggestion had a basis of truth, but it was not meant for public discussion, nor was it suitable table-talk. Even in business he liked small, innocent jobs. For example, he owned an oil-well from which even the most diligent engineer could not extract a drop of oil. Jakub decided to sell the well. Since, however, it was to be presumed that no one would give a penny for it, he had the inside of the shaft cemented, and at the bottom, deep down, had a cement floor laid; this pit was then filled with oil. Jakub offered it for sale to the Parisian, Rothschild, whose representative came, inspected the well, and reported what he had seen with his own eyes—that every hour a considerable amount of oil was extracted. Rothschild paid the desired price and could not understand why from the very next day the well did not yield another gallon of oil. When the trickery was discovered, Rothschild's representative demanded the restitution of the money, but quickly waived further claims when Jakub explained to him that one usually paid for such a ridiculous demand with one's life.

Since Rothschild was a foreigner, nobody blamed Jakub for the transaction. With natives, however, he was more careful. There, like might be paid with like. Nevertheless, he performed extraordinary deeds here too.

He had an arch-enemy, who had sworn deadly vengeance. Jakub rode to this man, brought him presents, and begged for peace. The whole matter took place in the interior of Azerbaijan, where such a visit certainly demanded more than commonplace courage. The man was so much moved by the visit, by the presents, and by the plea for peace, that he forgot his old malice. Jakub equipped himself for the departure, and the reconciled enemy wanted to escort him to the nearest city so that he might not be attacked by robbers on the way. When both had left the village, Jakub drew his dagger and nonchalantly stabbed his new friend. "I did not trust him," he explained later. "Who knows—perhaps he would have stabbed me otherwise?" These are but a few fragments of Jakub's biography: for a complete picture of him, it must be added that when he visited Paris or Petersburg all regarded him as the perfect gentleman. In Baku several particularly shrewd methods of oil-graft were named after him, but Paris did not know this!

During the revolution Jakub was imprisoned, and shared a cell with a dozen criminals. When they found out that their companion in misfortune was the oil-magnate Jakub, they demanded that he should give them a thousand tumans; in return, they would not make life hard for him.

"Do I owe you anything?" asked Jakub.

"No, but if you don't give us the money, we will cover you with dirt!"

"Good," said Jakub. "You can splash me with dirt, but you won't get money."

And so it happened. Jakub spent a month in prison, was splashed with dirt from head to foot every day, and till the end firmly refused to pay the paltry sum. Later he was beaten thoroughly and thrown out of the cell because the criminals could no longer bear his presence. Nevertheless, even today he is proud to remember that he did not pay a single penny unnecessarily. "I didn't owe them anything," he adds in a matter-of-fact tone.

He was undoubtedly the worst of the owners in Baku. Today he also lives, as I do, on the Kurfürstendamm in Berlin. Recently he visited me, complained, as always, about the dishonesty of his fellow men and about barbaric Europe, in which all profitable dealing is forbidden. In conclusion he said: "It certainly is strange that there are so many dishonest men who are well off, and I of all people must get along so badly."

Jakub was the most outstanding of his kind; still there were many others who ranked only a hair's breadth below him and did not permit themselves the luxury of being honest. These, together with the honest ones, formed a caste, which left nothing to be wished for in barbaric luxury, debauchery, despotism, and extravagance. But not a single oil-magnate was ever ruined by extravagance. It was simply impossible for an owner of oil-fields to spend too much. The liquid gold covers all expenditures. The most gigantic sums were squandered in the building of palaces which reflected the fantasy of the magnates in a grotesque manner. Thus the pompous oil-lord, Isa-Bey, erected for himself a three-storey building in the shape of a house of playing-cards. On the front wall was written in huge golden letters: "Here live I, Isa-Bey of Gandja." The house was equipped with all the refinements of modern interior decoration, but, according to the express wish of the owner, had no lavatory, for Isa-Bey considered himself much top genteel to suffer such an indecent room in his residence. The toilet was situated in the remotest corner of the court, of which the great lord was quite proud. Today the Oriental propaganda division of the Third International is situated in the card-house. Since Isa-Bey had won these laurels, one of his neighbours had no peace. He built himself a palace in the shape of a giant dragon, taking as model a huge prehistoric beast which he found pictured in a book. The entrance represented a gaping jaw into which the guests marched. From the nostrils extended two lanterns which provided illumination in keeping with the whole scheme.

The streets of the oil-city were not lacking in other oddities of architecture. All styles were represented. Moorish palaces stood next to Gothic buildings, and a Byzantine cupola arose next to a rococo pavilion. The palaces were the hobby of the oil-lords, and each sought in his own way to realize some strange dream of his soul.

Mr. Musa-Nagi, a member of a Persian sect, who owned more gold than the Shah of Persia, chose the easiest way. He decided to build a house of pure gold so that he might thus surpass all that already existed. It was with great difficulty that the architect convinced him of the impossibility of carrying out this undertaking. Finally Nagi insisted that at least all the outer walls of the house should be covered with thick gold plating. When the house was finished, he did not like it. The rooms were too large; the air undoubtedly felt different from that in his own dwelling—unventilated for many years; the gold was too tempting for housebreakers, who, indeed, had no need to break in at all, but only to break off something for themselves. With quick decision he gave the house to a philanthropic association, which had no idea what to do with it. Unfortunately the precious monumental structure was destroyed by the Armenians during a street battle with the Mohammedans.

The most notable sight in the city, however, was the club-house of the oil-magnates, which had cost countless millions and contains probably the most beautiful social rooms in the Orient. Since the owners could come to no agreement as to the style and execution, they simply secured a European authority, who was given orders to build something extraordinary on an enormous terrain regardless of the expense.

First the expert had a park laid out on the desert sand. That alone consumed incredible sums. It is not easy to transform a desolate oil-field into a tropical garden. Then the building began: the architect dropped no hint as to the style, and only after several years was it finished, becoming, in the meantime, the centre of heated debate. The club-house, of white marble, is twice as large as the Berlin Reichstag. Its classic, simple lines did not, however, please most of the oil-lords, and to satisfy them a luxurious Colonnade was built in the park, and the corridor walls were lined with endless mirrors. Only the owners of oil-fields had admission to the club. There, in complete peace and among themselves, they could follow their business affairs or their dreams.

It was easy for anyone who was not a member of the guild to arouse the anger or love of an oil-prince, and both were equally dangerous for the one concerned. Beautiful women who strayed to Azerbaijan were abducted or disappeared without trace in the mountain villages or strongholds of the oil-lords. Now and then the breakers of the Caspian Sea threw up the corpses of men who had placed themselves in the way of an oil-prince. And the wild guardsmen attacked and stabbed their masters' opponents in the narrow alleys and corners of the city. In broad daylight shots were fired when enemies encountered each other by chance on the street. Sometimes the great ones would ride into the desert or sail out upon the sea in the grey dawn, after fantastically spent nights, to greet the sunrise with revolver-shots. In short the native oil industry flourished and bore fruit.

All these are only the unfavourable aspects. Inside the great palaces, in the spacious rooms with servants and Persian rugs, there was no more oil. In undisturbed peace another life bloomed here.

Women and children lived in the palaces, watched over by the sinister oil-guard.

In the evening the people sat on the level roofs and played with tame parrots. They listened to blind musicians, singing the Bajads—the Persian love-songs. On the small gay carpets Circassian girls danced their mountain dances, flirting with the men.

In the daytime one remained in the cool apartments, played Persian games, lazily chewed the chalwa, the lukum, and the candy nuts which were shared with the parrots. Nothing reminded one of blood, oil-dregs, shady transactions, and strange adventures. When one was tired, the eunuchs came, carried one to bed, and at the same time murmured old fairy-tales and wise sayings. When the children went out for rides, the eunuchs carried them to the street and carefully laid them, on the soft cushions in the carriage. The veiled women were also escorted to the street by the eunuchs.

The boys, when in the street, felt like men and heroes who protected their small sisters and cousins, while they themselves were being guarded by a few bandits. They carried golden daggers, and, from the time when they were about ten years old, small Brownings that looked like toys. The guard was there for protection, but the children were to become accustomed to real firearms at an early age.

At home revolvers were not needed. At home the eunuchs took care of everything, slept in the same room with the maids, and endlessly nibbled sugar-candy. Sweets are the only pleasure of a eunuch, who often takes the place of a nurse and has the advantage of dependability, because he never disappears to a rendezvous.

The oil-lord himself was usually at home only for a few hours in the night. He lived at the office, dined at the club, spent his free time in the small villas which he owned for special purposes. They were situated in remote regions among the gardens, far outside the city. At home very little was seen of him. Small maid-servants and wise fairy-tales, the Oriental calm, endless squabble. That was the other phase of the oil-city, idyllic and accessible to but few.

CHAPTER 5

OLD AZERBAIJAN

Not everything in Azerbaijan is ruled by oil. Baku and its surroundings and the whole railroad to Georgia and Russia are under the sway of the liquid gold; but where the city, the oil-desert, and the railroad end, there begins the unexplored country, which is still in the true sense a terra incognita. Unknown clans live there, nomads, descendants of the old Assyrians and the crusaders. Among the mountain rocks and the oases are lords who resisted the lure of the oil, and have remained sole rulers over their land and their people. Foreigners seldom come into the interior of the oil republic; from their point of view no good business is to be found there, no profit—only dangers, long hardships, and a population which has little inclination to exchange habits of living thousands of years old for the transitory charms of Europe. Often, all too often, Azerbaijan is visited by strangers. Writers, journalists, scientists of all kinds come by train to the capital, view the oil-derricks, gaze in wonder at the eternal fire and the old ruins, find out that there is "nothing doing" in the interior, and go on to Russia, to Georgia, or to Persia, with the sincere conviction that they have learned to know Azerbaijan.

The tiny clans which dwell in the rocky mountains, however, have remained hidden, as well as the courts of the princes, the nomads, and the ruins of the holy shrines. During thousands of years of history, foreign conquerors crossed Azerbaijan, seeking the way to Europe or Asia. Remains of strange peoples were forced back into the mountains and, even today, form the small ethnographic island in the sea of the present population. The world of science knows nothing of these little nations. An "International Society for the Exploration of Azerbaijan" is trying to open up the land, but, up to now, except for a few ruins, they have "discovered" only the temple of Zarathustra (which for years has served as a Sunday excursion for the inhabitants of Baku) and the nation of the Jassaians, whose existence was never a secret to the Azerbaijanians. The discovery of the Jassaians was celebrated with great pomp in the world of science and in the Press, for new nations are seldom discovered nowadays—few of them are left.

Smaller and smaller becomes the number of mysterious white spots on the maps of Africa, Asia, and America. Smaller and smaller become the dark regions of the earth which geographers and travellers have not yet explored. In the meeting-halls of the scholarly societies hang large maps with small white surfaces, on which is written, "unexplored territory". Geographers and students regard these maps and apprehensively look forward to the time when there will be no more work for them.

I should like to tell the reader what I know of the Jassaians from my own experience. For this nation is extraordinary, as the "Society for the Exploration of Azerbaijan" may have suspected,

The Jassaians live in the north of Azerbaijan, in the district of Sakataly; yet the dark canyon in which their settlements are found has no name, nor have the settlements received any name up to the present.

The neighbours simply call the people "the nation of the virgins" or "the nation that does not know its past". For the Jassaians know nothing of their past; they have none at all, just as they have no administration, no authorities, and, of course, no writing. Only a few traditions determine their life. According to these, the hands of the Jassaian men may do no work. "Our fathers did not work, and we may not work either," they usually say; and, in fact, they do not work; they spend the whole day stretched out under large nut trees, gaze up at the sky, and meditate on the wisdom of their ancestors, who forbade them to work. Once in a while, however, the Jassaian goes fishing, when he is tired of lying still endlessly. He does not go for the sake of gain, but only for pleasure, for working for the sake of profit is a terrible disgrace to a man, a shame, an unlawful action, for which there is no forgiveness. Work, any kind of work, is the exclusive province of the woman. And the woman is also the first who forbids her husband to work, who casts him out and mocks him, if he begins to work; for it is "an insult to a woman if her husband works", says Jassaian wisdom.

Frequently the neighbouring peoples try to change this regime; but all attempts are frustrated by the opposition of the women. In the dark chasms, in the small, miserable Jassai huts, in the forest and at the river, one can see the Jassaian women at work. They do not veil their faces like the other women in the Orient; they carry daggers and axes and are more warlike than the men of other tribes. Woe to him who attacks either them or their husbands! Like knights the women defend their lazy idlers. It seems that everything feminine is foreign to the women of the Jassaians. And when they do the most feminine thing of all—bring a child into the world—they hide in the forest, hide from the eyes of their fellow-humans; even their husbands may not follow them, for they are "mundar" (unclean).

Only once in the year may the man work; on the day before the New Year festival he takes his wife's weapons, goes hunting, and, upon his return home, lays the game at the lady's feet as a token of thanks for the work of the year. Then he again stretches himself under the branches of the nut tree, until another year is past.

The woman, who carries the weapons, chooses her future husband herself and makes the marriage proposal. She refuses to give up to her husband the least of her rights and duties. She does not like to permit him to leave the village and go abroad, so that it is seldom that one sees an "idler" in the cities of Azerbaijan, isolated and reserved, they live in their settlements in the dark chasms near Sakataly.

However, it can happen that the woman becomes weary of happy married life; and then there is a divorce. Nothing is easier than to be divorced in the canyon of the Jassaians. Two witnesses are called, and the wife says in their presence: "Bir talach, iki talach, ütsch talach", that is; "Go from me for the first time, for the second time, for the third time", and the divorce is legal. For the law of the fathers says: "It is a sin to live with a man of whom one has become weary."

In most parts of the Orient, the woman is a slave even today; she is

41

veiled and hides timidly when a strange man approaches her. In the entire Orient, the men carry daggers and defend their wives. Who knows how it came about, that just in Azerbaijan–in the ravine of the Jassaians–women grew up who took the duties and rights of men and themselves came to be like men? No one will ever be able to find out, for the Jassaians have no writing and no traditions; they have only their wives, who work for them, and their nut trees, under which they spend their days.

In contrast to these, another small, remarkable nation, the Ossetians, has traditions, authorities, and writing to excess. They dwell in Azerbaijan, but mainly in the mountains of Daghestan, and form a little mountain state "Ossetia", barely 130 square miles in extent, with a population of about 65,000. Not all are pure Ossetians; frequent mixtures with other mountain peoples, with the idol-worshippers, the Ingushes, and the Mohammedan Tschetschenes have occurred. Only in certain especially hidden regions can one find the pure stock, and it is there that one encounters the most remarkable thing. For the pure bred, who form the nobility of the ruling class, in contrast to all their neighbours are blond and blue-eyed like northerners. It can be assumed, therefore, that the present Ossetians are not aborigines of the country, but immigrants. If you ask one of them about his descent and the past of his race, he answers calmly that he is descended from mighty knights, from the "Alleman".

When I heard this answer for the first time, I was amazed; for "Alleman." in every language of the East means "German". I repeated the question: "Just what are the Alleman?" The Ossetian smiled at my ignorance: "The gentleman does not know who the Alleman were? The gentleman is very ignorant. The Alleman were great knights from the Land of the Crescent, from Syria and Palestine. They were brave warriors and mighty heroes, but they had many enemies. They fought among themselves and with the strangers. Part of them were driven back out of their country and then sought a new home, came into the mountains, conquered the savage peoples and adopted their language. The descendants of these knights are ourselves–the 'blue-eyed Ossetians'."

Statements like these—which are remarkable enough, if one remembers that the Ossetians could hardly have had an opportunity of finding out anything about Germany—are to be heard all over in the mountains. Even the enemies of the Ossetians confirm the fact that these strange immigrants come from Syria, from the Land of the Crescent. In the individual families, too, evidence is present that their fathers really immigrated from these countries. However, since an explorer attempted to purloin these proofs for his private collection, the Ossetians have become more careful and produce their scraps of evidence only after long hesitation, and then only to people who enjoy a good reputation in the mountains. Articles they can show have already roused the imagination of many a scholar; for they are genuine weapons of the German crusaders, old swords, rusted shields and helmets. Documents are also present, which, however, contain no Gothic symbols, but are in Syrian script and contain, among other things, names of Syrian princes of the time of the crusaders. This, by the way, is all that the blue-eyed Ossetians can produce in the way of evidence. Their main proof is the stubborn conviction that they are descended from German crusaders, a conviction shared by their neighbours.

To science, the Ossetians are still a riddle in many respects. It is only known that their language—which they may have borrowed—is a branch of the Indo-European, like their mythology. The strongholds which are erected on their cliffs remind one of the German castles on the Rhine, also of the strongholds of North Africa when it was conquered by the Vandals. Perhaps the Ossetians are descended from the Allemann! As to religion they are undefined, neither Mohammedans nor true Christians, rather idol-worshippers. Some of the Ossetians now live in the cities, where they become Europeanized quickly and abandon the customs of the mountains.

That is all that science can report about this mysterious nation. Possibly some day a serious-minded scholar will prove that the Ossetians are not descended from the crusaders. In any case this old legend, which has existed in the mountains for centuries, will remain remarkable—the dark secret of the crusaders, of the mighty knights from the

Land of the Crescent, of the "Alleman". The Jassaians, Ossetians, and their neighbours in the north of Azerbaijan are not the only remarkable people of my home awaiting more minute investigation.

To describe all these fragments of the old migrations, would fill a whole book. In the south, too, on the borders of Persia, in a region which few deem worthy of a visit, the strangest customs are hidden, the queerest races, who only occasionally amaze a curious traveller. There, for example, live the Aisors, who number barely a thousand in Azerbaijan, and are regarded as the last descendants of the old Assyrians. They speak a Semitic dialect, are Nestorians (a Christian sect), and are of a decidedly Semitic type, such as one finds on the Assyrian reliefs. They are among the most peaceable people in the world. The pure Azerbaijanians in the south are also interesting ethnographically, for some customs have been kept up among them which originated when Alexander the Great conquered the land of Zarathustra. For example, in Azerbaijan the well-known horn head-dress is worn; that is, the hair is shaved away from the forehead to the neck in a straight, broad line, and on the right and left it hangs down uncut. It is combed so often that it hangs to the front and looks like two bent horns under the little black fez which covers the shaved skull. Alexander is known to have adopted this style of head-dress after his Persian campaign, to the great indignation of Macedonia. His curls resembled horns particularly (the Azerbaijanians have no curls), and so even today Alexander is called "Iskender Sülkörnei" in the whole Orient, which means "Alexander with two horns".

One of the most curious customs of this region, which I have often visited in the summer, is the wedding ritual.

During the ceremony the couple are separated by a rug that hangs down from above, so that they do not see each other. The bride appears for the first time during the wedding dinner and must then be "gilded". Her face and hands are covered with gold paint, which gleams fantastically in the sunshine; this corresponds to the current idea of "gold-radiant beauty". Before she goes to her husband, in the presence of all her relatives and guests, she must stamp to pieces with her boots a mirror that lies on the floor. This is a symbol that her old life will not be reflected in her married life. The better and more vigorously she crushes the mirror, the happier her marriage will be. In some principalities it is also customary for the guests to wait for proofs of the bride's virginity. And they do not leave the house satisfied until they have incontestably convinced themselves of her innocence.

The single khanates of the south form a chapter of their own. They and their khans are forgotten by mankind and the neighbouring governments to such an extent that some of them have preserved their independence until now. In these small states, which are connected somewhat loosely with Persia, truly medieval conditions reign, and with their grotesque sovereignty and isolation from the rest of the world they could become a true El Dorado for adventurers, if these suspected their existence. Unfortunately the country is seldom visited, but what does happen when a stranger comes the following story may illustrate.

CHAPTER 6

THE CONQUEST OF SWEDEN

In the south of Azerbaijan, where the semi-independent principalities of Maku and Choya are situated, there ruled more than fifty years ago the wise and mighty Feth-Ali-Khan. He was a true potentate with a palace in which bed-bugs and fleas fought for supremacy, with a harem which resembled a hen-house, and with real court poets and court painters, the dignity of whose appearance made up for their questionable skill.

The court of the khan was a caricature of the court of Teheran; his courtiers were pale shadow-figures in comparison with the dignitaries of the realm, and yet he, like every prince in Persia, had absolute power in his dominion, for which the great "king of kings" could envy him.

One day the capital village—one cannot call it capital city—the residence of the khan, was visited by a remarkable stranger, golden-haired, tall, fair, and with a leather trunk that resembled the throne of the khan. The stranger rented a house, and on the very next day he was invited to appear before the khan, because of his peculiar appearance. The khan pityingly regarded the light eyes and blond hair, and expressed the opinion that a man who was so ill-treated by fate certainly needed his protection; for blond hair is looked upon in the Orient as a sign of the disfavour of Allah.

The stranger thanked him heartily, and said that he had come from Sweden to Azerbaijan in order to study this holy land. The Swede stayed in the village and chatted with the khan every evening in a horrible mixture of Persian, Turkish, Arabic, and Russian, and finally even became prime minister, travelled about in the whole region, and made some kind of charts, which filled the population with fear and dismay.

Three months later he appeared before the khan with an enormous contract, written in French, which he laid before the ruler to be signed. It is said that the Swede had actually found traces of oil, and now suggested to the owner of the land—the khan—a contract for the concession.

In private life the khan was a good-natured person, a calligrapher, who had mastered the most beautiful ornaments of the Eastern styles of writing with artistic perfection. (Calligraphy is an important branch of graphic art in the Orient.) He did not read the contract, would, in fact, hardly have understood it; but he took the greatest pains to inscribe his name on the paper in inimitable Cufic writing, thus to grant the request of the agreeable Swede. Apparently the Swede did not need more. He remained in the village about a week longer and mysteriously conversed with the guardian of the honour of His Highness, an obese eunuch. At the end of the week he paid his rent, bought a few gay Persian rugs, and took leave of the khan, who presented him with three of the best horses in the royal stable as a remembrance. The direction in which the stranger set out was unknown. The same day the favourite daughter of the khan also disappeared. At first no one suspected that the two events might be related. They searched for the daughter in the nearest villages, at the houses of the chiefs of the nomadic clans, and in the harems of the local Don Juans; no one thought of the pitiable stranger with the blue eyes. Not until six weeks later was the khan to find out the truth. Through a camel-driver he received a letter from Russia from his Swedish friend. The Swede again thanked him for the hospitality which he had enjoyed, and expressed his regret that as a man of honour he was forced to abduct the daughter of the khan. He excused himself by saying that on the one hand, as a stranger, he could not expect a paternal blessing, and on the other hand the circumstances made desirable as quick a legitimization of his love as was possible. Moreover, he hoped that the khan would not refuse his consent now, especially since he—after the sale of the oil-concession to a Russian company—attached no importance to a possible dowry.

The khan received the letter, read it once, read it again, did not believe his eyes, nevertheless had to believe them; and had the messenger of ill-fortune arrested; then let him go again; and finally sank into deep silence. He planned a vengeance which was to surpass anything experienced by mankind up to that time. After three days he ordered the court painter to come to him and acquainted him with his plans.

The painter bowed, expressed his admiration of his sovereign's wisdom, and began to prepare himself for the execution of the plan of vengeance. Soon the order of the bloodthirsty khan was fulfilled. In the main hall of the palace, opposite the throne, the latest creation of the great artist was fastened to the wall. The picture showed several riders with barbaric expressions on their faces, who stabbed down thousands of white-clad foot-soldiers. In the background were depicted burning villages, weeping women and children. At the head of the victors, on a fiery steed, rode the khan. Under the heels of his horse lay the corpse of one who had been beheaded. The head of the dead man was portrayed very clearly in the foreground; it lay in a pool of blood, the face turned towards the spectator, and had magnificent blond hair and large, blue eyes, from which dripped tears of blood.

Under the picture this inscription could be read: "The conquest of Sweden by the troops of the mighty, invincible guardian of the faith, Feth-Ali-Khan. His Highness beheads the crafty King of Sweden."

CHAPTER 7

THE OIL-GUARD

I was not ten years old when my father showed me our oil-guard for the first time. It consisted of a few dozen well-built Azerbaijanians, armed to the teeth, who came from the mountain villages, belonged to one and the same clan, and looked quite sinister and brutal. These people were the most pampered children of the oil industry; everything was granted to them: furlough, money, presents—even women, for it was owing to this guard that a certain degree of peace reigned on the oil-fields and in the works. Few owners could afford a guard of their own.

Most of them were dependent on the so-called Kotschis, who forced their services on their employers and fixed their own salary. These Kotschis are deserving of a more detailed description. A Kotschi is a prince who has lost his land on some occasion, yet kept a few subjects, whom he must now support, according to the law and tradition. The subjects do not leave their prince and demand of him that which one usually asks of a good sovereign—work and wages, with which they can pay him the taxes. These last subjects are for the most part former courtiers of the prince, and would die of hunger without him, for no one in the entire Orient would support the courtiers of a strange prince. Consequently the impoverished prince and his court form a whole that cannot be divided, and in other Oriental countries it would form the nucleus of a robber-band. In Azerbaijan, where there is more profitable work than plundering, most of the princes renounce this branch of trade and proceed with their dozen vassals to, the oil-city, and begin their extortions from the oil-princes. The Kotschi inquires for the owners whose guards are related to him and so will not enter into competition with him. Then he proceeds to the office of the magnate, where he gives his well-sounding name and is usually admitted to the private sanctum at once.

In the course of years, the conversation that now develops between the Kotschi and the oil-owner had become a stereotyped form which was kept up for the sake of etiquette. After the customary formulae of greeting and commonplaces about the weather and the bad condition of the oil industry, the Kotschi pulls a long face and says: "Dear friend, I am really very sorry for you, for black clouds are gathering above your illustrious head." The oil-owner must then ask about the origin of the clouds, whereupon he receives the following answer: "Your enemies want to kill you; although I know it, it is hard to undertake anything against these enemies." Now, if the oil-owner is an inexperienced foreigner, he is seized with a disquietude that is easily understood. The initiated native has no such feeling, but simulates it nevertheless, because it is the thing to do. In the meanwhile the prince continues to lament: "No one in the whole world loves you as much as I. I knew you when you were still a child. I was a friend of your grandfather, and now you must die." He sobs for a while, drinks a glass of water to calm himself, "yet I will try to save you, even if I perish myself in the attempt. I must save you because I love you. What would one not do for the sake of friendship! Just cover part of my expenses—which will ruin me."

Nothing is left for the befriended owner except to come to terms as to the monthly sum which he must pay to his protector. If he refuses he is murdered by the Kotschi, who then runs through the whole city and wails: "I said so from the beginning; now he is dead."

The Kotschi usually has from eight to ten clients, who pay him a monthly sum of from five hundred to a thousand roubles. On the first of every month he collects his money, supports his subjects with it, and with the rest plays a part in high politics. Yet he is by no means a parasite; he makes himself worth while, performs priceless services for the owners, though often these services are of a very questionable character. He is the only one who may abduct a beautiful girl without attracting notice, or, without wasting many words, kill the mortal enemy of his friends. He guards his master in the daytime and at night, and protects his money shipments, fights with his competitors, and does all this as modestly as possible. Officially he is a "financier", lives in grand style, moves in the best society, and is perfectly aware of his important role as protector and saviour.

Clashes between the Kotschis of two hostile owners often occur. When the owner meets an enemy on the street, he tells his Kotschi, who is escorting him. The Kotschi immediately draws his revolver and fires a few shots at the Kotschi of the enemy (not the enemy himself); the shots are answered conscientiously. He shoots at the enemy only if agreed upon before. Sometimes, when two mighty Kotschis fight for the favour of an employer, it comes to regular battles, which take place on the outskirts of the city and are meant to decide who is to have the honour of protecting Mr. X. A few foreign oil-owners, for example Rothschild, did not want to have anything to do with the Kotschis in the beginning, but later repented bitterly; for hardly a night passed without a burglary or some sort of damage at Rothschild's house. When Rothschild finally wanted to hire a Kotschi, it was too late. These gentlemen were accustomed to plundering him, and did not want to protect the "miserly" foreigner. Only with great difficulty was a Kotschi to be found who would undertake, for a double salary, to protect the magnate from at least the largest robberies.

The best trait of the Kotschi was his absolute loyalty to his master, who was never betrayed, even if it would have cost the Kotschi his own head. If the master had no more money, the guard sought a new employer, but continued to perform the old services gratis for his former master, because of loyalty and in the hope that at some time he might still be rewarded.

Occasionally, as in a workers' strike or a revolt, the Kotschis united, and then they became the terror of all Azerbaijan. No one could take up the battle against their fierce hordes, and undoubtedly they would some day have become the true rulers of the oil-land if they had not carried on constant feuds with one another. Often a Kotschi asked for a furlough of several days, giving as a reason that he must kill a personal enemy somewhere—usually another Kotschi. Only the many-sided duties which they had to perform continually restrained them from general anarchy.

The master also had certain duties towards the Kotschi. If the man was imprisoned, his master had to free him and make his flight possible. The Kotschi was indispensable. For example, he possessed a list of all the people who owed his employer money, carefully watched that they did not run away, and gave timely notice if the business standing of the debtor became doubtful.

Upon the Kotschi and his subjects one could depend absolutely in all difficult emergencies of life, and they could be entrusted with the strangest commissions, which would be carried out in the shortest possible time. For example, during the revolution my Kotschi succeeded in procuring for me a rare book, which could not be bought anywhere, and of which I told him only the title. When I asked him how he had obtained it, it turned out that he had simply pilfered it from a private library. I read the book, and the Kotschi was very much surprised when I later commissioned him to return unnoticed it to the owner—who was a good friend of my father.

In Europe this oil-guard would have been impossible. But I really do not know what would have become of the oil industry if these sympathetic braves had not been at the disposal of the owners at all times.

CHAPTER 8

THE FIRE BREAKS OUT

Thus the owners of oil-fields lived; thus I lived; and thus we might have continued to live until today, surrounded by Kotschis, adventurers, primitive clans, and workers' settlements. But there came a change. From the West came ruin; turmoil, chaos started in the East. Robbers, criminals, and thieves made demands; murder and plunder, which had been the prerogative of a few, became general. Nations began to hate each other. Barbaric nationalism shot up wantonly everywhere and led the nations to hunger, war, and destruction. Uncertainty, fear, and desperation also entered the oil-land. The "great bloodless revolution" started, as Kerenski had named the chaos which he called forth, and which set the entire Orient afire.

First came the war. We hardly noticed it. Azerbaijan was united with Russia, but, according to the clause of a complicated pact, was not required to send men into the field. Nevertheless there were enough volunteers to constitute a national corps, which, thirsting for the blood of the enemy, fought with the others at the front. Later this "national corps" played the main part in the well-known Korniloff uprising.

In Georgia, the representative of the Czar resided; he protected the Caucasus in the name of Russia and at the same time observed Azerbaijan. Russian troops marched through Azerbaijan to Persia and to the Turkish front. A few prisoners had the good fortune to come to Baku and to be employed on the oil-fields. The prices of oil rose enormously. We did not see much more than this of the war.

During its first months an interesting incident occurred, which took place in our house, and caused us to be decried as friends of the Germans. You must know that in the beginning of the war a decree was issued that all German citizens—men, women, and children—must be delivered up to the Russians. The unfortunates were penned in ships like cattle, exported and taken across Astrakhan to Siberia. The whole thing did not concern us much, for there were practically no Germans among our acquaintances. But one day a German who had been born in Azerbaijan, and so could not be exiled, came to us and told the following story:

A young German student came to Caucasus in the summer of 1914 to visit her relatives there. The news of the outbreak of the war reached her in Tiflis, where the police informed her after only a week that, as a German, she would be sent to Siberia with the very next transport. Her relatives were naturalized and might stay in Tiflis. The German girl, who was only nineteen years old and came from an officer's family, knew that exile to the snowy wilderness meant death for her. During the night before her banishment, she left her relatives and, dressed in the costume of the men of the Caucasus, fled to Baku in the hope of remaining there unnoticed by the police. She was mistaken. The police found her, and took her for a German spy who had to be locked up temporarily, to be transferred later to an especially rigorous camp in Siberia. Only with the greatest effort did a naturalized German who went bail for her persuade the police to let the girl go about free until she was to be deported. Thus she was in Baku entirely without means, avoided, by way of precaution, by all, even by the Germans, marked by the police as a dangerous spy—and waiting for the Siberian prison-camp. Her German friend described to my father the girl's desperate position and begged him to do something for her. It was clear that the Russian authorities could not be influenced. My father considered a while, and then said: "She shall come to my house. She shall remain here as long as she wishes, and no one will dare to molest her." When the German left, my father ordered that two rooms should be furnished for a guest who would stay with us for an indefinite time.

On the same day the girl appeared and introduced herself as Fräulein Grete K. of Königsberg. She was very pretty, but appeared shy, harassed, and weary. As she did not understand the languages which my father spoke, I had to act as interpreter. She told us that she was studying music, knew nothing about politics, and would like to die. My father calmed her, and assured her that she would feel at home with us. However, she amazed us vastly when she asked what work would be assigned to her and what her duties would be. To us a working woman of good family was a phenomenon which disconcerted us completely.

"You do not need to work," said my father. The girl from Königsberg, on her part, could not comprehend our viewpoint. "But I must do something, if I am to live with you," she maintained.

At last we agreed that she should hold the position of music teacher; whom she was to instruct in music, however, was never made clear. Months passed. She realized that her task consisted of playing something to us now and then on the piano which was bought in her honour. The remaining time she could practise her music, and for that she drew a salary suitable to her rank.

The news that a German spy was living in our house spread throughout the city. When the day came on which Grete was to be taken to Siberia as prescribed, the police appeared and demanded that my father should dismiss the girl. My father drove them off and had the house garrisoned by our entire "oil-guard". The police surrounded the house to arrest Grete as soon as she should go out. However, she calmly went out walking with me, accompanied by twelve Kotschis, who looked sinister enough to frighten anybody. The police did not do more than besiege our house, as entering the home of an oil-magnate by force would have meant big street-battles, perhaps even a small civil war. In their distress they applied to the Russian military commander. He put on his gala uniform and proceeded, his breast decorated with orders, to the "espionage nest", as our house was called. My father received him with all due honours, offered him coffee and sweets, and chatted about the weather. But when the governor began to speak about the delivery of the "spy", my father said that was a coarse breach of the laws of hospitality, and in respect to them he would refrain from answering.

The governor then began to threaten with his military power, roared, spoke of seizing the oil-fields of the pro-German, and the like.

Upon this my father rose, called a Kotschi, and said to the governor in his presence: "The young lady of whom you speak lives in the women's quarters of my house, therefore belongs to my harem. In this country the attempt to force one's way into the harem or to carry off one of its inhabitants is punished by death. Since your Excellency has offended against my harem right, I find myself forced to put the matter into the hands of my friend, the Kotschi."

Then, my father went into the next room, got the statute-book, and showed the governor the paragraph which gives the master of the house the right to shoot within its walls the invader who attempts to abduct a woman from the harem. "The Kotschi," said my father, "is witness that you are seeking to abduct an inhabitant of my harem, and through that have deserved death."

The governor, who understood nothing about laws and only saw an armed bandit before him, wanted to call his guard, but his attention was drawn to the fact that in the case of a planned attack the law also recognizes the castration of the ringleader.

"You wouldn't dare to attack me," he finally shouted in a fury.

"That is not essential," responded my father, "the important thing is that tomorrow the whole country will find out that Russian generals invade native harems and are caught by the oil-guard. You will have to resign. Besides, you will not leave my house before you have granted the German girl free residence in the city. For the sake of security, you will sign a paper, in which you admit that, against the law, you wanted to force your way into my harem."

The governor, who had been surrounded by the Kotschis, had no alternative but to sign and solemnly grant Grete residence. The general assured the police that he had convinced himself of the harmlessness of the "German spy". But he had to resign, for soon the news spread in the Russian Press that the military governor had been bribed by Azerbaijanian bandits and often visited the native harems.

I must mention the fact that there had been no harem in our house for years. But that was none of the governor's business.

So Grete remained with us during all the war years, for which reason my father was designated from time to time as a "suspected pro-German". Since, however, nine-tenths of the natives were suspected pro-Germans, he worried little about it. Later, when the Germans had conquered Azerbaijan, Grete was able to return to Germany unhindered, and there I found her again after many years as a married woman.

The arrival of the German girl was the only event that brought the war close to me. Not until the outbreak of the Russian revolution did the actual disintegration begin which affected the whole of the East. How the revolution began, what causes brought it about, no one in Azerbaijan knew. In the last analysis, we were indifferent to those causes. One day the notice simply came that the Czar had abdicated and his brother would occupy the throne. This news was received rather diffidently. Everyone in the Orient knows that monarchs renounce their thrones from time to time for enigmatic reasons. The Turkish Sultan did it, the Shah, too—why shouldn't the Czar abdicate once, also? In his place will come a new Czar, without any need for his subjects to become excited about it. In any case, for them nothing would change in the slightest degree.

But when it was proved that Russia no longer had a Czar, that there would never be one again, great disquietude began. Who would take the place of the Czar? Had Russia become an empty space, which concealed a riddle within itself and could bring forth God knows what?

One began to become fearful. In the bazaars people spoke of the huge land that was left without a "host". The owners of oil-fields doubled their guards. Soon, however, it was noticed that the old Russia need no longer be taken seriously. The Russian military governor was most politely expelled from Baku; in Georgia the representative of the Czar disappeared, and the Russian soldiers began to kill their officers. In Georgia a new native government was formed which condemned everything Russian. Azerbaijan joined. Nothing came of this government. It consisted of Georgians, Armenians and Azerbaijanians who combated each other and were unanimous on only one point, their hatred of all that was Russian. Their greatest worry was clearing the land of Russian troops, which mutinied, deserted from the front, and gradually began to grow savage. In the interior of Azerbaijan the clans staged for them a true massacre of St. Bartholomew. Tens of thousands of mutinous soldiers were attacked, disarmed, and slaughtered in a brutal manner.

Since, however, new Russian bands kept streaming into the country, the government began negotiations with the German-Turkish troops, who were to take the land under their protection. But there was no unity in the government, and therefore the negotiations lasted several weeks and led to the ruin of the Georgian central government. Thereupon the Azerbaijanian and the Georgian local governments independently concluded treaties with the Germans and the Turks. When these treaties were finally completed, both countries were already in a state of total anarchy, by which Baku was particularly afflicted. It took months before the government of Azerbaijan, supported by the Turks, could restore peace—that is, the might of the oil-lords. Let me describe this time of anarchy, of ruin, of fierce battles.

Baku was an industrial city, the only industrial city in the country. Her hundreds of thousands of workers were most eagerly encouraged to revolt by socialists of all degrees. The first encounters came about in the workers' settlements. To Baku, from all corners of the country, streamed Russian and Armenian bandits who had visions of good business in the rich oil-city at this time. First they contented themselves with simple robberies of harmless passers-by on the streets; later they ventured to attack the oil-lords, and soon began to play a part in politics. I, too, suffered at their hands in rather a mild way. Later the situation became more critical. Peace was over in the East.

CHAPTER 9

THE THIEF IWAN
AND THE ROBBER IBRAGIM

One day my father received a letter. It was short and unambiguous. It contained only two lines: "I shall come tomorrow, and you will give me a hundred thousand marks; otherwise we shall kill your son." It was clear that the letter came from a foreigner; no Azerbaijanian would have thought of writing to my father thus. When I learned the contents I said: "If the man comes tomorrow, take a revolver and shoot him down; otherwise I will do it myself." At first my father refused and wanted to have the man killed by a servant. I explained, however, that the killing by a servant would be murder, but killing by me only self-defence. We debated for a while; then my father agreed and instructed me the whole morning in the art of shooting, for it was to be my first murder. We also ordered our boat for the evening and, of course, unofficially, informed the coast-guard, that during the night we would throw the corpse of a Russian (we were convinced that it could be only a Russian) into the sea. The coast-guard promised to raise no difficulties.

At four o'clock in the afternoon the stranger appeared. He was a pale youth, about twenty-two years old, in khaki suit and trousers. We received him and asked whether he came to call for the money, and when he said that he had, we—my father, I, and two servants—drew our revolvers and commanded: "Hands up!" The youth turned still paler, obediently put up his hands, and his teeth began to chatter. I wanted to fire, but my father ordered that the man should be searched first. He was stripped, and nothing was found on him but a pocket-knife and a few pennies. His emaciated body was tattooed, which aroused my particular hatred, "I will kill you," I said, "because you are a thief and wanted to kill

me". I determined to wait five minutes so that the man could pray a little, and then to fire. My father, too, seemed to consider that right. But
before the five minutes had quite passed someone knocked at the door;
my aunt, an elderly lady who had read Tolstoy and no longer wore a veil,
entered. She looked at me and my revolver, then at the naked man in the
corner, approached my father and said excitedly: "As long as I am in the
house no one shall be killed here. What has the man done?"

"He wanted to kill me," I shouted angrily, for I saw that my aunt
wanted to cheat me of my pleasure. And that she did. She talked endlessly, saying that one might not kill a young man so informally, that it
was a crime, and so on. I responded that I, too, was a young man, that
one might not kill me either, and that at last I must learn to kill a person. The role of the wise Solomon was played by my father, who let us
finish talking first and then gave his verdict, saying: "Get our neighbour, Ibragim!"

Our neighbour, Ibragim, a powerful Azerbaijanian with an incredibly
long nose and melancholy eyes, was a robber chieftain. Everyone knew
that he stabbed the competitors of the oil-magnate, Musa-Nagi, at his
command, that he had found the fugitive banker, Swei, in the desert,
taken from him the stolen money, and killed him—and done many other
heroic deeds. He was a man who was sought after, earned much money,
and knew every scoundrel between Constantinople and Bucharia. He
came immediately, listened to the whole story, and asked us to leave him
alone with the young man. When we left the room, we heard the thun-
dering curses with which our neighbour began the conversation; then
came some blows; unintelligible murmurs from the one who was struck.
Ibragim flung open the door, came to my father, and said: "He is just a
fool. Let him go." My father went back into the room, ordered coffee,
gave the man who had been beaten a cup of coffee, too, and began to
converse with him. For two hours my father talked with him, preached
all sorts of virtues; finally gave him money, a written recommendation to
a friend in Russia, and ordered him to leave the country immediately.
The fellow assumed an innocent expression, pocketed the money, and
went. Our people reported that he had actually gone; but from the bor-

der he sent back a picture postcard: "You are good-natured savages! Thief Iwan." When the robber chief learned of this, he only laughed. "He will never again come to Azerbaijan," And he was right; for we, the owners of the oil-fields and our amiable neighbours, work better, more skilfully and inconspicuously, than any European police.

Ibragim, the melancholy bandit, was my friend; he did not belong to our guard, but has often given us valuable advice in regard to the general state of the robber business. He himself was leader of the body-guard of the oil-prince, Musa-Nagi, but also had incidental earnings which enabled him to spend long hours in leisure and chat with me about the advantages of European culture. In spite of his profession, Ibragim was a confirmed friend of Europe, wore only European clothing, shaved daily, had European coachmen, a dwelling equipped in European style, and a European mistress, of whom he was especially proud. When I visited him, he always spoke of the "backward superstitions" and "insufficient progress" in the country, which made him extremely unhappy. By superstition and backwardness he meant very curious things indeed. For example, when it was prohibited to fire at the passers-by on the street on the occasion of any happy event—which had formerly been the custom— he wrote an outraged letter to the ministry, maintaining that this was an interference in the private affairs of citizens which would never be tolerated in Europe. He also regarded punctuality as a superstition, which was superfluous in the age of machinery that took care of everything itself. These advanced views, however, did not prevent him from considering his profession something most necessary and valuable. According to his viewpoint, he, the upholder of culture and leader of bandits, was the pillar of the oil-industry, which he protected from ruin and anarchy— and in part this was quite true. "In Europe such a man as I would be the pride of his fatherland!" he used to say. In his profession he was a model of excellence. The oil-lord, Nagi, could sleep peacefully. His oil-derricks were safe from all incendiarism, and every enemy was sure of speedy death. Ibragim always called Nagi uncle—in order to avoid saying "master"—was on good terms with him, and laughed at his proverbial miserliness, which he himself surely never felt.

He treated his mistress, a blond Pole, with great respect, introduced her into society as far as it was possible for him, but considered it necessary to influence her educationally from time to time, lest it should occur to her to regard him as an inferior Asiatic. More than once I witnessed his educational efforts. They usually began by an effort to make his advantages clear to her. As he usually did not succeed in this, he finally was overcome by deep melancholy, looked at the Polish girl with pity, and rang for the maid. When the maid, dressed in European clothes, appeared, he pointed sadly to the woman and proclaimed with dignity: "Girl, remove this dark spot from my dwelling", or if he was very much irritated: "Girl, carry this dirty heap out!" Whereupon the maid curtsied and answered: "At once, Mr. Ibragim." Then he sank back into his easy-chair with the self-satisfied expression of a European who is conscious of his duties as an educator. The Polish girl, accustomed to such flourishes, usually fell asleep.

As a consequence of the revolution, Ibragim was forced to flee. He now lives in Constantinople, where the surroundings are scarcely favourable for the practice of his profession. The Polish girl has left him and lives with a rich merchant. However, she has not forgotten Ibragim. Once a month she receives him in her salon and writes him a cheque, which suffices for his support. The retired robber is very proud of this, and regards it as a result of the ideal education which she received in his house.

He was the only robber who knew enough to give up his honourable trade in Constantinople, whither they all fled. All the others, who had not realized the change in their circumstances, are now in prison. Ibragim, however, remained a polished European, who had an inclination for culture, the theatre, the ballet, and even for literature. I have heard that he has opened a cabaret at the Galata Bridge, with the slogan: "The Window to Europe!"

CHAPTER 10

THE ABDUCTION FROM
THE SERAGLIO

Our amiable neighbour, Ibragim, expert on robber-affairs, could not, however, save me from a fate which then overtook many. One day I, too, was kidnapped, as were many other oil-princes in Baku, among them even Musa-Nagi, the owner of the best body-guard in the land. It happened on a warm summer afternoon, when I had left the house to enjoy the pleasures of a rendezvous in an obscure lane. Since the two members of the body-guard whose duty it was to accompany me everywhere were by no means to be eyewitnesses of my lyric, erotic excursions, I ordered them to become absorbed in the complicated fortunes of a game of chess in a café near the old castle of the khan, and proceeded to the lane, where a charming maiden was to await me in a hidden nook. I noticed that several passers-by seemed absolutely determined to accompany me, and I stood still. They approached, and asked in an earnest and sinister tone whether I was the person for whom they took me. I answered their question in the affirmative, and full of curiosity awaited the rest. "Then we must arrest you," said one, a swarthy Armenian with hollow cheeks and close-cropped hair. With a view to the rendezvous I protested vociferously, without success. The passers-by, whose numbers grew larger and larger, put me in a black-lacquered carriage, the door of which was decorated with the state crest.

Thus began my dime novel, which was distinguished from thousands of other dime novels neither in style nor structure. The only difference is that mine actually took place, once again bearing witness to the sad fact that life very rarely surpasses the level of a dime novel.

The state crest reassured me; I already saw myself at the police station, where the chief of police would ask pardon for the small misunderstanding, for such it must be. The trip to the police, however, seemed to be indefinitely long. Endlessly we circled through the streets, which I could not see through the curtained windows. At last we stopped, and my neighbour, who until then had not spoken a word, drew a piece of cloth from his pocket and with it firmly bandaged my eyes. We got out, and I was led into a house. I could tell by the air that we were outside the city, which made the desired meeting with the chief of police, to say nothing of the rendezvous, appear highly improbable.

When the black cloth was removed I found myself in a small room, hung with Persian rugs, with no window of any kind. The man who had taken off my bandage disappeared through a small door without bothering about me any more. Left alone, I still could not grasp the meaning of all that had happened. I approached the door and—since I had no idea who had really arrested me—began to swear loudly in Azerbaijanian, Armenian, Persian, Georgian, and Russian. My stock of Asiatic curses exhausted, I switched to the European dialects, without materially improving my situation. When I had stopped cursing and began to thunder at the door with my fist, it opened gently, and a middle-sized man wearing a black mask entered the room, holding a revolver, its muzzle levelled at me. Locking the door behind him silently, he leaned against the wall and remained in this position without putting down the revolver.

I now stopped announcing my dissatisfaction, sat down on the pillows which lay on the floor, and began to brood over abstract matters, a practice which has usually soothed me in unpleasant situations. Thus several hours passed. The man held the revolver, I brooded, the girl in the obscure lane and the servants waited. At last the door opened a second time, and a fat gentleman, also masked, but without a revolver, appeared on the threshold. The fat gentleman came towards me, greeted me in the most amiable manner, and sat down by my side. "You dare to sit down with me?" I asked angrily. The man rose and said with a pronounced Armenian accent but in the tones of a cultured person: "I can also stand. That makes no difference to me. How do you like your room?"

"I had a different idea of the police station," I answered. Thereupon he began to laugh, and I did likewise, for I had long come to the conclusion that this comfortable apartment had little to do with the police. "We have stolen you," he exclaimed at last, "and I believe our trouble has not been in vain." It was an Armenian band that had kidnapped me in the hope of receiving a rich ransom; for the liberation of my modest person.

We began the negotiations. I was to write a letter home in which I asked for the payment of a certain sum. At first I refused, assuring him that I could not possibly define my own value, that his valuation of my person rested only on unfounded goodwill, and that the sum which he named to me was indeed fantastic. I was never worth 500,000 gold roubles. But the man would not hear of less. I was worth much more, he said; it was only because of exaggerated modesty that I would not admit it.

Thus we talked till late in the evening, exchanging endless compliments without arriving at any result. As I became hungry in the course of the conversation, the man had a meal brought in which would have satisfied the most pampered appetite, and was served on silver plates. At last, after the excellent food I declared myself ready to write the letter home.

The negotiations which my father was now forced to carry on with the Armenians lasted five days. The messengers who demanded 500,000 roubles were thrown out. The leader of the band came to me and said that my father would not ransom me; I must write another letter, for otherwise they would be forced to, kill me. First, however, he only wanted to cut off one of my ears to send it to my father and thus prove how serious he was. But I was uncompromising. I knew that upon my pleas, I should be ransomed at any price; yet the consequence would have been that my father or some cousin of mine would have been abducted the next day, to get another 500,000 roubles. I knew, too, that the band would take good care not to harm me; after all, they were Armenians who still had countrymen to lose.

Those five days I spent in the small room in the company of the sinister Armenian, who stood at the wall with the revolver in his hand. I was treated very well. The bandits were obviously concerned for my well-being and took the greatest pains to make my stay as pleasant as possible. Each morning one of them appeared and asked what menu I deigned to order for the day, and whether I had any particular wish as to reading-matter or service. All my desires except one—that the man with the revolver should finally disappear—were granted. The man had to remain in order to shoot me, as they said, in the case of an outside attempt to liberate me. On the third day of my imprisonment the fat gentleman came and even asked whether I longed for the society of ladies, since my stay might possibly be protracted. He did not wish me to suffer from involuntary asceticism. However, I declined, in view of the man with the revolver, who did not resemble a eunuch in any way. The fat man chatted a while longer and complained that my family wanted to pay but little for me, although I had been lodged in the best room with the best of care. Only highly esteemed people were kept in this room; for people of inferior means they had other accommodation. This class distinction in the robbers' den touched me, and I assured my captor that he would get his money's worth in the end. At last the bandits came to an agreement with my father. My value was set at 100,000 gold roubles plus the 5,000 which the people demanded for my maintenance, that is, 1,000 roubles a day, which, no doubt, was a little too much.

I was led out of the house, again blindfolded, entered a motor-car, and was set free at the edge of the city, after the bandits had heartily shaken my hand at parting and, as a remembrance, had given rne the books which I had read during my imprisonment. We parted almost good friends, and when I arrived at home, they even rang up and inquired whether anything had happened to me on the way. Not till later did I find out who these robbers were. They were Armenians, members of a radical party, who needed money for their political battles at home. After a year I heard, to my immense gratification, that they had been hanged in the village square in Gandja.

This method of raising money for election campaigns and propaganda was general among the political parties of the Orient, even if, all too often, the money which had been so raised disappeared in the pockets of the party-members. The best expert in such financial transactions was, in his time, the Georgian, Joseph Dzshugaschvili, who was then just exchanging his notorious revolutionary pseudonym "Nischeradse" for the simple name Stalin. There are probably few wealthy people in the Orient who were not forced now and then to place their moneybags at the disposal of the aims of some revolutionary band. But this "expropriation" or "exing"; as these feats were called, was best organized among the Leninite Marxians and the Armenian Duschnaktjutjun. Unfortunately I cannot boast of having fallen into the hands of Stalin. When I was abducted in 1917, the communist party needed no "exings". Besides, Stalin had more important things to do; he was General Secretary of the party and an intimate friend of Lenin and the South Russian journalist, then even more famous, Leo Bronstein Trotski.

In Azerbaijan deep calm still reigned at that time, as far as this idea was reconcilable with Azerbaijan. Fleeing Russian troops still camped peacefully in the neighbourhood of Baku, and the Armenian party, Duschnaktjutjun, without attracting much notice, organized an army that had to depart for Armenia to defend the country. Their leaders were Prince Andronik and Stepa-Lalai. The two did not reach Armenia, however, for the three bloody March days were nearing during which the fate of Azerbaijan was decided in street-battles, and 30,000 corpses covered the squares, roofs, and alleys of Baku.

Prince Andronik and Stepa-Lalai became immortal during those days.

৵

CHAPTER 11

THE MASSACRE

General Hadschi Seinal Abdin Taghi-Sadé was the most highly esteemed man in Azerbaijan. When he appeared at any meeting or came on a visit, all present arose, and everyone felt honoured if the general extended his hand to kiss. Every word he spoke was considered law in the country, and he was regarded as a being of a higher order by peasants, workmen, robbers, and even by the shrewdest oil-well owners. How the general attained such prestige is a riddle. He erected a prison, a school, a theatre, and a mosque for his people; but many other owners did the same. Though very rich, he was by no means the richest man in the country and bore the title of general without having been in the field. The reason why he was so honoured was probably that he usually made only honest deals, literally was analphabetic, and passed for the wisest man in the East. In the case of General Taghi there could be no question of aristocratic descent. In his youth he was a mule-driver, who advanced laboriously to the position of a camel-driver; through various oil transactions he later succeeded in laying the foundations of his riches, which, nevertheless, he only increased to a certain amount. One day he estimated his wealth and ascertained that he owned nearly forty millions.

Then he liquidated all his business, except that which served the good of the people in general. He built the theatre, a spinning-mill, a school, and other institutions Beneficial to all; this won him the halo of a saint. He could not read or write, but had definite office hours, during which he dispensed wise advice, entirely gratis, to all who wished it.

When he was eighty-five years old, he decided to marry again, which increased his prestige considerably; for a man who marries again at eighty-five is looked upon in the Orient as a particular favourite of Allah. The lady of his choice was a Circassian of rare beauty, who had not yet reached the age of eighteen. At that time General Taghi had sons who were twice as old, which however, was also an honour. The wedding was celebrated; the young bride, who was treated in the European manner, moved into the palace of the general, and the peaceful married life of the newly wedded pair began to develop according to all the rules of Eastern wisdom.

But soon it came to a catastrophe.

The oldest son of the general had a foster-brother by the name of Prince Bebutoff, who had the freedom of the house, since foster-brotherhood was considered a very close relationship. Prince Bebutoff was young and handsome, and passed for a favourite with the women. Whether he fell in love with the young wife, or whether she conceived a liking for the prince will certainly never be fathomed. Probably there was nothing that mattered at the bottom of the incident, for otherwise the young lady could scarcely have remained the favourite wife of the general. But the fact remains that the wisest Azerbaijanian called Prince Bebutoff into his private chamber one day. The conversation that took place between the two I give word for word.

"How are you?" asked the general.

"Very well," answered the prince.

"Look me in the eyes."

"All right."

Then the general rose and announced: "I have always been your benefactor, and now you say rude things to me and look at me askance." He clapped his hands three times, and armed servants entered the room. Hadschi Seinal Abdin Taghi-Sadé, the wise general, beckoned to the servants and commanded: "Deprive him of his sex!"

What happened then is hard to render. The prince roared, the general cursed, the armed servants obeyed their employer. The son of the general hurried to the assistance of his foster-brother, but was beaten and driven away. As if by a miracle the prince succeeded in tearing away and running down the steps. There he was attacked again, but was able to attract the attention of his servants, who stood in the street. Now it came to a regular battle between the servants of the prince and of the general. Passers-by, who did not want to let the opportunity to take part in the battle slip, interfered so that the prince could be dragged away; but the fight, which had then lost its purpose, lasted for several hours as a pure practice of the art.

Whether the general's attempt on the virility of the prince had succeeded could never be determined definitely. On the very same day Bebutoff was shipped off to Paris by his relatives; he never returned to Azerbaijan. From that day he also refused to make any utterance about his injury or its cure.

The case came to court, and it was a Russian court, as the prince was a subject of that country, and the general was knight of all the Russian orders and a Russian privy councillor. At first imprisonment was suggested; but that would not do, since the prison had been built by the general, and was, so to speak, his private property. The best lawyers of Russia defended the "Azerbaijanian eunuch-maker", as the Russian press now called the general. Nevertheless, his case seemed precarious, since the whole matter not only appeared to the Petersburg judges as a cruel bodily injury, but also meant an incredible disgrace to the princely crown of the Bebutoffs, the most aristocratic pro-Russian princes in the Caucasus.

At this crisis the general dictated to his secretary a long letter to the Czar. What was written in this letter is not known. Nevertheless, the general again proved his wisdom irrefutably, for after the receipt of the letter the Czar personally commanded that the proceedings against "His Excellency, General Tagm" should be discontinued, and the honour of the family Bebutoff should be considered unimpaired. At that time the Czar's word still counted. Bebutoff's honour was saved; and after this event the prestige of the general rose even higher in Azerbaijan.

This amiable, kind, and wise general had a favourite son named Memed, who was a good friend of mine, and became the indirect cause of one of the worst massacres that the Orient has ever known. Memed was a queer fellow, not a rare case among the sons of the owners. He was gloomy, melancholy, and, of course, tired of life. When he reached school age, the general decided that he should learn something. Up to then his only occupation had been to smear the wallpaper with cherry juice and applesauce. No English, French, or German teacher could get along with my friend for more than three days. His education had remained in the initial stages. At last the general hit upon a truly brilliant idea. "You must go to school," he said to Memed. The latter had various objections to make to that.

In his opinion, every school in Azerbaijan had its bad sides. For the foreign institutions, on the other hand, he felt a burning hatred. The general listened attentively to his offspring, then considered, and finally built him a school of his own in the most modern style of architecture, and with an equipment that met all the demands of modern European pedagogy. Today the first university of Azerbaijan has its home at this school.

Memed went to school, learned quite well, became modest and subject again to melancholy. In 1918, shortly after the Russian revolution, he left, and became an officer in the famous "Wild Division", which then was the object of my longing, too (but I was five years younger than Memed). The "Wild Division" consisted of representatives of the best families of Azerbaijan, and was notorious for the fact that the members (officers and soldiers) not only fought in the battle with bayonets, daggers, and other weapons, but also knew how to bite through the throats of their opponents by a particular trick.

Memed entered this division. He put on a handsome uniform, sauntered about the streets for a few weeks, and let all his friends who had not advanced as far as he admire him. He finally rode to his division, stationed in a little hamlet. Several weeks passed; then news came that he had shot himself with his gilded, jewelled Browning. The burial, of course, was to take place in Baku, and the whole "Wild Division", armed to the teeth, accompanied by machine-guns and field-guns, proceeded to the city to pay the last tribute to the officer.

At that time, as I have said, the remains of the Russian army were encamped near the city. In the city, the Duschnaktjutjun were organizing an Armenian troop. The communists from the workers' quarters, Armenians and Georgians, carried on ardent propaganda among the Russian soldiers, who were greatly demoralized by war and revolution, not without results. They looked greedily at the palaces of the owners, got drunk in the saloons, loudly reviled capitalists, and roared "Hurrah!" when one of the communist leaders, the Armenian Schaumjan, or the Georgian Djaparidse, showed himself anywhere near. For the present, however, absolute calm reigned in the city, which was protected by the scanty guard of the owners of the oil-wells. The Armenian nationalists, Prince Andronik and Stepa-Lalai, who were organizing their army, did not interfere in the inner affairs of the government, which was making the greatest effort to persuade the savage Russian hordes to return to Russia. Then there came to the city for Memed's funeral the whole "Wild Division", the only purely Mohammedan army in the country. It obtained quarters inside the city limits, and thus became, besides the Armenians and Russians, the third danger of the oil-land.

It certainly was not easy to keep these three armies that hated one another from bloody encounters; nevertheless, before the burial all three parties restrained themselves from any great excesses. After the funeral representatives of the Russian soldiers' councils and of the communists appeared to the leaders of the Mohammedan army and demanded that the "Wild Division", before its departure, should deliver its arms and ammunition to the communists; otherwise the communists, supported by the Russians, would force the "Wild Division" to give up the weapons. Of course the delivery of the weapons would have meant annihilation for the division. Their leaders now applied to the heads of the Armenian non-communistic organizations, whom a similar fate might threaten. Prince Andronik agreed to drive out the communists with his battle forces and the "Wild Division" together, so that later they might peacefully settle the boundary controversy. One could also be sure from the very start that the Armenian-Mohammedan army, supported by the owners, would easily overpower the communists. Thereupon the division informed the communist leaders that they were prepared for a street-battle in Baku to protect the oil-wells from fire. Two hours before the beginning of the conflict, when the plan was already worked out, the parts distributed, and the Russians were nearing the city, the Armenians broke their promise to fight on the side of the Azerbaijanians. Stepa-Lalai, an Armenian leader, had sworn mortal vengeance against the Mohammedans twelve years before. Many of the Armenian soldiers, too, did not want to fight for the Mohammedans, who were known as friends of the Turks. In this decision it was also a consideration of weight that the majority of the communist leaders were Armenians, thus countrymen, partly even blood relations, of the Dashnakes.

Supported by the Armenian inhabitants, Andronik and Stepa-Lalai decided to take revenge now for the last Armenian massacre of 1905. In an appeal to all Armenians in the city who were able to fight, they demanded the extinction of the Mohammedans and aid for the Armenian-Russian communists. Since every peaceful inhabitant of Baku is armed, this appeal was received with enthusiasm. Of course, at the last moment, the Mohammedans also summoned the Mohammedan inhabitants to the battle. Since it was now less a matter of a communist attack than a battle of the Mohammedans against the Armenians, in which the communists supported the Armenians, the uninvolved inhabitants—Russians, Georgians, Jews, and foreigners—were hastily notified of the impending events, and advised to remain in their houses and give no sort of assistance to the members of either party.

Then the street-battle began.

I was sitting on the balcony of our house when the first shots were fired. In the street were still some passers-by, among them veiled women. I saw one of them fall just as my father called me away from the balcony. We had remained in the house alone, we and the women and children who lived with us; the men-servants fought for us in the street. Even our eunuch, the most peaceful person in the world, took a curved sabre and disappeared in the mêlée, eager for the battle and glowing with pleasure. Not until several hours after the beginning of the affray did our friends appear and set up on the edge of the level roof of our house a machine-gun worked by several men. Our house stood in the midst of the disturbance; it was situated at the gates of the old stronghold of the khan, which was occupied by our friends. The Armenians fought especially for the advantage of the stronghold. For a whole day they were kept back by the machine-gun on the roof of our house. Not until Stepa-Lalai took possession of our house after a violent struggle and levelled the gun against the stronghold, did the defence become hopeless.

The houses of the owners of oil-fields are carefully prepared for such occurrences. In almost every one there is an underground dwelling which serves as hiding-place for the women and children. In our house this refuge consisted of several well-furnished rooms, separated from the rest by a steel roof and steel doors. A few barred and hardly visible holes in the roof led to the court and ensured a supply of air. In the rooms were telephones, electric light, and running water. In spite of the most violent street-battles the electric light and the telephone remained available; which was a good thing for both sides, especially for the owners, who, whether Mohammedans or Armenians, had to control the situation on the oil-fields,

At the beginning of the struggle we withdrew to these rooms. There were about fifty of us, mostly women and children, many of whom I had never seen before in our house. They came creeping from all corners and presented themselves as blood and foster-relatives, or even as servants, and, of course, had to be admitted. A few neighbouring owners, who were not as well prepared, also fled to us to hide and to remain in contact with their fields by means of our telephone. My father did not fight; he and the other owners had to be ready to carry on peace negotiations in a case of necessity. Above all the peace on the fields had to be kept up during the battle. In spite of their burning desire neither of the parties dared to set fire to the oil-derricks of an enemy owner, since the fire would undoubtedly have destroyed those of his own side, too. Although the Armenian owners were on the side of their countrymen—Stepa-Lalai, the hero of the day, was also a well-known oil-magnate—they were forced to come to an understanding with us, their mortal enemies, during the street-battle. The derricks, indeed, were the only sanctuary which might not be injured even during those days. The oil-derricks rose above all parties. They continued to spit out their black gold and had to be protected, cost what it might.

Our telephone was constantly in use. Soon the Armenian owners called us up and informed us almost hysterically that their derricks were being threatened by Mohammedans. At that we had to warn the leaders of the Mohammedan uprising so that they would send dependable people to the derricks. Then we were again called up from our fields, which reported that Armenians, on their part, were killing the Mohammedan engineers and throwing them down the shaft. This news we telephoned to the Armenians, who in their turn took the necessary precautions. The management of the oil-fields worked feverishly. Among the workmen there were also both Armenians and Mohammedans. Death ruled at the derricks; fourteen of our engineers were murdered. Workers bit through each other's throats. Nevertheless the bloody days passed comparatively peacefully for the oil-wells, thanks to the owners who trembled at their telephones. The Armenians and Mohammedans could still remember the massacre of 1905, when almost all the derricks were destroyed by the flames.

A communist who reads this will say, perhaps, that here the solidarity of capital won a victory over the national hatred of the individual capitalists. He is wrong; for people protected the oil-wells without knowing whether they would come out of the battle alive themselves. More than one owner was killed; the national hatred that raged in the streets spared no one. The Armenians, who were victors this time, took the bloodiest revenge for 1905.

Women, children, and aged men were killed in their homes. In the mosques, where the inhabitants sought refuge, massacres took place. Stepa-Lalai, communist and oil-magnate, searched the whole city for Mohammedan children, grasped them by the legs, whirled them through the air, and dashed their skulls to pieces against the paving-stones. He killed a hundred children in this way, and after every murder he yelled: "Revenge for my parents!" They had been stabbed twelve years before by Mohammedans. Only six hours the battle lasted; then the Mohammedans were conquered.

Twelve deputies, among them six clergymen, proceeded to the enemy camp with white flags to make peace. They were shot by the Armenians in spite of the white flags. For three days blood flowed in the streets of Baku. Corpses filled the roads and houses. Pregnant women with bellies cut open lay in front of the mosques, Armenians forced their way into the courtyard of our house; through the airhole I could see how they threw two children up into the air—both together were not ten years old—and caught them, on their sabres. Many Mohammedans who had lost all in the battle put on white garments and flung themselves unarmed against the daggers of their opponents. No one was spared; even physicians, usually considered inviolable everywhere in the Orient, were killed.

Every Armenian had to take part in the battle. Captured Azerbaijanians were now brought before Armenian children whose parents had formerly been killed by Mohammedans. Daggers were forced into the children's hands. Taking revenge for their dead, they slowly had to cut through the throats of the captives. Unceasingly machine-guns shot at the Mohammedan houses, in which no defenders were left.

Thirty thousand Mohammedans were dead. Stepa-Lalai was celebrating the victory.

And in the midst of the battle, in the cellars and rooms that were safe from the enemy, the oil-owners sat trembling—Mohammedans, Armenians, Russians, Jews—the telephone-receivers pressed to their ears, and guarded the black gold. Their wan faces glowed with fever, with oil-fever.

Three days we spent in our retreat. The telephone kept us informed of everything that happened in the city. We knew our losses even before we saw them. In the night of the first day our house was occupied by Stepa-Lalai, who tried in vain to force his way into our cellar. He had to content himself with stabbing women and children to death in our court before our eyes. The first two days I stood it and tried to read or to sleep. On the third day it was no longer possible. It was the first great massacre that I had experienced. I admired the men, who, accustomed to everything, amid blood and death critically compared this massacre with the former one; I could not stand it any more down there among howling women and children, and I begged my father to allow me to go out; I no longer wanted to hear about the blood over the telephone, but wanted to see the blood and murder with my own eyes.

My father only laughed. "The time for the battle of vengeance will come, never fear," he said, "for the present just stay quietly in the cellar".

Not until the night of the third day did we both leave the house to sneak in the dark to our office "building, from where we hoped to get a better view. Accompanied by crying and moaning, we left our hiding-place and stepped out to the blood-covered street. What I first saw was corpses with severed ears and noses, with severed sex-organs which were stuck into the open mouths. They lay there, and no one made any effort to remove them. Only on the next day vehicles began to work, carting the thousands of dead bodies out of the city; the whole day long wagons rolled through the streets. The people who drove them searched the pockets of the dead ones. That was their remuneration. They threw the dead into the wagons by dozens and then drove slowly through the city—without covering their burden in any way—in the direction of the oil-desert, where the corpses were buried in the sand.

For a few days longer we had to stay in hiding in the office. Gradually our servants and the guard, as many as had remained alive, gathered together.

And friends also appeared who, at present, helplessly faced the new condition of the country. For in Baku, at the oil-wells, in the factories, in the country up to the border of Georgia, the new rulers played havoc—the communists, Lalai and Schaumjan. Prince Andronik, the nationalist and Armenian, was forced to flee.

CHAPTER 12

THE REVOLT OF THE LEPERS

Two incidents from the time which immediately followed the street-battles have remained especially clearly defined in my memory: the revolts of the lepers and of the wild Jews in the province of Kuba. Leprosy, the most horrible disease in the world, seldom occurs in Azerbaijan, but often lepers escape from Turkestan and Persia. It is hard to recognize them, as they usually hide their wounds and lodge among healthy people in the poorer districts of Baku. A leper whose leprosy is not yet advanced and whose limbs are not yet deformed can live for years among healthy people, thus spreading the horrible contagion unnoticed. He does not suffer any pain, is able to do any kind of work, and is exposed only to the gradual decay of his body. That may last for decades. Meanwhile, at intervals of several months he cuts off rotten flesh without suffering any pain.

The recognition of his condition is made more difficult by the fact that skin diseases occur very frequently in the Orient, and that the lepers declare the police—who have very little medical knowledge—that they have a harmless syphilis which needs neither to be controlled nor isolated.

But whenever a leper is discovered or the disease has progressed so far that it can no longer be hidden, the leper is taken to the leper-colony, where he is supported by the government until the end of his days. The leper-colony was situated in the desert, near the city. It was guarded by disabled soldiers who deposited provisions at the entrance, to be fetched by the afflicted ones. The guard itself lived round about the colony and avoided any contact. When one of the lepers died, his body was buried by the other victims within the colony. The soldiers were free to shoot anyone who stepped over the boundary marked by a wooden picket-fence. Within the colony the lepers were permitted to marry, to beget children, to build huts, to transact business, even to be merry.

People who have suffered from leprosy for years become accustomed to their rotting bodies and do not think of the disfigurements. As a rule they do not die of leprosy, but of old age. Only those who have been newly consigned to the colony rave for some time, until they, too, have learned to bear their lot.

After the street-battles, after the revolution, the organization of the control and guarding of the colony degenerated. The disabled soldiers disappeared. Revolt and hunger reigned throughout the country. Nobody thought of providing the leper-colony with food. Its very existence was forgotten; it was hoped that perhaps all the lepers were dead.

Suddenly the revolt of the lepers broke out. The starving, rotting people with green festering faces and limbs organized, elected a sheik, broke out of the colony, and plundered the adjoining villages; then they approached the oil capital. Panic-stricken, the villagers left their huts when they heard of the impending attack. They knew that they themselves would become leprous should they come into hand-to-hand combat with the lepers. In their fear the fugitives from the villages who came to the city related all sorts of horrible tales; for instance, that the lepers were equipped with machine-guns and that they formed ten divisions of a thousand men each. Every day the number of lepers increased; no essential facts at all were known about them. It was said that the lepers preached a new social order, that they intended to burn down the oil-derricks and infect the entire population. In a session of the revolutionary government it was decided to declare the revolting lepers to be "adversaries of the world revolution" and remnants of "the old regime", and to fight them ruthlessly. The execution of this wise decision, which was debated bitterly (not everyone wanted to consider the afflicted ones adversaries of the revolution), met with many a difficulty.

No leader of the Red proletariat cared to take command over the anti-leper troops. Also, the revolutionary troops refused to fight against such a horrible enemy. Panic was already growing in the city; the enemy was but a few miles away when Kaschi declared himself prepared to lead the troops for love of the revolution.

His task was no easy one; for the troops would march to battle only if he, the leader, actually led them, that is, marched in front of them all and, if necessary, would be the first to come in contact with the lepers. He consented, was appointed Minister of Social Welfare, and proceeded to the scene of his future heroic deeds, with a hundred soldiers and ten machine-guns.

When the lepers, who were but primitively armed, spied the government troops, they immediately hoisted the white and red flags, as a sign of their surrender and their revolutionary partisanship. However, as soon as the bearers of the flags of truce made signs requesting a hearing, the Minister of Social Welfare gave orders to get the machine-guns ready. The distance between the government troops and the lepers was no longer great; none of the rebels could escape. They all were killed because, as the Minister claimed later on, they had sold themselves to the "oil-sharks". Their corpses were left to the jackals and dogs, who are known to be immune to leprosy.

The inhabitants of the plundered villages refused to re-enter their communities. By order of the Minister of Social Welfare, who enjoyed great prestige after the suppression of the leper revolt, the houses which had been entered by the lepers were drenched with petrol and burned down as a public reassurance.

Thus ended the revolt of the lepers. It was perhaps the strangest revolt that ever took place. From that time the leper-colony remained uninhabited; the state budget derived the benefit of this. Two years passed before the leper-colony was again put in condition for new colonists.

CHAPTER 13

THE WILD JEWS

Much more dangerous was the uprising of the wild Jews in the district of Kuba. In individual regions of Azerbaijan, in the steppes and on the summits of the stone masses of the southern Caucasus, one often sees small, half-dilapidated settlements without the customary minaret, without the cross of the Christian Church. These are the Auls, the temporary or permanent settlements of the "Kipta" or the "Bani Israel", as the Jewish clans of Azerbaijan are called. The inhabitants of these settlements, like the nomadic brothers of their race, wear the usual costume of the country, are always armed, and, at the best, work at agriculture. Where agriculture is impossible, these Jews, like the other clans of the country, are shepherds, nomads, warriors, at times even robbers, who plunder the caravans of the merchants at the border of Persia together with the Mohammedans.

Their neighbours look upon the Jews as aborigines of the country, not as strange immigrants. They were in Azerbaijan even before the present Turanian population migrated from the deserts of Turkestan and Mongolia into the land of Zarathustra. According to old legends the first Jew of Azerbaijan was a certain Schambat, who fled from Babylon to Armenia centuries before Christ. His successors were commanders-in-chief and aristocrats of the old Arsacid kings, and one of them, Schambat Bagarat, even became hereditary "Tagadir"—the courtier who placed the crown on the head of the new king. From this Bagarat originates the mighty Caucasian race of the Princes Bagration who were later related to the Russian house of the Czars.

Another legend tells that the "Kipta" lived behind a golden wall many thousands of years ago, where they waged war against seven kings, and finally, having been conquered, migrated to Azerbaijan. During the Middle Ages the chieftains of the Jews were independent vassals of the Shah of Persia, proud families of princes, who still exist today in part, and, several centuries ago, even founded a mighty kingdom, in which, however, only the fighting caste, the nobles, and the king were Jewish.

Judaism was at that time the religion of the privileged classes. When the Czars had conquered the southern Caucasus, where part of the "Kipta" lives, these Jews demanded equality of rights with the remaining inhabitants of the country, freedom from the restrictions of the other Jews of the Czar's empire, arguing that they had emigrated from Palestine before Christ and so were not responsible for the crucifixion. Although this could hardly have been true according to the evidence of science, the Czar granted the demand of the warlike people, perhaps to avoid revolts.

These Jews now have little comprehension of the past glory of their race. The majority of them are illiterates, rough warriors and cowherds, who differ from all other Jews in the world in their peculiar customs, usages, and laws. The laws which the "Kipta" obeyed till the last were proclaimed in the twelfth century by the Azerbaijanian ruler, Rustem-Khan. According to these laws the Jews were completely independent in their affairs of the interior.

In conflicts with Mohammedans the "Adat", the Azerbaijanian prescriptive law, and not the church law, "Schariat", was generally decisive. Only a few questions were regulated separately; for example, the atonement for the murder of a Jew. The murderer, even if he was a Mohammedan, had to tear the skin from the body of the murdered, fill it with silver, and surrender it to the family of the dead as the price of his life. This mandate was seldom followed, however, as the Jews, like the other Azerbaijanians, usually insisted on mortal revenge.

Mortal revenge, which was officially permitted for the Mohammedans and Jews until 1920 (not for the Christians, to whom it was forbidden in consideration of their religion), was carried out among the "Kipta" with definite ceremonies, and under the supervision of the elders of the villages and the rabbi, who were responsible for the procedure.

After the murder all the blood-relatives of the murderer were notified that they would be abandoned to the revenge of the family of the murdered after three days. The relatives used these three days to withdraw to some stronghold and there unitedly defend themselves against the attack of the hostile family. If the relatives of the murdered could take no revenge within three weeks, the elders of the village and the rabbi then had to take a hand, according to the law, and they set the price of life and reconciled the families. The guilty had to kiss the dust from the feet of their opponents at the scene of the reconciliation. The murderer himself was exiled for two years, then returned to the village, and to a certain extent as a substitute for the murdered, had to enter his family, where be became from that time the favourite son of the house.

Towards the foreign, especially the Russian Jews, the "Kipta" are inimical. The language difference may play some part in this. The Jews of Azerbaijan speak Tatish, a mixture of Persian, Azerbaijanian, and Hebrew. Above all, it is the natural hatred of the naively pious nomad for the foreigner and city-dweller, a hostility strengthened by the fact that the latter attempts to pass as his fellow-believer.

For example, a foreign Jew is never admitted to the native synagogue; also, marriages between the native and foreign Jews occur very rarely. The "Kipta" despises the white Jew. He considers him corrupt, inferior, and of lower social rank, a feeling that finds its explanation in the Russian laws for the Jews. The free nomad does not want to recognize a Czar's Jew, without any rights, as his brother in faith.

With their neighbours, the Mohammedans and Christians, on the contrary, they live in the best imaginable relations, as far as it is possible with the constant small marauding expeditions. Very often the so-called blood-brotherhood occurs. A Jew and a Mohammedan exchange weapons; then each slits the left arm of the other and sucks blood from the wound. After this ceremony they are called "Karadaschlar", are considered brothers, and are treated as such. Until not long ago it was still customary to lead the new brother to one's mother, who gave him the breast as a symbol of admission into the family. Now this custom is seldom observed. Once it happened that a Mohammedan clan of three thousand—the Andi clan—closed a pact of blood-brotherhood with the Jews.

Polygamy is widespread among the "Kipta"; it occurs among them even more often than among the Mohammedans. But usually there are only two or three women who have the same husband. The household is then always separated; the women live in different houses far apart from each other. Unmarried men are despised by the Jews just as by the Mohammedans, and are not looked upon as full-fledged members of the community. They are also prohibited from carrying weapons.

The "Kipta" are very pious, obey all the precepts of their religion, but have taken over, besides, all the superstitions of the neighbouring Mohammedans, Christians, and idol-worshippers. Strange to say, the Mohammedans regard them as former Moslems, who became Jews through some "error", therefore, too, the name "Kipta", signifying "those who err". Beys and khans even today strive to set the erring ones on the right path, for which they would receive the title of sheik and the dignity of village elder. However, the contrary often happens, Christian and Mohammedan clans becoming Jews.

The insurrection of these Jews, which set the whole Kuba district ablaze, was an event that would have taken its usual course in normal times. In an onset of insanity, a Jew named Baba-Ogly began to throw silver coins from the roof of his hut down to the street. A crowd of Mohammedans and Jews gathered in front and eagerly collected the money. Naturally a fight soon started, in the course of which the house of Baba-Ogly was plundered. Since, after the revolution, not a single government official, not a single soldier remained in the entire district, the natural consequence of this event was that on the next day the Jews robbed a Mohammedan house. In the course of a week the whole region was in flames. Mohammedans attacked the Jewish clans, and robbed them of fat sheep and girls. Jews attacked the Mohammedans, and both parties together attacked the Armenians, who soon had to suffer most.

For months anarchy reigned in Kuba. All fought against all. No one let this favourable opportunity slip by.

The communist government made a few attempts to send government troops to Kuba; but the combatants then united and drove home the troops, which were not particularly eager for battle. The inhabitants of Kuba just wanted to be left alone and not to have their pleasure spoiled by anyone. This situation in Kuba—the few Europeans who lived there had long since fled—would have lasted even longer, if a telegram had not come from Moscow, from Lenin personally. It read as follows:

"Have heard that persecutions of the Jews are going on in Kuba. The revolutionary proletariat must put an end to this medieval condition."

Thereupon the search for a suitable leader began in Baku. No one wanted to venture to Kuba, for, in any case, even if the revolt were suppressed, the leader would be decried as an anti-Semite. Besides, the probability of success in view of the generally known courage of the Kuba people was very slight. But something had to be done, for the original idea of distributing communist hand-bills in Kuba, with the exhortation to be calm, could really have none but a theoretical value. Daily communists were insulted in public meetings because of Kuba. In the morning one found on the house wall, written in coal: "What is going on in Kuba?" and similar sneers.

My father, who generally had nothing to do with the communists, remonstrated with the new authorities about the situation in the Jewish villages, with the result that he was offered, in all seriousness, the position of Governor-General of Kuba. "If you are so sorry for the "Kipta" said the communists, "then take our soldiers and suppress the pogroms."

At last the decision was reached to entrust the fate of Kuba to a Jew, an Armenian, and a Mohammedan, a triumvirate of communists. As troops they were given Russian sailors, who might be considered impartial.

Nevertheless, weeks passed before the three commanders-in-chief succeeded in introducing the Soviet regime there; and even then they

succeeded only officially, for in spite of the suppression of the disturbances—in which at times very brutal means were used—the communists did not dare to leave the city of Kuba and to make peace among the
clans which were scattered throughout the country. Fundamentally the
province remained as good as independent during the communist
reign, and it was left to its own statesmanship. That, of course, resulted
in utter confusion.

In spite of this, the government in Baku soon telegraphed to
Moscow:

"The revolutionary proletariat has suppressed the pogroms with a
hand of steel. Red Kuba sends greetings to the leaders of the world revolution."

CHAPTER 14

THE FLIGHT

For months we lived under the rule of the communists and Armenians; our friends and followers had long been beyond the border, in Turkey, in Persia, or Turkestan, from which we could expect help. We, who had stayed in the city, also did our best, conspired with our remaining followers, built up connections with the neighbouring countries, and attended to propaganda. At that time the communists themselves were uncertain of their power. The Cheka did not work well enough yet; general instructions from Moscow came but rarely.

The possibility of combating the communists still existed. Revolts raged throughout the country; there were battles in every village; and only the Armenian population, for whom indeed there was no alternative, conducted themselves with loyalty towards the new authorities. In the city, however, not only the Armenians and communists ruled, but also hunger, true Oriental hunger, of which even the war-conditions in Germany can give no conception. In this it was not merely a matter of a scarcity of provisions, but simply the non-existence of everything eatable; the bazaars had been swept clean. For weeks it had been impossible to buy anything that might have resembled food at all. For right behind the city, behind the district of the oil-derricks, the domains of the rebels started, of the "bands", as they were called, who prevented the importation of any provisions. Even the farmers refused to supply the city. What was going on at the other shores of the Caspian Sea remained unknown. No merchant from Persia or Turkestan was prepared to sell provisions to the government of Baku. Every day reeling figures could be seen, faces swollen with hunger; people fell in the streets, nobody paying the slightest attention to them. In the morning one could find emaciated corpses at the entrances of strange houses. Only the government and the government troops possessed just enough provisions not to die of starvation. We, too, in spite of all connections which we had in the interior, could hunt up but little food. Our diet was curious; it consisted mainly of sweetish camel meat, peanuts from which bread was prepared, raisins, and—caviar in unlimited amounts. Caviar was the only edible on hand in the city; the finest, dearest caviar in the world was distributed on the streets. For weeks I ate nothing but nut-bread and caviar. Ten years have passed since then, but even now I still become nauseated when I see caviar exhibited in the shop-windows of Berlin.

Worse than the hunger was the life in the Bolshevik oil-city. Militarism reigned. Daily parades were organized in the large square in front of our house. Tattered soldiers marched through the streets barefoot, sang newly coined revolutionary songs and abused the passers-by. Daily there were revolutionary meetings, in which Armenian commissioners exhorted the hungry people to the last battle against their exploiters—the khans, the beys, and oil-sharks. Since I had nothing to do, I regularly took part in these meetings, sang the Internationale, quoted Lenin, and fought against the oil-sharks.

The meetings were conducted by Armenian communists, who also appeared as speakers. Sometimes younger communists who had rendered service to the revolution also took the floor. Among the latter a nineteen-year-old Armenian boy, who was unusually capable of rattling off startling nonsense, attracted attention. At that time he was still lean, modest, and stupid; he did not become clever and fat until later, when he, Comrade Mikoian, had become Stalin's private secretary, Minister of the Interior of the union, and second most powerful man in Russia. Many suspicious people became communists at that time. A former inmate of a lunatic asylum, for example, who became Minister of War, seriously made the suggestion of electing a donkey to the government as representative of the oppressed animals. The care of the public welfare was given to a well-known procurer, and an illiterate, a sailor, supervised the schools. A relative of mine also became a communist leader, to the indignation of our family. He often visited us, and my father once asked him why just the most impossible people were in the government. "Because no one else will join us," answered our relative. "If you wish, we will name you Minister of Finance tomorrow."

But my father would not. Such suggestions were not scarce. The commissioners ran about the city, looked up the "oil-sharks" and offered them the best positions in "The First Soviet Republic of the East". Of course, no one accepted, which again was called the "sabotage of capital". As yet they did not dare to arrest the leaders of the old regime, though this was being done in Russia. The workmen threatened with strikes in that case; therefore for the time one was content with insults, threats, and announcements of victory from the front, which began behind the city. The strangest thing of all was that no one knew at first against whom he was fighting. The government itself did not know and simply called the unknown opponent "bands". Only some time later was it discovered that the mysterious bands were under the leadership of Kress von Kressenstein, the German general. Gradually the revolution began to develop, and it showed in the growing restlessness and the increasing uncertainty. The general mood during this period of the revolution may be gathered from an example. Opposite our house was situated the largest jewellery store of the city. The shop was on the ground floor; on the first floor lived the jeweller and his family. Of course the place had steel doors which were locked and bolted each evening. One night—I happened to be sleeping on the roof of our house because of the heat—I heard loud curses and the clear sound of striking metal from the street. I looked down and saw a dozen armed people making the greatest effort to break into the shop with iron bars and hammers. The windows were closed tightly, but I saw the proprietor standing on the roof of the house and gazing down at the street. I awakened my father, who told a servant to notify the police. At the corner he met a revolutionary guardian of the peace, who also seemed to be observing the incident. When the servant informed him of his suspicions regarding the questionable activity of the dark figures, the policeman said: "They want to break into the jewellery shop. That does not concern us at all. They are surely armed, and it will be best for the jeweller not to pay any attention. After all, life is more precious than stones." Until early in the morning the robbers worked at the steel doors, none daring to interfere. When they gave up, failing to break or penetrate the protecting doors, they angrily fired a few shots into the air and, cursing, left the scene. This time the treasures of the jeweller were saved.

From day to day the restlessness grew; even in broad daylight it was endangering one's life to appear on the street. We were afraid of the government, and the government, in its turn, was afraid of us. Each overestimated the strength of his opponent. Then the government, after lengthy telegraphing back and forth to Lenin, decided to follow Russia's example and for a start to arrest "ten former blood-suckers" and shoot them. The list was determined during a night meeting, and the arrests were made on the following day. My father was one of the ten. Our relative—the communist—took part in the night meeting. Immediately after the meeting, thus even before the arrests began, he hurried to us and informed my father of the decision of the government. It was about three o'clock in the morning, when I was awakened and had to prepare for flight with my father. We decided to go alone and to leave the servants, women, and children behind. First of all, they were threatened with no danger, and secondly, stealthy flight with a following of thirty people was quite impossible. We had no time to pack anything, and left the house without any sort of baggage, in ordinary street clothes, as harmless strollers. Our way led to the harbour where we hoped to find some sailing-boat piloted by countrymen. We hired a tiny boat for ourselves with the excuse that we were exhausted by the heat and wanted to cool off on the water, as was the general custom in Baku during the summer. When we had left the harbour my father asked the Mohammedan seaman whether he knew us. It turned out that the seaman had been a sailor on one of our steamers before he had made himself independent. Then my father described our situation to him and said: "If you return to Baku now, the government will reward you; but if you take us to a strange harbour, Allah will reward you, then you will be doing a good deed." In any case, we naturally had revolvers in our pockets to force the men to sail on, if it should be necessary; but it did not come to that. The seaman bowed and said:

"Master, I have eaten your bread. At which part of the coast do you want to land?" That we did no yet know ourselves.

Our pilot was not certain that he would be able to take us to the right spot without fail. Besides, we did not know which governments were in power in the different towns on the Caspian Sea. I wanted to go to Persia, where there were surely no communists; my father, on the other hand, did not want to enter the district of the English occupation. At last we decided to make for the shores of Turkestan, where we hoped to get more detailed information about the situation of the country from the ships which we certainly should encounter.

We landed first at Mardakjany, the summer residence of the oil-princes, near Baku, to procure a supply of water and food; then began our real voyage. Fortunately it was summer, so that we had no fear of storms. On the fourth day the coast of Turkestan appeared. We had no difficulty in ascertaining that we were not far from the city Kizil-Su, which was free from communists, at the entrance of the great desert country of the world-conqueror, Timur. Unhindered we reached the shore.

PART II

ON THE TRACKS OF
THE LAME TIMUR

CHAPTER 15

THE CITY OF THE RED WATER

Only twelve hours at average steamer speed separated us from home, but the great pond which lies between Azerbaijan and Turkestan divides two worlds—the green world of the Transcaucasian steppes and the age-old, dark world of the deserts of the "black and of the red sand".

The city of the red water, Kizil-Su, is situated by the oil and filth-covered waters of the Caspian Sea. It is the most god-forsaken, dirtiest city in the world. High masses of stone rise about it, and from three sides crowd it against the seashore, which steams with heat. In the daytime one cannot go through the streets unshod—they would burn one's feet. Only the camel-drivers dare to bathe in the foul water. In the evening when the sun sets, the masses of stone which enclose the city glow; the heat which they have stored up during the day now sinks in stifling waves of oppression. The camel-drivers, who are indifferent to everything, are the only ones who can sleep. It is horrible, the city of the red water.

Immediately behind the city, behind the thin wall of rocks, the "Kizil-Kum", the desert of red sand, begins. The nomads who inhabit this are narrow-minded, simple savages; they know nothing but their sand and the distant city, "Kizil-Su". And to this dirty city the children of the desert dedicate their hymns and songs of praise: "Thou Pearl of the Desert", "Thou Queen of Cities".

This bastard among cities with ten thousand inhabitants was then a free, sovereign republic with a Social-Democratic government at its head. How these extreme Social-Democrats arrived in the desert of Turkestan, no one could discover. They were just there, like the sun, like the sand, like the rocks. The republican population did not care.

We landed; a government official approached us, and in view of the peril of troublesome foreigners, asked which of the esteemed citizens of the republic knew us personally. The question sounded rather firm. But who in all the world on this scrap of rock could belong to our circle of acquaintances? Several years before, indeed, my father had acquired a few houses in Kizil-Su for reasons which have remained puzzling to me until today. Someone or other took care of these houses and no doubt wrote once every ten years that unfortunately the property brought no rents as yet. My father had never bothered about this property: now he remembered it, and mentioned the name of the manager to the officer, being somewhat surprised when the guardian of the socialistic peace suddenly changed his tone to the humility of a servant. It turned out that our trusty manager had as a secondary occupation the position of republican Minister of Foreign Affairs, and was persona grata in the local political circles.

We told the officer to call him, and admired his alternating facial expressions of diplomatic dignity and eagerness to serve. "Naturally, Sir," he whispered, "the houses are in order. I will also put a dwelling at your disposal immediately, don't worry." Aloud, however, he said, casting a side-glance at the crowd that had gathered about us meanwhile: "Citizens, the free republic, Kizil-Su, greets you and grants you hospitality and protection."

When I think of this scene now, I always regret that no camera-man was at the disposal of the republic. The minister with his civil virtue, the ragged citizens about him, and the officer with his bandit's face should have been immortalized. Unfortunately, I did not think of this at the time. I suddenly felt a pain, which had been unknown to me till then—the bite of a bed-bug. The bug came from the minister's sleeve.

Oh, Turkestan, "Land of my Fathers"!

We established ourselves in the residence which the Minister of Foreign Affairs put at our disposal; but we could not stand it there long. I could not become accustomed to a life among mosquitos and unwashed women. Soon we found a better house; it is deserving of mention.

In my life, I have seen the most varied sleeping-quarters and accommodation. I knew a pastor who had rented a room in a brothel in Odessa because of scarcity of lodgings, and chastely covered his ears when the free corner of the room served the purpose of the house. I have slept on billiard tables; under the belly of a Karabachian donkey; on the humps of a camel; on the desert sand under the open sky; and in a synagogue. Nevertheless, the lodgings into which we moved in Kizil-Su are the most beautiful memory of my youth.

We rented the motion-picture theatre, perhaps the only one between the Caspian Sea and the grave of Timur. The performances, which did not take place any too often even at other times, had to be discontinued, and we settled in the large, cool room which was the only one in the city that had an almost European toilet. Soon, however, difficulties arose.

The people demanded picture-plays. The governing body appeared to us, and, in the name of the people, with a view to possible disturbances, asked for permission to allow this source of public amusement to be used from time to time. We bowed to the will of the people.

CHAPTER 16

THE REPUBLIC KIZIL-SU

The life in the republic of the red water was boring and monotonous. We were cut off from the whole world. At rare intervals some suspicious-looking Turcomans appeared in the city, who related all sorts of fantastic tales about high politics and the last harvest; for example, that the Turks, aided by the Germans, had built a cannon with a range from Constantinople to Baku. The cannon had to be buried half-way in the earth so that it should not recoil to the Mediterranean at each shot. The Sultan already wanted to give the command to fire, but the Sheik-ul-Islam had persuaded him to spare the lives of the Mohammedans in Azerbaijan for the present.

Besides, it was said that in Russia the rye grew from the earth red, because of the great amount of blood spilled, but still was edible; furthermore, that the Soviet government had decided to introduce the harem and the Islamic prohibition of alcohol into Russia.

That was the news service of the republic Kizil-Su. The government consisted of foreigners, of a few Russians, Persians, Armenians, and Georgians, who had seized control of the power. The natives did not worry about the politics of their fatherland, which they were willing enough to leave to anyone, even, for example, to the only European, the representative of the white race, who had his residence in Kizil-Su.

This single European was, strange to say, a German, and indeed a hundred per cent, genuine German, who bore the proud name, Baron von Osten-Sacken, and so was Baltic. Why this man lived in voluntary exile in Kizil-Su I still do not know; I only know that he, this sole cultured person, without being bound to the place in any business way, spent thirty years in retirement in this nest with his German wife. He did not associate with any "coloured" person and seldom left his house, in which, on the wall above the desk, hung the Gothic inscription: "May God protect this home."

When I visited him, he told me about Germany, but never spoke of the city of Kizil-Su or Turkestan, as if this country in which he had been living for thirty years did not exist for him at all. I was afraid of him, and used to prefer to occupy myself with the politics of the government. Shortly before our arrival the republic declared war on another republic situated somewhere beyond the desert, whose dominion, was unknown to the government itself. At the front from five to six hundred mercenaries were fighting with a like number of mercenaries of the opponent; neither side, fighting for the freedom of all mankind, would hear of peace.

A tacit agreement on both sides ensured that not much blood should be spilled. When an officer from Kizil-Su lost his life one day during an attack on the enemy, the indignation was so great that it almost led to a real war. Words could hardly be strong enough to censure the opponent who had murderously sent an honourable republican officer to his death during the execution of his professional duty at the front.

Unfortunately these idyllic conditions soon changed.

The main worry of the government was the question of finances. Money, that is, real money, the government did not possess. At the edge of the city indeed there were alabaster quarries, but first of all they had belonged to my father, and secondly, because of the scarcity of purchasers—Azerbaijan was closed off—nothing could be brought in. The income of the government consisted of Persian furs, which were taken from the nomadic clans and delivered to the Persian merchants for ammunition and bread. For domestic commerce paper money was printed on the only printing-press in the country. Since ink had to be saved, the front side of this paper money showed the crest of the republic, the indication of the value, and the inscriptions, "The state guarantees" and "Forgeries are punishable ..."; the other side was white and I used it for scribbling satiric poems.

And yet enterprising people were to be found who considered this money worth forging. The forged notes were printed in Persia, and could not be distinguished from the genuine ones. To put an end to this impossible situation, the Minister of Finance issued a statement with the help of which one could distinguish the true banknotes from the false ones without further difficulty.

The decree stated: "Dampen the suspected note with water. If the colour does not fade the banknote is forged." The genuine banknote lost its hue immediately upon contact with any sort of liquid. That sounds fantastic, but it is true. The false banknotes were better made than the true ones, which the state guaranteed.

Moreover, the banknote with colour that can be washed out was by no means the most ludicrous thing.

At the same time the Russian robber chieftain, Machno, who ruled a region of the size of Germany in South Russia, printed paper money which bore the amiable inscription: "Good forgeries are permitted and will be accepted by the government." Little Father Machno was an anarchist and could not manage to prohibit any "free action", even if it were forgery of money. In Siberia the big merchants printed private paper money in times when notes were scarce. On the front of these notes the face and signature of the merchant in question were usually reproduced. Above the signature was written: "Guaranteed with my entire private fortune." The back bore the inscription: "I will prosecute forgeries with my own means." The "own means" were also portrayed; they were usually two large fists of the merchant and grim faces of the employees of his house. This money enjoyed great popularity.

In a Moscow museum, paper money could formerly be seen that had been distributed by fugitives from the prison during their flight. These notes had the following text: "I, the thief Iwan, have forged this three-rouble note to buy myself vodka and sausage." The illiterate peasants of Siberia gladly accepted this money, too. So the accomplishments of the Minister of Finance in Kizil-Su are by no means the peak of wisdom in financial politics. Personally, however, I paid little attention to the financial achievements of the republic, but occupied myself with the inspection of this unique desert city.

The population of Kizil-Su—nomads who had become rich, Sart merchants, begging dervishes, and people for whom one can name no occupation at all—led a life which bordered on idiocy. Nowhere, either in Europe or the Orient, have I experienced anything comparable. The place was cut off from the whole world, though at other times, as Turkestan's only seaport connection with the Caspian, it kept in touch with civilization. But now for weeks no steamers came. The only one which happened to enter the harbour was detained by the government for any emergency. Only the tiny Turcoman boats sometimes sailed off to Persia. The cities in the interior of the land belonged to a hostile government. A few oases and nomad tribes of the desert formed the dominion of the new republic. I found one amusement in Kizil-Su that the revolution did not destroy: the buck-fights which took place every week on Friday in the square in front of the government building. In Europe bull-fights are known, in North Africa cock-fights, in India one is acquainted with the elephant-fights at the courts of the maharajas. In Turkestan there are no elephants, cocks are expensive, and the bulls weakly; therefore buck-fights have been customary for thousands of years, in the absence of other amusements. In Turkestan the ram is fat, stupid and above all cowardly; he has long, bent horns, which serve solely as ornament. He fights with his forehead, which is apparently impenetrable. The fight goes on in the following manner: Two rams are led to the middle of the square. The owners make speeches before the people, in which they praise the qualities of their animals. Bets are made; the high clergy and members of the government are present; the suspense grows. The rams stand quietly in the middle of the circle and contemplate each other with kind, stupid eyes. At last someone begins to encourage them to battle; they are pushed towards each other, screamed at, scolded. The rams run around in a circle, and each persistently avoids his opponent. The crowd begins to rage. Finally the animals run at each other; but shortly before the collision they stop short, shake their heads, and return to their owners. They refuse to start the fight. Often red-hot iron spikes must be brought, with which they are singed on the leg. Not until then, mad with fear and pain, do they begin to fight. Soon their foreheads are bleeding; still they run at each other, shake their horns, and bleat. Very rarely does the fight end with the death of the opponent. When things become too bad, one of the animals usually struggles through the crowd and, fleeing, leaves the field of honour. The victor is decorated with wreaths and flowers.

Except for the rare motion-picture exhibitions, that is the only entertainment of the people of Kizil-Su.

Years later I saw prize-fights in the Sportpalast in Berlin. Involuntarily I thought of the fights at the Caspian Sea.

CHAPTER 17

THE STORY OF THE TWENTY-SIX

The republic Kizil-Su no longer exists today. It disappeared in the revolution with many other new states, and its territory now belongs to the Soviet republic Tadjikistan, which is hardly more fit to live than Kizil-Su. Most of the republics of that eventful time are forgotten; no one recollects their past glamour or fame. Kizil-Su, on the contrary, is not forgotten.

Once a year, in the whole territory of the U.S.S.R., this republic is lifted from its oblivion and ceremoniously condemned, to be forgotten afterward for another year. Every workman, every unionist, every party-member in U.S.S.R. knows the republic Kizil-Su (in Russian: Krasnovodsk, today: Türkmenbashi), knows "the crime of the socialist of Kizil-Su", knows the bloody story of the twenty-six who fought for Marx and met their death in the sand of the red desert. These twenty-six are avenged today; monuments are erected to their memory; thousands were killed for them in Kizil-Su and Baku; every single one received a biographer and a place of honour in the pantheon of the "Red heroes and martyrs".

I was in Kizil-Su on that warm winter day when the fine nose of the Prince Alania scented the twenty-six. I was the first to be notified of their arrival, and I recall the cold night in the desert when twenty-six shots drew a bloody line under a chapter in the history of the greatest of all revolutions.

As perhaps the only impartial one who remained alive, I may tell the story here:

As the reader probably knows, in March, 1918, twenty-six Armenian and Caucasian communists seized the control in Azerbaijan after a cruel massacre These twenty-six were members of Stalin's famous body of followers, the Transcaucasian Activists, who terrorized the whole Caucasus in the years 1917–18. Actually there were twenty-seven of them. The twenty-seventh, the Armenian Mikgan, survived by chance and later became dictator of Armenia and leader of the Cheka of the Caucasus.

When the German-Turkish troops occupied Azerbaijan, the communistic government shut itself up in Baku, where it could rely on about 100,000 men. The Transcaucasian Activists, these most intimate friends and assistants of Stalin and Lenin, soon proved themselves to be bad labour-leaders. Vain were the appeals which Lenin wrote to "the proletariat of Baku", vain the greetings which the government sent to the first "Soviet of the East"; the workers turned away from the "Liberators of the East", as the twenty-six were called in the official reports. While Baku was already being besieged by German-Turkish troops, the revolt of the trade unions against the communists began in the beleaguered city.

The twenty-six leaders, who were no longer sure of their lives as a result of the siege, left their adherents and took refuge on a steamer that was to convey them to Russia. Officially it is now said that they wanted to make themselves secure for the sake of the world proletariat; at that time, in everyday language, it was called "desertion".

The ship with the communist government aboard steamed off; the twenty-six sang the Internationale and ordered the sailors to steer their course to the mouth of the Volga. However, the Red sailors, the nucleus of the Soviet power, suddenly refused to obey the command of the government. They did not want to return north to the great Soviet country; they did not want to offer their help to the bleeding, starving, murdering Volga-Soviet. For the twenty-six who sailed to meet their fate, cowering together in the dark cabins of the freighter, freezing and trembling, this meant a death sentence. Except for the coast of Azerbaijan, except for the mouth of the Volga, only two coasts came into consideration: the coast of Persia, which was occupied by the British, and the sandy harbour of Kizil-Su.

At that time, in 1918, the English, especially in the colonies, were frankly opposed to the communists, particularly if they belonged to the Oriental race. Pity, or even mere imprisonment, could not be counted on. The entire dialectic of Marxism was now employed to persuade the sailors at least to choose the harbour of Kizil-Su, if they absolutely refused to go to Russia. It still might be expected of the grotesquely uninformed government there, that they would pay no especial attention to the arrival of the twenty-six commissioners. The sailors allowed themselves to be persuaded. In fact they were no opponents of Marxism; they just did not want to go to the Volga. They were ready to sail to Kizil-Su, and they even took the fleeing Marxists under their protection. The twenty-six commissioners were put on sick beds, covered with bandages, and entered in the ship's list as wounded sailors. The steamer steered its course towards the glorious capital of the water.

In the republic of the red water there was only one man who deserved the title of ruler—the mister of Police, Prince Alania, a Georgian who for years had voluntarily placed his fine instinct at the service of criminology. He hated the communists for three reasons: firstly, as an extreme Social-Democrat; secondly, as a prince; thirdly, as a Georgian who could not forget his communistic countrymen's "betrayal of the war of liberation". It is strange that, although only twenty-four hours separated Azerbaijan from Kizil-Su, the communists were ignorant of the fact that Alania, the notorious Alania, was Minister of Police in the land of the red water.

We—the prince and I—were standing on the seashore, when the oil-transport steamer appeared behind the island along the coast. "A steamer from Azerbaijan," said Alania.

Immediately he put the prehistoric machinery of the republican custom and coast-guard into operation. At first I thought that some refugees from the communist city might be on the steamer—no one yet knew of the *coup d'état* of the unions; therefore I suggested that I should be the first to board the vessel in order to receive from my countrymen, whom I hoped to find there, the latest news from the scene of the German-communist war. Alania accompanied me. To our amazement we found not one single fugitive on the steamer. The sailors who received us explained that they themselves had fled from Baku from the communists with wounded comrades and, for the present, till the recovery of the wounded, wished to remain in the port. Then they showed us their companions in battle, who were bandaged up to their eyes. They pretended that they knew nothing definite of the outcome of the fighting in Azerbaijan. Without putting any further questions, we left the boat.

On shore, when I wanted to take my leave, the prince looked at me, smirking, and said: "Do you know who is on that steamer? The communist government of Azerbaijan!"

Two hours after her arrival, the whole military power of the republic appeared. The steamer was searched, the Bandages torn off the "wounded comrades"; the twenty-six had to leave their last place of refuge in chains. I saw them being marched off; I accompanied them as far as the stinking hole called the state prison. When the door closed behind them, I remained standing at the wall and listened; suddenly I heard dull sounds. One blow after another followed pitilessly, unceasingly, the horrible thud of the butt-end of a gun; then I heard, at first softly, then louder and louder, the crying and screaming of the people who were being beaten. The preliminary examination began. Three hours later I met Alania. He smiled and rubbed his hands.

"What will become of the communists?" I asked. "Still uncertain," he answered; "perhaps a funeral at the expense of the state."

In the evening it became known that the government had decided to dispatch the fugitive government into the interior of the country and deliver them to the English or even to the Russians at a suitable opportunity.

But things turned out differently. Late at night, when we were sleeping in our cinema-dwelling, there was a knock at the door. Prince Alania entered; his expression was serious but satisfied.

"Do you want to come with us?" he asked.

"Where to?"

"Into the desert; we are all going, the government, fifty soldiers, and I. A place is reserved for you too."

"What are we going to do in the desert?"

Alania's face became solemn; he bent down and spoke softly: "The twenty-six will be executed today. You want to be there, don't you?"

My father jumped up. "You are crazy," he shouted. "Send them back to Russia. What else have we to do with them?"

Aiania shrugged his shoulders, but remained polite, "I need their blood. I thought you would be the first to welcome this deed. The twenty-six have earned death a hundredfold."

He went. Naturally I could not fall asleep again. I silently condemned my father; for were not the twenty-six the inciters of the Azerbaijanian massacre? At that time I considered unwillingness to kill a weakness. Not until later did I realize that murdering and not murdering mean neither strength nor weakness. For most people it is merely a simple movement of the body, for few hard to execute, and only in exceptional cases impossible for anyone.

At that time I was still young and had never yet seen an execution; I have seen dozens since. Then, however, I was curious. Unnoticed, I crawled out through the window and ran to the prison. I was in time. The condemned—who could only guess the verdict—were being led out, one behind the other, handcuffed, each between two armed natives. Most of them were pale but calm. They had been rulers long enough to know what such a nocturnal deportation meant in the Orient. Only one—he was a relative of mine—did not want to go; the soldiers had to drag him by the collar like a steer to the butcher. Every three steps he stood still, and said monotonously, distractedly, dully: "I won't—I won't—I won't." I can still hear those soft words today, their tortured, no longer human, almost beast-like sound.

I did not ride into the desert. I lost all liking for it. Later I found out how the twenty-six had to dig their own graves in the sand, and how one after the other was shot and thrown in.

Until the early morning I ran through the streets of the city. When the sun rose, I stood in front of Alania's house. A lamp was still lighted in his room; he was sitting at the table writing. I knocked at the window.

"To whom are you writing, Prince?"

"To my little bride. She is in Persia; I want her to come here. I should like to celebrate the wedding as soon as possible." Suddenly he sighed deeply and added : "She is the best girl in the world, small and dainty. I wonder if she still loves me?"

The wedding did not take place. Two years later in Daghestan he fell into the hands of the wild mountain tribes, who happened to be communists. They cut open his belly, put sand and stones in, and sewed it together again.

Dead also are all those who were connected with the murder of the twenty-six, even the sailors of the steamer; also their brothers, cousins, and friends. They all died in the revolution. They were killed by the bullets of the Red troops, which later came

from the north.

They lie in the sand like the twenty-six.

CHAPTER 18

THE MONARCHIST "COUP D'ÉTAT"

About a hundred years ago the desert of the red sand belonged to the khan of the Teke people; the Teke are nomads, who, like all nomads, recognize only the power of the father of the family. The chief khan of this very numerous nation was an esteemed, but in no case omnipotent ruler, who stepped forth as leader of the people only on rare occasions of danger, at the attack of hostile troops. A hundred years ago the last khan of the Teke was captured by Russians and taken to St. Petersburg, where the Czar allowed him an annuity as a guardian of the monarchial principle.

The people of the Teke, however, forgot their khan, as nomads forget everything that does not particularly stimulate their fantasy. The flight and imprisonment of one of their khans was an everyday experience, hardly remembered after a hundred years. The son and grandson of the last khan had grown up in Russia, strange to their people, and even in their own country aroused merely the moderate attention which is given to everything exotic.

Now they suddenly appeared in Kizil-Su—the son and the grandson, who still bore the title of the Khan of Teke. No one paid any attention to them, least of all their former subjects, who had substituted an imported republic for the monarchy of their fathers. Not even the government took notice of their sojourn, although a few of the ministers were soon on good terms with the khan, who conducted himself very modestly and amiably.

The nation of the Teke, who were peacefully raising their sheep in the desert, gave little thought to their legitimate potentate. When the khan travelled to any oasis, fat wethers were offered to him—just as to every other stranger; a few especially shy people no doubt kissed the hem of his silk chalatt, which they also liked to do to others. However, the dispassionate nomads wanted to know nothing of his monarchistic plans, about which he tried to speak to influential tribal chieftains.

"The times are hard," they said; "everywhere people are fighting. One does well to withdraw quietly to the steppes."

The khan, who in the hurly-burly of the revolution had lost his sense for realities, would not renounce his throne. He only changed the scene of his activity. "The bearer of the political power is the army," he said to himself. From that time on, with touching unselfishness, he began to take an interest in the life and activity of the republican troops. Soon he discovered the most heartfelt longing of the modest desert children. It was for red trousers: trousers of some bright red material, that seemed to the nomads to be an indispensable part of military dignity. For red trousers they were prepared to sell their fatherland, to recognize the khan, perhaps even to accomplish deeds of real heroism. The government also knew their wish, but could not fulfil it, as the red cloth that was still to be had in the country would have sufficed for only a third of the troops. The necessarily unjust distribution of the cloth would have led inevitably to a civil war. So this much-disputed material was conveyed to the coast-island Chaleken, and kept there temporarily in the storerooms of the government.

Chaleken, which is about fifteen minutes from Kizil-Su, belonged to the Azerbaijanian oil-magnate, Gadschi, who lived somewhere in Persia; his investments had depreciated during the revolution. He himself had no interest in the swampy island where the presence of oil was uncertain.

The Khan of Teke was attracted by the stores of the island, which contained the material and therefore also the ardently longed-for crown. With his son and a few friends, he removed to Chaleken, where the first preparations for the *coup d'état* were made. During the night the pretender to the crown sneaked to the storerooms, broke into them, took part of the red material, and carefully locked the door of the state-chambers behind him. No one had noticed this act, so dangerous to the state. With the greatest speed the trousers were now finished by His Highness in person. One day when a rather large squad of the government troops were billeted at Chaleken in passing, the grotesque *coup d'état* began. The khan put on his most expensive silk gown, wound a snow-white turban about his head, and appeared before the troops accompanied by his friends, who dragged along the sacks filled with the trousers. The khan made a speech, talked about his high-born ancestors, about the art of governing which he had learned in Russia, the holy war, and the decadence of the world today. In conclusion, he quoted a few verses from the Koran in Arabic, which were to make a particular impression on the shy mind of his listeners. When his stock of rhetoric was exhausted, he began with the main subject. As khan with a fatherly love for the people, he promised to respect even their slightest wish, and was already bestowing on his faithful troops as a proof of this—the longed-for red trousers. This address was effective. In no time the republican convictions and the achievements of the revolution were forgotten. The troops threw off their blue trousers and delighted themselves with the long-desired symbol of monarchy, the red trousers of the khan. The government officials, who had hurried to the scene, were arrested, and the khan was proclaimed autocratic monarch of Chaleken.

Thus happened the monarchist plot, which, however ludicrous it may seem, did not differ fundamentally from other upheavals in the world. I have experienced the fall of many a government, seen many an overthrow, and could never get rid of the feeling that in each revolution some sort of red trousers were at the root of the matter.

At first, when the news of the upheaval spread in Kizil-Su, people did not want to take it seriously. But when they heard what an impression the bestowal of the red trousers had made on the troops, when they considered that the entire government stock of red material was now in the hands of the monarch, they began to be seriously disturbed. A meeting of the cabinet was hastily called, in which the fate of the republic was discussed. As my father and I were very much interested in maintaining peace in the city, we attended this historic gathering. It turned out that the condition of the republic left much to be wished for. The situation at the front was not gratifying. The republic was still carrying on war for the liberty of mankind. The troops could not be depended upon after the *coup d'état* of the khan. The treasury of the government was empty, the importation of provisions unorganized. The Minister of Foreign Affairs held the floor; in his address, teeming with socialistic catchwords which were incomprehensible to me, he suggested the customary procedure in such cases—to ask a neighbouring government for assistance under certain conditions. The suggestion could have but one interpretation. It could only be a matter of the English troops which then occupied all Persia as far as the shores of the Caspian Sea. But at that time we already belonged openly to the German-Turkish party and did not want in any circumstances to take part in the "appeal to the English".

We left the meeting, the outcome of which had been clear from the very start. After all, we could not take it amiss that the government, in their need, wished to ask for English help without consideration for our own party-membership. The Minister of Foreign Affairs was commissioned to proceed to Persia. Inexcusably—probably for purposes of representation—the whole contents of the government treasury were left in his hands. He went to Persia and appealed to the English, but never returned. The treasures of the government were modest, but for him they sufficed. Even before the English troops had left the Persian harbour, we began to equip ourselves for the journey. Nevertheless we still suffered from the breakdown of the monarchy of Chaleken. A few dozen English soldiers came into the territory of the Khan of Teke. Under their escort was an authorized agent of the oil-magnate, Gadschi, the rightful owner of the island. The khan had to flee; the private owner was reinstated in his rights, and if it had not been for the revolution, would have been able to continue to exploit the oil-riches of the island. This private owner and the heir-apparent who was driven out by him were bitter enemies then—as rivals. Later they were reconciled. Ten years after, I saw them both sitting at a table in the *Café de la Paix* in Paris, chatting with a fat Englishman. For a fantastic price, the oil-magnate offered to sell to the Englishman the entire oil constructions of Chaleken. For a much smaller price the khan also wanted to put all his claims to the throne, together with his possible subjects, at the disposal of the Englishman. That is what we all wanted at that time ...

Our departure was delayed; we did not know ourselves what course to choose. We did not dare to linger in Kizil-Su under the doubtful protection of England. In Azerbaijan the revolt of the rabble was raging. We could not reach the regions in the west which were occupied by German-Turkish-Azerbaijanian troops, so we decided to travel into the interior of the desert, through the republican front, to reach Samarkand first—the seat of our family—and then the court of the Emir of Bucharia, where we had many friends. About the conditions in the country we knew nothing definite; the news was contradictory. Only one thing was certain, that the only railroad in Turkestan was occupied by disorganized bands who made communication impossible. These bands, members of the former railroad unions, were the only ones in the country who were familiar with the management of the railway, and terrorized the whole region about the line. They overthrew the governments, interfered in all questions of administration, and were a true plague of the population. Their members consisted of skilled workmen, who, in spite of the incredible conditions, kept up the communications at least for their purposes. As all the oil-wells were shut down for the time, the railway was in danger of being stopped. In Russia, in such cases, one resorted to wood-firing; at some part of the journey passengers usually had to alight and saw wood in some nearby forest under the supervision of the conductor. The whole trip took place with the slogan: "Who does not work, cannot ride". Since there are practically no forests in Turkestan, the railway-men had to discover other means.

It was decided to fire the locomotive with dried fish. The dried and salted fish, which are hard as stone and which no European stomach can digest, existed in Turkestan in great quantities. They were confiscated by the railway management and turned out to be quite fit for raising steam in the boiler. A few even claim to have seen the chimney of the locomotive throw out *en route* fat roasted fish, which were consumed by the starving population of the country. I personally never noticed it, but consider even that possible.

We did not want to trust ourselves to these vicious railway-men and their fish, and therefore decided, as conservative politicians, to choose the way which, though somewhat out of date, was less dangerous for us personally—the route by caravan. The wild tribes of the desert, the sandstorms, the seasickness on the humps of camels, the great thirst, were all to be preferred to the railroad, not to mention the fact that our planned flight over the front could succeed only with the help of the nomads.

For me this venture into the desert was a great joy; though it became less attractive during the ride, I longed for variety. The journey of several months, which took us through the desert, oases, and cities of Turkestan and Persia, started from west to east through Aschkau-Abad, Merv, Samarkand, then to the south to Bucharia, and in the end over the border of Persia, and north to the port of Enzeli on the Caspian Sea.

Seldom during the journey could we use the railroad. By far the greatest part we had to cover on camels or even on donkeys. We avoided the larger cities as much as possible where the influences of the communists made conditions unsafe. In the wilderness, under the protection of the "robber bands", which were feared in the city but were in truth rather peaceful native clans, we felt safer.

The nornads and "savages" dwelling there knew us, or had at least heard of us; in speech and religion, too, we were close to them after all. In various regions, where neither we nor our families were known, our arrival was announced by the messengers of our friends, which immediately secured for us the best reception that can be imagined. This hospitality of the desert helped me above all to endure the almost unbearable difficulties and hardships.

The desert is boring, infinitely poor in events and adventures, and offers new and unexpected things only to the stranger. I was a stranger, yet its charms soon disappeared for me, and I recognized its true, unveiled nature, its tediousness, melancholy and suffering, derived from hunger, work, and disease. Therefore, in the following account, I shall not describe chronologically the most wearisome journey of my life; I shall rather portray the details of the desert life, its tribes and customs, the old cities and palaces of Turkestan, the princes, saints, and beggars, as I saw and learned to know them.

CHAPTER 19

THE CONSTITUTION OF THE DESERT

The endless sand-deserts of Turkestan and Persia are not wild regions in which man is delivered powerless to the elements; they may be compared to an orderly establishment. The constitution, the organization of the desert, is known only to the natives, who, merely because of the language, rarely disclose the principles of this constitution to foreigners.

To get lost in the desert, to lose the way once entered upon, is impossible for the nomad; for infinite distances he feels a contact between himself and all the oases and clans. For example, at all times he can determine the position of the caravan exactly through slight changes in the colour of the sand, can even discern events which have taken place a short time before. I have seen experienced caravan leaders who lost their way among a few houses in Kizil-Su and yet were able when looking at the surface of the desert to read it as an open book. The caravan leader, the "Chalwadar", is really the ruler of the desert; he knows all its secrets, knows its moods, feels safer in the ocean of sand than the European within his four walls, and can be replaced by nothing, not even an aeroplane. This "desert expert" is to be compared with no man; even among the nomads he occupies a special position and is prepared for his profession from early childhood. In my eyes the Chalwadar is hardly human; he possesses more animal than human characteristics. His profession is the peak of human specialization in the sense that, in the course of generations, he has probably replaced several attributes of man with qualities pertaining to animals. To a stranger the caravan leader may sometimes appear to be a magician; to the nomads, who in other cases believe in magic only top gladly, he is merely a well-paid expert, who can be of use to his fellow-beings through experience, schooling, and talent. He always walks ahead of the caravan. Only when the goal of the day's journey is in sight does he take his place of honour on the humps of the first camel. During the journey he is the sole ruler who has control of absolutely everything: the liberty-loving nomads must obey his every command.

In Persia, where our caravan consisted of fifty camels, this supreme position of the leader led to many unpleasant experiences. At that time we were travelling with several Russian families, who wanted to go through Turkestan to Northern Persia. Among them were a few ladies, who, till then, except for the desert scenery of the imperial opera, had seen nothing of the Orient. The fifty camels were tied to each other and surrounded by Turcoman riders as guards. With every five camels came a second in command, who had to report each event, even the smallest, to the Chalwadar. In no case were the camels allowed to slow down the pace, to say nothing of standing still altogether. Thus, if one of the ladies wanted to dismount from the camel, she had to inform the second in command of her wish, giving reasons. Through a Turcoman rider he sent the news of the lady's desire to the Chalwadar, who then usually gave the whole caravan the command to halt. Thereupon the particular second in command had to force the camel to its knees, and the lady could then dismount. The desert is flat, without any vegetation. The fifty camels, the escort, and the fellow-travellers would wait gloomily and patiently till the lady again mounted to her seat.

These are the small vexations of the desert ride. The greater ones, for example the scarcity of water, rarely occur under the guidance of a good Chalwadar. With animal-like instinct the leader can literally smell the presence of water at great distances. At first I thought that he determined the location of the existing well by his knowledge of the section of the country. But I was wrong. The face of the desert changes daily. Where there is a level plain today, hills can rise tomorrow. The caravan leader pays no attention to the exterior appearance of the desert, for all exteriors are deceitful.

I noticed myself that when the supply of water was running low, he stood still a few minutes and turning his face in all four directions breathed in deeply. "I am looking for water," he once explained to me. And he would change the course of the caravan, although the spring was sometimes not reached for several hours. The springs in the desert are sacred, just as the scraggy trees are. In the wars between the clans, water and trees are considered inviolable; girls may be stolen, herds of sheep destroyed, warriors killed, often in the most cruel way; but the spring must be spared. With loathing the nomads still tell the story of some Mongolian chieftain who centuries ago had the springs which were left behind poisoned upon the retreat of his troops, and thus rendered the whole region uninhabitable. The nomad is entirely incapable of comprehending such occurrences; he can accept any act of cruelty, sanction any crime, but not an infringement of this fundamental law of the desert. When any clan permits itself to be so carried away as to make a spring useless, the whole population of the desert rises against the guilty clan until it migrates to another country.

The actual danger of the desert, therefore, is not scarcity of water. Its dangers are sand-pits, hunger, robbers, and snakes. The sand-pits are a terror which the Chalwadar alone can avoid. At a distance he recognizes dangerous places into which the whole caravan might sink. For in a few sections of the desert the sand is too thin to bear the weight of the camels; they would sink into the depths, just as in water. Often whole divisions of troops have disappeared without trace in this manner. There can be no rescue out of such pits. I have seen, as we rode by the edge of a sand-pit, a dog drawn into it and lost. Naturally these pits are not marked in any way, and it is the task of the leader to escape such spots by detours. How he recognizes them is his business, but he does.

I often tried to start a conversation with the Chalwadar. During the pauses for rest I sat next to him, chatted about all sorts of philosophic topics, religion, war, beautiful girls, even literature, in the hope of finding out something from him about his method of guiding. I confess that I did it mainly through fear. I wanted to find a system in his guidance, to be convinced that the Chalwadar's dependability did not rest on chance. The interviews led to nothing. I have rarely seen such inaccessibility and reticence. It seemed as though he really possessed few human characteristics, and vegetated in dull omniscience, his whole attention centred on the desert. Questioned upon his method of recognizing the sand-pits or finding water, he answered, "Anyone can see", or "It's quite simple". Later I found that most Chalwadars really look upon their art as a matter of course, and that their primitive mentality can communicate it only to him who is born to be a Chalwadar like themselves.

The caravan is never dependent on itself. It enjoys the hospitality of the invisible desert people and the foresight of the hundreds of caravan leaders who have travelled on the same route. Unnoticeable marks tell the Chalwadar of the revolts and battles between the nomads, and may force him to change the course. He is the first to find out—God knows how—all the news of the desert. He knows what sheep pass at the horizon and what conclusions he must draw from this. He cares for the nourishment of his own caravan, and also of those that follow which might suffer from the scarcity of bread.

This care for the caravan which may follow is a touching example of the organization of the desert. During the halt in the evening when the flat desert bread was prepared of flour and water, the leader took a few fresh loaves, wrapped them in damp rags, and buried them deep in the sand. Then with a small stake he marked the place for an unknown caravan which might come from afar, lacking food. Such bread, wrapped in damp rags and buried, remains fresh rather long and is a true blessing of the desert. On the journey we continually came across such stakes indicating hidden provisions; sometimes the Chalwadar had them dug out and replaced by fresh ones. Certain signs agreed upon among the leaders are cut on the loaves to announce matters of general interest to the coming Chalwadar in a secret code. This is the newspaper of the desert, no doubt the most curious newspaper of mankind.

The general idea that caravans find their way by bleached human and animal bones is only partly correct. The organization of the desert is too perfect for very many of such signs: inexperienced travellers are usually led astray by these bones. Nothing is more accidental than the place of death of a human being or an animal, and the bones are easily covered or swept away by sand or storms.

A real Chalwadar who has never left the desert and who would be more helpless than a child in the city, has resources in his own element of which few have any inkling. He has his organization of welfare, his newspaper, his experience, and above all his animal instinct, which shows him the way to the distant oasis in the terrible desert gale.

CHAPTER 20

THE PEOPLE OF THE BLACK SAND

How do the nomads live? Like the Saracens of the days of the knights? Like romantic heroes of Kipling? Or like animals without feeling for anything beyond their herd of sheep?

The nomads are wild, diligent, poor, and live in the constant hope of becoming settled some time or other; and if they do not succeed in that, at least of destroying all the cities and villages in the world. The nomad's hatred for the city is rooted mainly in the envy aroused in him by the city-dweller, who accomplishes things which he cannot. Several times the nomads (just a short time ago, the Kirghiz) have handed in a petition to the government in which they declared themselves willing to work at agriculture if land were put at their disposal. Where that was done they have gradually become industrious farmers. They are awkward; they need the city-dweller, even though they are superior to him in some things, in physical fitness, for instance, and in certain enigmatic qualities. Strange to say, the nomad is conscious of his inevitable inferiority, sometimes even too conscious of it, which leads to passivity. He simply does not consider himself capable of escaping the spell of habits thousands of years old. He is ashamed of some customs because he, too, feels that they are barbaric, but does not know how to change.

In a desert camp, where a festival was held in our honour, the inhabitants did not want to kill their sheep in our presence for some time. "Perhaps you will not like it," they said. Not until I answered with an old verse in which I praised the beauties of the desert customs were they reassured—the nomads love poetry. They had reason enough to be shy. The slaughtering is accomplished in an extraordinary way. The sheep is thrown on its back and held fast by several men. The butcher cuts open the animal's belly, puts in his hand, pushes it up to the heart and grasps it. The sight must be horrible to a European. The nomads, however, follow the incident with indifferent glances.

When the sheep is killed, it is cut up into very small pieces, which are roasted on spits. The festival banquet in honour of the guest takes place in the tent, where all the members of the family sit on the floor, forming a circle. When the kettle filled with roasted pieces of meat is brought in, not one of those present moves; nor must the guest be first to taste the food. He must put his hand into the kettle, take out a piece of meat and hold it. The oldest of those present then creeps up on all fours, opens his mouth, into which the guest puts the meat; then swallows the meat, and returns to his seat still crawling. Not until after all the members of the family have been fed by the guest in this manner does the actual feast begin.

Besides mutton, certain fruits, rice, and bread, the ocean of the desert knows only sweets that are imported from the oases. As a drink mare's milk is used, which is fermented and then is an intoxicating beverage, passed round on every opportunity. When a strange rider approaches the tent of a nomad, the owner of the tent offers him a goblet of mare's milk even before he has dismounted. Sitting in the saddle the guest empties the vessel, but must take care that a few drops of the drink fall on the mane of his horse. These drops are licked off the mane by the host, which is an indispensable act of courtesy. Another form of politeness which is often hard for a guest to follow is belching after the meal. The host feels deeply insulted if the custom is disregarded. To him it is a proof that his guest rose from the meal not completely satisfied.

The nomad, who is condemned to spend the greatest part of his life in the fresh air under an open sky, hates both air and sky, and prefers to spend as much time as possible in his tent. The tent is dreadful. Sewed together of some questionable rags, carefully made tight to exclude all ventilation, it is one of the most terrible dwellings of mankind. In the evening the whole family—ten, fifteen or even twenty people—gather in a little tent no larger than a small bedroom. In the middle a fire is built, the smoke having but a scanty outlet through a small opening in the ceiling. On the fire mutton fat is fried or tea is prepared in the most horrible way. A piece of pressed tea—which is regarded as coin in Mongolia—is thrown into the kettle filled with water; then plenty of mutton fat, butter, and salt are added. The mixture must stand on the fire for half an hour, and is consumed with every sign of pleasure. Of course the stuff is totally unpalatable to a stranger. After the varied culinary experiments the air in the tent attains the right chemical composition which makes sleep possible for the nomad. This atrocious atmosphere is a symbol of domesticity to him.

I know a nomad who became rich and erected a palace for himself in Baku. He and his family could not become accustomed to the comfortable bedrooms. Every evening they crept into a small, dirty garret where they all spent the night together. They asserted that the air in the large bedroom was unhealthy. Undressing before sleeping is also an unnecessary luxury. Nevertheless sometimes the nomad of Turkestan will undress and even wash himself, which never happens among his colleagues in Siberia. The Siberian nomad is sewed into his furs and wears them until they fall from his body in rags. Under the legislation of Genghis-Khan it was absolutely prohibited to rid oneself of a dress before that. Washing is also forbidden to the Siberian, for reasons of religion. In the water lives Su-Tengri, the water-god who is insulted by the pollution of the water. According to a law of Genghis-Khan washing in water was punished by death.

The nomad of Turkestan rarely washes himself with water; not for religious reasons but simply because the water is too precious. He washes himself in the sand; he rubs his hands and face with desert sand and then feels cleansed, by all the rules of Oriental hygiene.

In private life these wanderers, the terror of the country, are modest, polite as far as they can be, and almost bashful in association with women, especially their first wives.

The oldest and usually very ugly wife is the mistress of the fiercest robber chieftain. He trembles before her, fulfils her every wish, has his ears boxed by her and takes it as a matter of course. If one asks him why he permits his wife to ill-treat him, he answers good-naturedly: "She beats me because she is clever and because she thinks that I do not love her enough."

The younger women who are sure of the love of their husbands are treated much worse than the older wives. At the meal the young wife must stand with a towel behind the man, who dines with the older woman. Each time the man has put a piece of mutton

with rice into his mouth, he lifts his hand back over his shoulder and has it wiped off by the young wife. The young woman must also do the dirtiest tasks of the household, the argument being that it is what she is loved for. However, a woman is never beaten, neither in the desert nor in the whole Islamic Orient, not even in the case of adultery.

For this the nomads in Southern Turkestan have, besides the customary death penalty, quite unusual methods. If the husband discovers that his wife has committed adultery, he takes her to the oldest woman of the clan who carries through a special ceremony. The woman is declared dead, wrapped in pieces of linen, and laid in the sand in some lonely region. For three days she must "play dead" while the oldest woman unceasingly sings the death lamentation to her. Then she may return to her husband, receive a new name, and be considered pure. Nevertheless the husband has the right to kill the unfaithful wife on the spot.

The birth of a child is also regarded in a strange way. The nomads are convinced that at the birth every woman curses her husband as the cause of her pains and swears never again to have children.

Amends must be made for the sin. After her recovery a wether is killed; the woman pours the blood into a bowl, and with this blood she sprinkles the couch of her husband and children.

The children of the nomad are his riches. The wealth is estimated by the number of sheep and children, for both can be sold—especially the girls. Still, it is considered unfair to ask a particularly high price for one's daughter; that would be usury. According to law, at the sale of a daughter the father may demand the sum that the rearing of the child cost him, and an additional charge for beauty determined by the head of the tribe. If the buyer has a goitre the additional charge is dropped. A man with goitre is marked by Allah and is therefore held in high esteem; one must not extort from him.

Thus the peoples of the desert of the black sand live, thus they have lived for thousands of years. They complain of their poverty, breed their sheep, sell their girls; and if they have the opportunity to slay a stranger who comes uncalled for and without recommendation in the same manner as they kill their sheep—they cut open the belly, put in the hand, and so forth—they are happy.

On the whole, however, they are kind-hearted.

CHAPTER 21

THE ENIGMA OF THE HAKIM

I recall a small oasis in the heart of Turkestan, where I stood barefoot on my father's naked back and danced on it and sang verses. This pastime, however, in no way indicated poor breeding or despotic inclinations which might have awakened in me. On the contrary, people stood at the doorway of the room, looked at my father enviously, and whispered: "What good fortune to have such a son!"

For my questionable gymnastics were nothing but the expression of dutifulness, of sacrifice to the welfare of the inhabitants. I was the hakim, the physician, from whom the population sought aid against the epidemic, the great plague which was worse than the revolution.

In the oasis, in the desert, even in the cities, death reigned. The Spanish flu for which no wise man, no dervish, no khan knew a remedy, had come. When the disease would not stop in spite of all the arts of these people, the people came to us, bringing mutton, rugs, and melons, and begged my father to name some remedy for the influenza. He was a wise man, they said, was highly honoured by the people of distant lands, and must know some secret formula against the flu. My father tried to get out of it, and explained that he was a modest traveller and feared the epidemic himself. The men, however, were not to be turned away so easily. If the illustrious gentleman knew no cure, then his son, who knew the language of the desert, the language, of the city, and even the language of the unbelievers, who, wise as a Hafiz, had penetrated into the depths of learning, must be the saviour of the Moslems. That seemed plausible to my father; he called me and asked if I did not want to prove my wisdom in practice at last. "The people here are dying," he said. "You know many things; perhaps you can really help."

I bowed to the men, touched the ground with my hand, requested them to allow me time to reflect until the next morning. The delegates bowed likewise, and the oldest of them, the mullah with the rosary and red beard, made a speech in which he tried to prove by means of quotations from the Koran that in times of need one Moslem must help the other whatever the circumstances. Then they went. I sat down on the ground and looked questioningly at my father. He also thought that I knew of some remedy.

"But I really don't know any," I asserted.

It finally turned out that even as a hakim my father was wiser than I. "The best cure for fever," he said, "is paprika and running about on the naked back. With these remedies you will protect me and the people from the disease from tomorrow."

And so it happened. Never before had so much paprika been swallowed in the oasis as on that morning when I announced my wisdom; never before had anyone walked about so much upon the backs of the inhabitants. The distinguished citizens and the mullah I had to treat myself, and that was no doubt the most agreeable occupation of my life. I did not hesitate—wasn't it the command of my father?—took off my slippers and danced on the strange backs, received the expressions of thanks, and generously refused presents. Then I watched while my patients ate paprika. Matters became bad only when my father began to try out his wisdom on me in his fear for my health. I let him run on my back but refused to swallow paprika. I did not become ill; nor did I unfortunately get any title of honorary citizen of the oasis.

Apparently my paprika helped, for gradually the epidemic abated. This flu was the only disease with which I had to deal. The native hakims, whose skill must not be underestimated, combat the numerous dangerous diseases of the country. Their ability is really great, especially in the treatment of the illnesses that occur only in Turkestan. Many a European physician studies under them when he wishes to settle in the country. These hakims, who are not to be confused with the ordinary magicians, are among the most interesting people in the Orient. Almost illiterate, they are irreplaceable in all questions of medicine, especially in the treatment of diseases peculiar to the desert; for example, in curing pindinka, the scourge of Turkestan.

Pindinka is a skin disease for which there are no remedies, according to European views. Its cause is unknown. On the skin, generally of the face, small red spots form, which grow for twelve months, always become more numerous, and in one year turn the face into a horrible red mask. The disease is contagious. European physicians do not know how to treat it. Only the native hakim knows a salve, which, if it does not cure the sickness, at least prevents its development. He treats the first red spot, after which no new spots form. The first becomes a small wound that disappears in a year and leaves behind only a deep scar. Pindinka occurs very often and usually attacks the Europeans who live in the cities. I know people who stayed in Turkestan only one day, returned to Europe, and within a week discovered the first red spot, visited the best European physicians, and still could not avoid disfigurement. Pindinka is the terror of the foreign quarters in the cities, for there is no preventive, and at best it leaves behind, as I have said, its scar. It is worst when it starts on the conjunctiva; then the eye is usually lost. The natives of the country regard pindinka as a necessary evil, as a small flaw in beauty, which is not to be taken seriously. The typical pindinka scar does not look nearly as bad on the dark faces of the natives as on the white skin of the Europeans. I had an insane fear of pindinka, but luckily was spared its suffering. The hakims are great masters in combating the eye-diseases which are extraordinarily widespread in the East. With the most primitive instruments they perform complicated operations, whose fortunate outcome no doubt is due partly to the Oriental's enormous power of resistance. The preparation of the hakim is essentially different from that of the European physician. It is medieval. He visits no anatomical institute, dissects no corpses; instead he studies much theology, literary history, logic, and grammar. The actual science of medicine he learns privately from some old physician, practises it first as a secondary occupation, and does not devote himself to it entirely till old age. Often he is a member of some pious society of dervishes, at times a student of the Koran and a poet.

The greatest feat of the hakim, one that has never been surpassed by any European physician, is the arbitrary change of the colour of the eyes. This secret of Turkestan, this hidden knowledge, the hakim guards as dearly as his eyesight. Never yet has anyone succeeded in probing this mystery, in discovering the means which enable the hakim to bring about this metamorphosis. Moreover, he seldom can be moved to this feat, unless he realizes that his help is urgently needed. The reason which seems sufficient to him is the women's fashion, which, in Turkestan, as everywhere else, determines the fate of people. The fashion of Turkestan, thousands of years old, demands that the woman's eyes be black. A light colour is inadmissible; it is considered a mark of Allah's displeasure, a punishment and disgrace. A girl of Turkestan who comes into the world with light eyes will be admitted into no harem; no one will marry her; parents forbid their children to play with her. She is avoided, and it is said of her that she has the evil eye. If she is born into a nomad family deep sorrow overpowers the whole clan. They would like to kill the child, but Mohammed has forbidden the killing of newborn girls, no matter how burdensome they may be. The parents hide the child of misfortune, are ashamed of her, and pray to Allah for one of his miracles. Usually they wait till the third year of her life. If the colour of her eyes has not changed by that time, the hakim is called and with the aid of Allah and his own ability causes the girl's eyes to become black. But before he begins all strangers must be removed from the vicinity; no prying person may watch and learn the hakim's art. For three days the physician and the whole family of the child fast; for three days they pray and beg for the favour of the merciful one. Then the doctor prepares a salve which he spreads over the child's eyes. The salve is made of unknown plants, boiled in a great kettle into which all sorts of ingredients are thrown.

After a few days the effect is seen. The eyes become red, begin to fester, soon look like large, pus-discharging wounds. For half a year the girl sees nothing; her eyes are covered with festering, tumour-like scurf. Then a dent appears in the loathsome scurf and gradually becomes a small opening. First one can see the pupils; very slowly the festering stops; the scab falls off. Larger and larger grows the opening through which the girl looks out into the world. When the scab has fallen off, wise men and curious ones come from the distant oases, from the cities and villages to investigate the miracle, for the girl's eyes, with which she can now look proudly and calmly upon the world, have become big and black, entirely black, as the fashion of Turkestan dictates. The hakim, the pious man, has again won a victory over the ignorant doctors of the unbelievers.

As I have said, no one has as yet discovered this secret of the hakim. It is age-old, as old as the dreams of the desert. Only if the girl has eyes of two colours, which happens very rarely, does the hakim refuse to try his skill. The woman with eyes of two colours is no creation of Allah; she belongs to the devil. It is a sin to touch her. She is treated worse than the lepers, is ostracized, must live on alms at the outskirts of the village, and may visit her parents only during the night.

The law of the colour of the eyes does not extend to men. The man's strength does not lie in his eyes. They may be grey-blue, even of two colours; no one pays any attention to it. If Allah has permitted one to be born into the world as a man, it is already a proof that he is not unfavourably disposed, say the people of Turkestan, who, in their deserts, pay no less attention to female fashions than the unbelievers in the big cities of the West.

CHAPTER 22

THE GRAVE OF LAME TIMUR AND HIS CAPITAL, SAMARKAND

Turkestan, the enormous land of deserts and steppes, lives under the spell of Timur, the lame world-conqueror. Timur is the myth, the legend of Turkestan, the fabulous figure for whose return the nomads, merchants, peasants, and warriors yearn. The squat, slit-eyed Timur is the symbol of the land, and his grave the most sacred shrine in a country which is certainly not poor in shrines.

The grave of Timur, which has been depicted a thousand times and has been included in all encyclopedias, I need not describe. As is well known, it is situated in his romantic capital, Samarkand, which owes its existence to Alexander the Great. The city is surrounded by gardens, is regarded in the whole Orient as the pearl of the world, and, besides the famous tomb, contains mosques, libraries, Islamic high-schools, and legends that intoxicated me. I shall not dishonour the memory of the great conqueror by describing the decline which is now taking place in the country; I shall not report in these lines the dirt and misery of Samarkand. Lame Timur, his deeds, and the legends which grew up about these deeds shall here form a chapter of the old, genuine Orient, which I love and which has sunk for ever into the sand-hills which extend about the city, Aschkau-Abad.

Timur! The word is like the blade of a scimitar; it contains within itself the legends of the slit-eyed people that came out of the desert, numerous as the gods of India, and overthrew thrones, destroyed cities, bathed in blood, and knew no other god than the tail of the horse of the steppes. Timur-Leng, the lord of his people, the grandson of Genghis-Khan, was short, slit-eyed, lame, and immortal from the time of his birth. When the nomads gathered about the fire in the evening

131

they would tell stories about him. These tales are melancholy, naive, and saturated with blood, as is all that comes from the desert; they are the mirror of the nomad people, who see themselves in it.

Timur was born with blood in his left hand, a sword in his right hand, and in his mouth the end of a horse's tail; therefore his mother was greatly tormented at his birth. On the day of his birth blood flowed in all the rivers instead of water. When his umbilical cord was being cut, he said: "I am lame Timur, who loves blood and hates the world", and all knelt down. Even the trees bowed, which until then had happened before to only three men—Mohammed, Jesus, and Oguz-Khan, the first nomad. Thus the nations of the desert describe the birth of Timur. No one can be convinced that anything in Turkestan was not erected by Timur. Even buildings barely fifty years old are stubbornly ascribed to him. All Eastern lands have some legendary figure to whom everything which seems out of the ordinary, or mysterious, is ascribed. In Azerbaijan it is Alexander the Great who has built everything. I know of a bridge in Azerbaijan, on which the words are chiselled : "Constructed by the General Prince Ziziani, 1805." Everyone reads the inscription, but no one believes it, for it is certain that everything in Azerbaijan, except the oil-derricks, was erected by Alexander. Turkestan, on the other hand, cherishes the name of the lame world-conqueror who rests in Samarkand.

Nevertheless Tamerlan did build many palaces, mosques, and bridges, even if he destroyed still more. The most famous of all are his square towers of loam which one encounters in ruins even today in various places in Turkestan and Persia. These towers are the most terrible monuments that a world-conqueror could ever erect for himself. Their idea is Timur's very own. It is said that his court poet, the wise Idrisi, told him one day how the conquerors of ancient nations had monuments of their victories composed of the ruins of the fortresses and marble palaces of their enemies. Timur liked this idea, but he looked for better material than the remains of the palaces of his conquered foes. He decided to use the living flesh of his opponents for the perpetuation of his fame. After every great victory the captives were separated into divisions of sixteen hundred, were chained, and laid in a square, forty men with ten on each side; lime and clay were poured over the living men. Upon the square of clay thus formed, a second layer of humans was laid and likewise covered till the square tower with forty layers of forty men in each row was complete. Then the name of the victor was displayed in huge letters on all four sides, and the conqueror marched on to further deeds of heroism. These towers are in ruins today; through holes in the walls and round about on the earth one can see skeletons. The nomads of Turkestan consider this idea particularly amusing. The stories of Timur's cruelty are inexhaustible and are told with pride by the friendly and peaceful nomads. It is notable that Timur is the only national hero in the world to whom—humanly speaking—legend ascribes no single good quality. The scientists were the first to discover human traits in him.

Timur's last campaign, during which he wanted to conquer China, is especially embellished with legends. During this campaign he died in the desert and was brought back to Samarkand for the pompous funeral. But tradition reports that he was led astray through the magic of the Emperor of China, and was intoxicated by Chinese dream-visions which tempted him from the right path in the form of naked girls. Then he came to the desert city of Aschkau-Abad, where he is held fast even now by a Chinese spell.

Aschkau-Abad means the "city of love", and is said to have been erected by a magic incantation of the Chinese Emperor in the form of a single harem of unfailing beauty and fascination, which caused Timur to forget his bloodthirsty plans. The city does exist, it is a neighbour of Kizil-Su, and owes its name to the famous girl-markets which were held there in former times.

The mausoleum of Timur in Samarkand is a tall, dome-shaped edifice which resembles a gigantic stone papyrus blossom. In the middle of the dark, cool space is the tombstone, a malachite the length of a man, the height and breadth of a bathtub. It is said to be the largest malachite in the world. Everyone who comes to Samarkand knows this stone, knows how it looks and how it lies. The stone might well be a real fact for the population of Samarkand and all Turkestan, and yet a few villages beyond Samarkand people begin to tell legends about it.

In many regions it is said that the malachite does not lie on the ground but floats in the air above the grave. When I tried to contest this legend and maintained that the stone which I had seen lying there myself could not possibly float in the air, an especially knowing man explained to me that the walls of the mausoleum were of magnetic rock which attracted the stone from all sides and in this way held it at a neutral point in the air. Since then I took good care not to contradict legends.

Opposite the grave a merchant lived who was friendly to us and had absorbed the wisdom of the old city. One day I visited him and saw that he and another merchant were about to divert themselves with the most expensive sport of Turkestan, the battle of the white cocks. White cocks which are able to fight are costly and are sacrificed only if the stake is very high. This time it seemed to pay, for the stake was a handsome eight-year-old Persian boy for whose favour the two honourable merchants were contesting. The fight was to decide to whose share the boy should fall. The boy himself had declared that he felt equally attracted to each of the merchants.

The white cocks—which were much more eager for battle than the rams of Kizil-Su—dashed against each other, crowed, and tried to pick out each other's eyes. The whole incident took place in the salon of the merchant. The two rivals sat opposite each other on silk cushions; in the middle the cocks fought, and the boy stood next to the fighters, watched them curiously, and at every successful blow slapped his thighs with his hands. In the background, through the window, one could see the mausoleum of the world-conqueror, to which the merchants looked up mutely when their cocks were faring badly, I took a seat on the side and regarded the truly gruesome scene; the cocks were flooded with blood. At last the one which belonged to the house-owner fell, after having lost both eyes. The victor jumped upon his body, picked the head to pieces with his beak, and crowed victoriously. He himself was thickly covered with wounds.

The merchant to whom the beautiful prize now belonged, jumped up, embraced the boy, condoled with the vanquished, and took his leave without paying any more attention to the actual victor, the cock. I stayed behind to console the host for his grievous loss. And soon he calmed down. "After all, there are enough beautiful boys left in the world."

We chatted about the world-conqueror, the cotton trade, which was slack, and the mosques which were falling into decay. The merchant became sad, inveighed against the unbelievers, and finally asked me to tell him something about the massacre in Baku. I did so, told about the corpses that covered the streets, about the raped women, and about the plundered sections of the city. He listened attentively. Suddenly he rose and asked me to follow him. We came to the court of the house where an old, worn-out sword lay beside the customary fountain. The merchant grasped it, looked at me pityingly and began to sharpen the sword on the stone threshold of the house. This was a polite gesture, and bore witness to his sympathy with me who had experienced the massacre. This gesture is the oldest custom of the whole Orient which still exists today.

I tell this little story of the staking of the boy and the sharpening of the sabre to bring the spirit of this interesting city of Turkestan more vividly before the reader.

Samarkand is surrounded by gardens which suggest the Riviera rather than the desert. In the small, narrow streets, past the house-walls, flow the Aryks, streams of water which were already dug in Timur's day. Thousands of such streams, tiny canals, cross the city, bringing freshness to the gardens, but causing malaria, from which every inhabitant of Samarkand suffers.

The pampered city of Timur is known throughout the Orient as the city of Epicureans and wise men. For thousands of years the people of Samarkand have known how to ensnare each new conqueror with women, verses, wise sayings, and songs of praise, to make him a slave of the effeminate garden city, and finally to celebrate a new victory of their culture on the ruins of his desert power. Not a single conqueror has escaped this fate; even the Soviets forfeited much of their original nature in the gardens of Samarkand.

The city of which Haroun al-Raschid dreamed, to which generations of poets dedicated their verses, has remained unadulterated till now. It did not become a museum of old ruins, nor a second Port Said or Baku, but has been able to incorporate modern Europe within itself painlessly, to become European without sacrificing the Orient.

When the railroad was built through Turkestan, the merchants of Samarkand immediately realized the usefulness of this undertaking. Yet they did not want their sybaritic peace to be disturbed by the whistle of locomotives and by the bustle of a station; so they decided to build the station two hours' distance from the city at the edge of the desert. In this way they secured a railway which, if they wished, they could ignore. From the town to the station an avenue of poplars was laid out, in the shadow of which mare's milk and rosaries are sold. This fairy city is separated into three districts. In one section, which is almost European, the government has its headquarters and trade is carried on; it has almost the atmosphere of the Wilhelmstrasse in Berlin. In the second quarter one amuses oneself without forgetting commerce. There is also the famous Bey-Kulak Street, in which nomads and traders from all Turkestan gather to sell beautiful girls to the patricians, who stroll pompously through the streets in silk garments and turbans, scented with ambergris, discuss politics and literature, and from time to time have the living wares displayed to them. The houses in the Bey-Kulak Street are by no means houses of pleasure (these are located a few streets farther on), but show-rooms in which one is entertained regally, drinks coffee, smokes cigarettes, and where one can examine the future slaves with the glance of a connoisseur, either naked, or if one wishes, dressed.

Officially the slave-trade is prohibited, so that these displays are called labour exchanges for maids and menservants. This, however, does not change the matter at all, for the sellers are mainly the fathers or brothers of the girls. The slave-trade is too sacred a tradition to be prohibited, for each nomad father considers it his natural right to sell his daughter. The slaves yearn but very little for freedom, since they are treated much better in a good Oriental house than the free servants of Europe. According to the Oriental idea, the master is answerable to God and man for his slaves. For example, he is security for the debts which his slaves make, is held accountable in court for their misdemeanours; and, if a slave wants to marry, is bound to give him a dowry suitable to his class. The slave is considered a child of the house, to be protected. An insult to a strange slave is regarded as an insult to the master, too; at least the owner of the slave reacts to such an insult as to a personal one. In the Orient, it is socially and materially much more agreeable to be the slave of a mighty gentleman than to be a small, free man.

In places where slavery is finally abolished, it is replaced by the relation of master and lifelong servant, which is exactly like the old connection. The master has the right to all his unmarried slaves; but the bedfellow of the master is always treated as his lawful wife. If she has a child she even takes precedence over childless wives and is entitled to an inheritance. Her children are considered legitimate and inherit the title and possessions of their father; the younger children who are born of a legitimate marriage are bound to obey her. Therefore it is no wonder that the nomads, who mainly come into consideration as sellers, are hostile to and incapable of comprehending the prohibition of slave-trade.

The street of girls, Bey-Kulak, is notorious for another reason. At the end of it lies the pleasure district of Samarkand. There one dances, sings, plays, and loves, according to the immortal example of the wise builders of the houses of pleasure, the old sultans. There are two pleasure districts; one for Europeans and one for natives. The houses for Europeans are visited by the drunken soldiers, railway employees, and travellers. They smell of dirt, liquor, tobacco; the women wear European clothing, and are mainly Armenians and Russians. The houses of pleasure for Orientals are either real brothels, where women provided with price-lists sit naked in the show-windows, or—it can easily be said—sites of culture, where the poorer inhabitants are deceived by the illusion of a harem of their own, with eunuchs, singers, dancers, and marble fountains. In the streets in front of the houses stroll ragged dervishes collecting alms, wandering poets, students who seek adventure in the madrasah after their work, jugglers, in short, all the persons whom the fantasy of Scheherazade included in the "Arabian Nights". The streets are narrow, and when a camel passes the poets and scribes must step back into the gateways of the houses to make place for the ship of the desert. This whole quarter, with its bazaars, slave-market, boys' dances, and houses of pleasure, is so deeply saturated with fragrance of the real Orient, so rich in mosques, mausoleums, and madrasahs of the past rulers, that I would term it the most Oriental spot of the world, if I had not known the third section of Samarkand, the "University quarter", which, along with the famous Al-Ashar in Cairo, is familiar throughout the Orient as a centre of Islamic spiritual life.

The University of Samarkand consists of a row of old buildings erected centuries ago, half of them in ruins; but in these, too, instruction is stubbornly continued. The instruction and the studies at an Islamic university are essentially different from those of Europe. The professors, for example, receive no salary, are poor, and may not use their knowledge for their own enrichment. Many of them live on charity, even though they enjoy incredible respect throughout the whole country. Their power and prestige are greater than that of the sovereigns; indeed a resolution of the university senate is even enough to dethrone a ruler. On principle no subjects are taught by means of which a person can acquire wealth. "Knowledge shall not lead to riches," says an Eastern maxim. The education itself lasts at least ten or twelve years, which is still considered too short a time, and it includes—besides theology—grammar, rhetoric, astronomy, history, mathematics, the art of versification, history of literature, poetry, law, geography, and metaphysics: of course, all from the religious point of yiew. The professors are free, may teach what they wish, and are subject to no control. The students, many of whom spend their entire lives at the university, are famous as the poorest people of the East. From early in the morning till late at night they sit in the court of the madrasah, reciting some tractate aloud. During the day they leave the building for only a short time to beg proudly for alms in the market-place, or in front of a house of pleasure, and they are never refused. The students, each of whom is learned enough to hold public office or the position of a clerk, are considered martyrs of science, and every father is glad to marry his daughter to a future wise man. Not until evening do they begin to resemble their European colleagues. No one in all Samarkand knows how to sing jollier songs, to stroll through the street more grandiosely, and drink coffee at the seat of honour in the coffee-house. The future of these students is very sad materially; they scorn to derive material benefit from their knowledge: that the foreigners or the merchants or the poets may do.

Occasionally a student may become kadi-judge; and from his verdicts there is no appeal. Most of them, however, spend their lives in meditation or as wandering wise men or honorary beggars; or they become members of some respected order of dervishes, or professors at the high schools. But whatever happens, they remain the most highly esteemed class, much more respected than the princes or the richest merchants. Of late these wise men have taken to journalism, because in this profession they can most easily and quickly popularize, their opinions. The power and prestige of these beggars is enormous, though they cannot be distinguished from illiterates and ordinary beggars in their appearance or mode of living. They bear the title of "hafiz", which corresponds approximately to the European doctor's degree. Considered quantitatively, their knowledge is very comprehensive; for example, one of the first steps of their wisdom is knowing the Koran by heart. I have heard a hafiz, speaking without interruption, repeat the entire holy book from beginning to end in twenty-four hours. How great the influence of these scholars of the scriptures is can be seen, among other things, by the fact that they can declare any law of the Shah of Persia invalid, free the population from the burden of taxation, and forbid the merchants to carry on any trade for months. They continually use their power for political purposes, and their dreaded utterance: "That is contrary to Islam", forms a constant danger for every Oriental government.

A peculiar branch of their wisdom is metaphysics and mysticism, or rather, the doctrine of demons and spirits, which in some respects recalls the cabbala. With the aid of this wisdom they can conjure spirits, spread bad or good fortune among the people, and work miracles. They are sternly forbidden to make use of their ability, however, in this direction. The power over the spirits is to serve simply as a step towards a more profound recognition of the nature of God. Whoever dares to misuse his knowledge for profane purposes loses his prestige and dignity, is cast out, and marked as a servant of Satan. It is strange, wandering through the madrasah, to see the row of students bowed before the master, forgetting everything in the world in unbelievably fanatic abandon to religion. The future poets form a special class of students, which may be mentioned later.

Except for the grave of Timur, the University of Samarkand is the most notable sight of the city; architecturally most (of these madrasahs are masterpieces of Oriental art, unforgettable monuments of the old culture.

Samarkand, the crafty, polished, dignified, royal city, was a stage of our journey. We stayed there a long time, for this city is the original seat of our family. Even outside the boundary of the city we were received by my uncles, cousins, and others of indefinable degrees of relationship. These relatives, whom I had not known at all till then and of whose existence I had only a faint notion, received us with a hospitality which far surpasses any Western ideas of that virtue. There were nearly a hundred and fifty people in Samarkand who considered themselves our relatives and took the greatest pains to prove it by presents, festivals, and the like. Their pleasure was all the greater because my father is the official head of the family. He had not been in Samarkand for thirty years, and relatives streamed in from all directions to greet him and to present those who had been born into the family in the meantime.

The reception into our family in Samarkand was an honour, at the conferring of which not everyone could have held his own. The great

fete at the home of one of my uncles, in his huge house, lasted uninter-
ruptedly for three whole days, during which all the hundred and fifty
relatives in order offered their good wishes. I sat next to my father in
the main hail of the house, surrounded by the elders of our family.
One after another the relatives appeared with their children and wives,
bowed before us and kissed us on the cheeks, upon which we had to
return the kiss. After all the relatives of the male sex had been kissed,
a vast crowd of brown, unveiled girls appeared in the room and were
introduced to us as aunts, nieces, and cousins. These greeted only my
father and remained standing shyly in the hall until I rose and kissed
each one on the mouth, a greeting to which they yielded with pleasure. That was, so to speak, the official presentation, after which the
actual festival began. It consisted of speeches, eating, general story-
telling, and protestations that the ties of blood-relationship are
stronger than any others in the world. I left my seat of honour and
went to the brown cousins, who, crouching together, stared at me curiously. These girls were almost all pretty, which filled me with pride.
Only with difficulty could I converse with them, since I understand
but poorly the dialect of Samarkand, which they spoke. They all called
me brother and did not display the slightest embarrassment. They had
thrown aside their veil and sat before me on cushions, wearing gay
slippers, full silk trousers, and small velvet vests. Each of them tried to
entertain me, asked me about my health, whether anything pained me,
or whether I had killed many people, and finally whether I was
pleased with them, my relatives.

I marvelled at their perfect courtesy, which went so far that, as I
made many mistakes in their dialect, they repeated the same mistakes
in conversation with me, in order not to offend me by their better
speech. Nowhere in Europe, I am convinced, can one find such polite
young ladies as| my brown cousins in Samarkand. Most of them were
not yet eighteen years old and had never left the place, but to my great
astonishment were familiar with the events of the outside world–revolution, war, and even the names of famous generals. All were friendly to
the Germans, mainly because there were German prisoners in the city,

a few of whom had been converted to Islam, bravely had themselves circumcised, and married brown girls. I myself have seen these people, who were admired because of the circumcision.

As I sat thus among my cousins, consumed enormous amounts of titbits, and chatted about war and peace, it occurred to me to ask whether they could read or write. It turned out that they could not only read and write, but were even very well informed in the fields of literature, music, and religion. Only they could not do arithmetic, which a girl in the East does not need to do; nor did they know any European language or anything about any science that does not serve for the enhancement of feminine charm.

"What have you learned besides music and literature?" I asked. The girls looked at me amiably and answered calmly and proudly, without blushing: "Besides that, we have mainly learned love." By that they meant the *ars amandi* of the East, the art of love, in which every girl of good family is instructed from childhood and of which she is always very proud. The correct education for love is the main distinction between a peasant girl and a girl who attaches any value to herself. Therefore one speaks with amazement in the East about any boy who marries a simple girl. One then says, "He took an uncultured girl, who was unversed in the art of love." The parents of my cousins in Samarkand, however, attached great importance to good education; hence the pride which showed clearly in the black eyes of the girls. As you see, Samarkand is the genuine Oriental city, where everyone learns that which is due to him and does without useless knowledge. The student learns the conjuring of spirits, the merchant the slave-trade, the warrior murder, the girls verses, music, and the art of love.

For weeks we lived in Samarkand, enjoying the fairy-tale life of its three sections, till the general restlessness Which kept growing in Turkestan forced us to continue our journey to Persia. Enemies advanced towards the city from all sides. Even the Emir of Bucharia and the Khan of Chiwa were not equal to them. The nomads became robbers; robbers became statesmen who did not wish to give up anything of their original nature. The desert threatened to conquer the cities; the eternal revolution in Turkestan's history again repeated itself. Later came the Soviets; in part they were already there. The desert was subjugated by the power of the red star. But it still lives; the nomads, the Basmatschi, as they are now called, awakened by the storm of the revolution, have not yet ceased to fight against the city. Since the Bolshevists rule the cities, they are called anti-communists. But they are really only nomads.

We fled from the disturbances—we had enjoyed them enough—and sought the shortest way to the border of Persia, that seemed like a paradise to us. Before that, however, I saw the sinister walls and palaces of Bucharia, His Majesty the Emir, who trembled for his throne, the famous criminals' tower, and a short distance from Bucharia the hungry steppes.

CHAPTER 23

BUCHARIA

Berlin; a ball at the Hotel Adlon. I stand at the wall and see how jazz and foxtrot vie with each other in fury. In front of me stands a young lady in a low-cut dress, her back turned to me. The back is beautiful—classic line, dark skin, but not dark enough to be striking ... The lady, whose face I cannot see, is chatting with her neighbour. I move nearer with shameless curiosity; I want to eavesdrop on the conversation of the owner of the classic back.

At last I am near enough to be able to hear the conversation in spite of the jazz. At first I cannot understand a word, or rather do not believe my ears; it cannot be true. Then my ear becomes accustomed to the half-forgotten sound of the language, the most unexpected language one can hear in Berlin at an artists' ball at the Hotel Adlon. The young lady is speaking Bucharian: moreover, not the ordinary Bucharian, but the select court-dialect of the Emir, the princes, the courtiers, and the harem. Bucharian court-dialect in Berlin! That leaves me no peace. I now try with the greatest effort to understand the conversation, too. And soon I succeed, for the lady is speaking loudly and clearly in the well-founded conviction that she will most probably not be understood in the Hotel Adlon. What she says is much more amazing than the conversations of Victor Margueritte's heroines. Every gentleman who dances past is nonchalantly, expertly undressed, put to bed, negatively criticized, dressed again, and dismissed.

A fat banker, who marches past smirking, is raised to the dignity of a eunuch, and a tender youth in dress-suit and monocle degraded to a Persian pleasure boy.

Suddenly the lady turns round; I see a pretty, dark face, large black eyes and hear the painted lips speak the innocent sentence: "And this one looks like my uncle's lover." Since this sentence obviously referred to me, I step up to the lady and say in the best Bucharian at my command: "I am really not your uncle's lover." Then I bow and continue modestly: "Since when do noble Bucharian women go about without a veil?" The effect of my words was just as it was meant to be. A scream, the friend runs away; but I grasp the other's hand and revel in her infinite embarrassment, "I did not mean you at all," she whispers at last, and as she sees my face that is none too stern, smiles with the corners of her mouth, bends her head, and says: "Please, oh please, noble cousin, don't say anything to my father." I consent generously, introduce myself, and find that the young lady is called Princess P. and is the daughter of the hereditary Minister of Finance of His Highness, the Emir of Bucharia.

"We are related," says the princess.

"How?"

"Most of the people whom I know are related to me."

There follows a rather long genealogical discussion, through which I learn that for centuries the Princes P. have married only members of the princely house of W.; the Princes W., however, are somehow related by marriage to my brown cousins from Samarkand. As a newly discovered cousin I am now ceremoniously led to the table of the father, who kisses me without formalities, in the middle of the great hall, and says that he arrived in Berlin a few days before with his four wives, eight sons and three daughters, and fourteen relatives. He speaks with especial pride of his youngest daughter—she is the one who suspected me of being her uncle's lover—because in his opinion she is the most Europeanized and for three years has worn no veil.

The next day the emancipated daughter, with whom I had made friends, called me up and asked me to visit her in the evening. She refuted my reply that I was no eunuch and so could not be admitted into the harem with the statement that firstly, I was her cousin, and secondly, she was emancipated. So in the evening I proceeded to Dahlem to the villa where the Bucharian family had taken up residence, without really being convinced that I should actually be admitted. That first visit—the others were not so exciting—I shall never forget. A Bucharian servant opened the door, led me into the reception-room, and announced: "The prince will appear immediately." However, I made a negative gesture and said: "I should like to see Princess Tamara", which was certainly monstrous, for one may not pay a visit to a lady of the harem. The servant turned pale, looked at me like an idiot, and disappeared, staggering. I waited patiently a quarter of an hour. Then the door opened, and on the threshold appeared a heavily veiled, but manifestly old woman, who looked at me a while without saying a word, and then ran away with a wild scream. Then a second door moved and I saw a pair of dark eyes look at me curiously. At last the princess came, excused herself for keeping me waiting so long, saying that the whole harem was in a state of great agitation. One of the old women had even become hysterical.

We sat and drank tea. From time to time a door opened and some veiled figures glanced at me fearfully from a proper distance. I felt that the whole affair was a demonstration of her "emancipation", but pretended that I noticed nothing. We spoke about Bucharia, in which the princess had spent her whole life and I only three turbulent days. I was in Bucharia during the worst time that the country had ever experienced, shortly before the deposition of the Emir and the proclamation of the republic. She, too, was in Bucharia at that time, but still remained in the harem, dutiful and veiled, and under the protection of the eunuchs. Our conversation was interrupted by the prince, who, no doubt at the command of his four wives, stepped into the room and acted as though my visit were a matter of course. He was very well acquainted with my father, who had visited him during our stay in Bucharia, and even asserted that he recalled my unworthy self. After he had made certain that I did not intend to rape his daughter immediately, he left the room and abandoned me to the protection of Allah and that charming lady. After his departure the whispering in the next rooms also ceased. We remained alone. I looked into the dark, excited eyes of the eighteen-year-old girl, stroked her black hair, which was not yet bobbed, and listened to her repeating Bucharian verses. The land of the Emir took form before me. ...

The dominions of princes and maharajas of India, the peacock-throne of Persia, the castles of Africa, are nothing compared to the dignity, the glamour, and the fame of the kingdom of Bucharia, the largest of the independent states of Turkestan. Old songs, popular in the entire Orient, praise Bucharia as the "only city worthy of a world-ruler". "If a king leaves Bucharia, then he is to be pitied," said the Persian poet, in the sense that a king who prizes Bucharia so little that he can leave it, is obviously to be pitied as demented. Until 1919 the throne was occupied by a direct descendant of Genghis-Khan. He knew how to govern his country with truly patriarchal sternness and dignity. An example of the Emir's patriarchal manner of governing is interesting even today.

A Persian merchant who wanted to take his wares to Samarkand was as good as robbed by the ruler in Chiwa. Chiwa is an independent state in the vicinity of the kingdom. The merchant thereupon proceeded to Bucharia, appeared before the Emir, and said: "Sovereign, the Khan of Chiwa was unjust to me. I beg you for aid, for otherwise I am helpless."

"I am not your sovereign," said the Emir. "Your sovereign is the Persian Shah. Besides, the Khan of Chiwa is no subject of mine; he is an independent prince whom I cannot command. Allah be my witness that I cannot help you."

Then the merchant bowed and said: "O lord, when I grow old and die, I shall come before the throne of Allah. The Lord of all lords will ask me: 'Merchant, how did you fare on earth?' Then I shall say: 'O Allah, the Khan of Chiwa was a mighty ruler; he had thousands of soldiers, armed and brave; he had palaces, gold, and women, and he was unjust to me. To the Emir of Bucharia you gave tens of thousands of soldiers and immeasurable wealth in addition, but he, too, would grant me no justice.' Then Allah will become sad."

After the Emir heard this, he declared war on the Khan of Chiwa and fought until the Khan richly compensated the merchant. This story, which seems like a fairy-tale, actually happened not so very long ago, and serves as an example of the Oriental art of government. This government has its bad sides, too. Several times a year, for example public executions were carried out in Bucharia in a very extraordinary manner. On the occasion of some, festival, the condemned were collected in the court of the Emir's palace. After a long prayer and the succeeding feast, the Emir appeared on the low terrace and greeted the condemned, who knelt before him in a row. If the number of the condemned was not large enough the ceremony was postponed; if necessary, a few more people were quickly sentenced to death. After the Emir and his court had looked at the criminals long enough, he gave the command to begin. The condemned crouched, chained, on the earth, their faces turned towards the Emir. The executioner stepped up behind the man on the right wing of the long row, stuck two fingers into his nose from above, drew his head back, and slowly cut his throat with a knife till the head separated from the shoulders. Then it was the tarn of the next, who had meanwhile followed the incident curiously. The ceremony was a highly appreciated diversion of the court society and the Emir. Very rarely the Emir would take his white turban off before the execution, as a sign that he pardoned all the condemned; if this happened it was only to show the tolerance of the Emir clearly to European dignitaries or princes who were there on a visit.

The famous Viennese Professor Vambéry, who explored Turkestan disguised as a dervish and finally came to Bucharia, came near to suffering this fate. He was received by the Emir, who was convinced that he was a real dervish. Of all the virtues that a man can possess the Emir valued most the high art of calligraphy, and so he asked Vambéry—the wise dervish from distant parts—to write a verse of the Koran. Vambéry's handwriting was atrocious; when the Emir saw his hieroglyphics he considered them a personal insult, and gave the command to behead the scholar. Vambéry, however, knelt down before the Emir and improvised a Persian poem that is still sung today in Bucharia. In English translation it reads: "O ruler, I know that my sins are greater than the Caspian Sea, In comparison to the breadth of your goodwill, however, they are thinner than a hair, O ruler, your power is unlimited, and only you can turn the worst of my sins into a bagatelle.

The Emir was moved and pardoned the wise professor.

There is another less cruel manner of execution in Bucharia, which is only granted to the criminal in very rare instances. In the middle of old Bucharia, near the bazaar, is the so-called tower of criminals, the Kaljan-Minaret, regarded as a marvel of Islamic architecture. The tower is notable especially for its height and the wonderful arabesques and carvings which adorn its walls. Those who were sentenced to death were dragged up to the roof under a large dome, unchained, and left. They had a free choice either to die of starvation up there or to hurl themselves down from the height to the market-place, where a curious crowd always hopefully waited. Many legends have originated about the tower of criminals, one of which is particularly popular. It tells how the daughter of the Emir fell in love with a simple poet. As a punishment for arousing the love of the daughter, the poet was sentenced to death and carried off to the tower of the criminals. The lovesick princess now sat beside the tower for days looking up yearningly. She was pretty, delicate, and famed for her tiny feet. One night, when no one could see her, she threw aside her veil and slippers, grasped the fine arabesques with her hands, put her feet into the decorations of the Arabic writing, and began to climb up the tower. Her feet were so small that she could use the finest carving as a flight of stairs, and so she reached her lover at the top, where they awaited death together. Whether the Emir pardoned them, whether the princess really died, or whether perhaps she quarrelled with her lover and climbed down again, the legend does not tell. But the tale of the princess's dainty feet, which climbed the tower of criminals, has become the most popular among the Bucharian poets, and is often quoted. I have even heard poems in which Lenin's heart is compared with the tenderness of the lady's feet.

The last Emir of Bucharia, who was dethroned and fled to Afghanistan soon after our stay in his country, was the best friend of the Czar all his life, and had been made a general in the Russian army. The Emir seemed to be much prouder of this title than of his crown and his descent from Genghis-Khan. Only in Bucharia, in the most intimate court circles, did he sometimes betray his true views about Russia, by virtue of which not the Czar, but he—the Emir—was the legitimate sovereign of all Russians; for the Ernir was descended directly from the Tartar khans who ruled Russia for centuries and to whom the grand dukes of Moscow had paid tribute. His hearers were at the same time expressly informed that the Emir attached no value to ruling a non-Mohammedan people like the Russians; that he left to his friend, the Czar. Outside these court circles the Emir was a friend of the Russians. He often travelled to Russia, on these trips always wore his general's uniform, and took great care that all military men saluted him as a general. His greatest worry was the activity of his neighbour, the Khan of Chiwa, who was likewise an independent potentate and Russian general. The Emir was officially called Highness in Russia and Majesty in Bucharia. One day the title of Highness was also bestowed upon the khan. The Emir flew into such a rage over this that one expected the beheading of all the subjects of Chiwa in Bucharia, until finally the title of Royal Highness was bestowed on him. For the increase of national pride, the Russian consul in Bucharia was also an authorized representative of the Czar and in Chiwa merely a government agent.

This constant rivalry benefited both countries. If the khan intended to found a newspaper in his capital city, the project of founding two papers was immediately considered in Bucharia. Russian engineers, architects, physicians, and all sorts of rabble streamed to Bucharia, where residence was forbidden all other Europeans. Palaces, European and Oriental, were built with the help of the amiable Russians who demanded no titles or honours in return, but only a salary. In the course of time a small Russian city arose in Bucharia, which was outside the jurisdiction of the Emir and was administered by the Russian consul. The Emir was a true friend of the Russians, was over his ears in debt to the Czar, and raised no obstacle to the spread of Russian culture in his country.

When the Czar was dethroned by the revolution, the Emir became thoughtful. He took off his general's uniform and called the royal council together. When the dignitaries had gathered, the Emir greeted them and ordered them to murder all the Russians in his country within twenty-four hours. As argument in favour of his sentence, he explained that Russia was now weakened and that there would scarcely ever be such an opportunity again. He was right; there was no Russian soldier near the border, and the number of Russian families in the country increased daily. All the members of the high council were happy at this idea, since the possibility of killing a European unpunished is always received with enthusiasm in the countries beyond the Caspian Sea. Only the Emir's Minister of Finance, the Prince P., the father of the cousin I discovered in Berlin, was depressed by the suggestion. He rose from his seat, approached the throne, knelt down, and declared that he would not stand up until the Emir had retracted his command. The Emir called an adjutant, ordered him to keep watch and to observe how long the prince would be able to remain in his kneeling position, rose from the throne, and left the hall. One hour after another passed, and the adjutant reported that the prince was still on his knees and had even received an addition in the person of the mighty aristocrat, Mirbadal, who, when he heard of the command, hurried into the throne-room and knelt down. The Emir then decreed that the execution of his order should be delayed until the two men had left their kneeling position. Panic seized the Russian families. The Russian quarter was already being surrounded by the armed soldiers of the Emir, who only waited for the two petitioners to give way in order to begin. Till then no Russian was permitted to leave the quarter or to communicate with non-Russians.

The relatives and servants of the prince and the aristocrat now hurried to the palace to support the two petitioners—in the literal sense of the word. Their backs could lean on the backs of servants. Their bodies were held erect by cousins, and their children, handed them food and drink. The sight must have been curious, for even the Emir appeared from time to time and watched the whole group. For three whole days and nights the two remained in this position.

Then the Emir's patience gave way. He again summoned his royal council, solemnly seated himself on the throne and repealed his command, whereupon the dignitaries were carried home by their relatives, exhausted. Both were too powerful representatives of the financial and the provincial nobility of the city for the Emir seriously to withstand their plea—which really was a command. So the might of the autocrat is not unlimited after all. Thus the Russians of Bucharia were saved, and the hereditary Minister of Finance, Prince P., is proud of the event even today. Nevertheless the Russian revolution had grave consequences for the Emir. Since its outbreak the Russian troops in Turkestan had stopped caring for the peace of the country. In the Russian territory matters were better. There were still some armed organizations which at least saved the cities from general plundering. In Bucharia, on the contrary, where, during the last decades, the Emir's defensive forces had served his private sense of beauty for the military and hardly sufficed for a superficial guard of the capital, brigandage began to flourish with an exuberance that had never really been present before. In this part of the world one soon becomes accustomed to the fact that some portion of the country is always occupied by bands of robbers; in Russian-Turkestan that was also the case. Usually a comparatively small part served as a sinecure for the robbers; in Bucharia, however, the whole country was delivered up to them after the disappearance of Russian protection. The Emir no longer had any authority; he had too long been a friend of the Czar. His descent from the idol-worshipper, Genghis-Khan, also no longer impressed his Mohammedan subjects. Soon he hardly even knew why Allah had granted him deliverance from the Russian yoke. Still there are rules of statesmanship in the Orient which even the greatest friendship for the Czar apparently could not blot out. The country was terrorized by robbers. The robbers were more powerful than the Emir, so one had to treat them as the Czar had been treated before; that is, with courtesy, with very particular consideration, and above all with understanding for their especial inclinations.

After this resolution—to treat the robbers civilly—had been passed in the royal council, the Emir sent messengers to all the important robber-chieftains in the country, with the polite request to appear at his palace for his birthday festival. Thereupon each robber sent the messenger back with the no less polite request that a hostage from the Emir's family should be placed at his disposal for the term of his visit. In Bucharia they know, too, what a St. Bartholomew's Eve is. The Emir wrote in reply that he had never intended to invite the worthy robbers without placing hostages at their disposal; he had considered it a matter of course. After the hostages had beendelivered, one after another, the birthday guests appeared.

They were received ceremoniously, washed, dressed in silk, and overwhelmed with all the products of Bucharian culture. The robbers yielded to everything, drank wine, were instructed as to the noble descent, merits, and connections of the house of the Emir, and, on their part, chatted of the loyalty, strength, and dependability of their bands; this apparently did not embarrass the Emir at all. At last the actual birthday fete began. In the gaudiest hall of the palace—the most tasteful would have appeared poor to the guests—an enormous feast took place.

The Emir, who never tired of offering wine, roast veal, rice, whisky, and sweets to his guests, presided. He and the courtiers made endless speeches about the noble qualities of their guests: the whole world marvelled at their courage, their deeply religious and patriotic attitude, which had at last given the country its long-desired liberty, and so forth.

When the right spirit had been created, came the climax for which the whole affair had been organized. The Emir rose, asked for silence, and clapped his hands three times. Immediately the door opened, and into the room streamed unveiled girls who boldly fell upon the necks of the dear guests. They were the daughters and nieces of the Emir, whom he was now giving to the robbers as wives. "You are worthy of being my relatives, and as such I raise you to the rank of princes of my house."

The very same night the weddings were celebrated, and the new relatives, who had not expected that, were appointed governors of the territories they occupied. The Emir, who had rid himself of his whole harem-stock in one night, was solemnly congratulated by all his honest subjects. The governors, then, did not need to return to their tribes at all; most of them stayed in the city and administered the provinces allotted to them through representatives suggested by the Emir. The Eastern art of government celebrated its last, unfortunately all too short, victory in Bucharia. Only a few months passed. When the communists became the lords of Turkestan, the days of the glory of the Emir were numbered. At that time I had long left Turkestan, but I can very well imagine how, with the help of a few hundred Soviet soldiers, Bucharia was made a free, independent, sovereign republic. The Emir fled to Afghanistan; the new and old princes, the ministers—among them my Minister of Finance—the courtiers, governors, each ran where he could. The palaces were plundered, and from the treasury of the Emir forty wagons with bars of gold and silver were transferred to the republican and later to the Russian state treasury.

The old neighbour, rival, and enemy of the Emir, the Khan of Chiwa, suffered a similar experience.

Thus two states which had lasted more than a thousand years in fame and glory have disappeared, and the last bearer of the crown of the house of Genghis has become a "troublesome foreigner".

The Minister of Finance also became a troublesome foreigner. He could find no peace in Berlin. The police looked very much askance at his four veiled wives, at the Bucharian passport with the seal of the Emir, and at his other Oriental surroundings.

After long deliberation he decided to move to London with his whole family, where he expected more understanding of his peculiarity from the enlightened seafarers than from the German police.

Possession of colonies causes obligations. In England his harem and he were regarded as a natural thing, about which no one wasted a word. I later found that a financier from Bucharia can also make his way in London. Today Prince P. is the owner of a large London colonial bank.

With still greater satisfaction I learned that the emancipated daughter renounced the traditional marriage with a member of the princely family W., which in the meantime also appeared in London, and in spite of the distress of the four wives of the harem, has become a junior partner in the prince's bank.

CHAPTER 24

ALLAH IS GREAT!

We left Turkestan to find refuge and protection against the threatening Bolshevist invasion in the land of the Silver Lion. Chiwa, Samarkand, the old glorious cities fell, one after another, and Russians, Turkestanians, Armenians, and Azerbaijanians fled to Persia, which at that time was aflame with civil war; but to us, who were turning our backs on a much worse civil war, it appeared like a paradise. The domain of the shah, the king of kings, the peacock-emperor, is one of the most beautiful, most interesting, and least settled countries of the world. Persia contains luxuriant gardens, fields and woods, tropical plants, palms, and endless deserts, and in addition the oldest ruins known to mankind, but few inhabitants in proportion to its extent: three times as large as Germany, it has not ten million people. One can ride for days and see only ruins of old cities, sand, dust, loneliness. Genghis-Khan, the Mongol, and his descendant, Timur, passed through the green land of the shah with their armies centuries ago.

Since then it has become a desert; since then the poet's voices have died out; since then there is no longer a Persia. The old kingdom continues to live only in the past, in its ruins, deserts, and the endless caravan trails.

Nothing is alive in Persia, neither the degenerate Kajar-princes nor the farmers who follow the plough and recite five-hundred-year-old stanzas by Hafiz or Saadi. It is the true country of the old poets and thinkers, considering its present tattered garment unworthy of a glance, and proudly studying the versification of the divine tent-maker. In Iran religion alone is alive, the Shiitic religion with all its branches, sects, dervish-societies. The "Shiah Ali" of the green flag of the Prophet's nephew is the immortal symbol of Iran. For in every village, in every settlement, wherever there are still people, the heretical saying of the Shiites sounds out, words which have in their time cost millions their lives: "lla Ali wesir ullah" ("And Ali is the true friend of God"). This saying, which is appended to the end of the Islamic creed: "Allah is the true God, and Mohammed is his prophet", explains all: the mysticism of the tent-maker, the holy Hafiz, the dervish-orders, the terrible mystery of Ramazan, the scholars of the scriptures, and not least the words of Goethe, who knew little of Persia, and yet could understand, when he wrote:

"O holy and reverend Hafis,
They call thee the mystical tongue,
But who of the words knows the purport?
There's no one the learned among."

Shiism or the party of Ali, which rules in Persia, still forms the life of the country and the emotional life of the individual.

Fifteen centuries ago Ali, the nephew of the Prophet, and Hussein, the grandson of Mohammed, were killed by the Omayyad calif, but according to the views of even the modern Persian theologians, a Shiitic heart must constantly bleed with sorrow over these two, even today. "Joy is the lot of the heretic, sorrow is the dignity of the Persian", says the dogma of the Shiah. For centuries the Shiite has been grieving, fighting the unbelievers, the Turks, Arabians, Hindus, scourging his body, founding sects, and in mystical ecstasy singing his sorrow to his fellow-believers. For it is an active grief that inspires the Persian, an inherent urge to disclose the secrets of existence, not through knowledge but through emotion, and to preach everywhere his conviction, which he has acquired through the feelings. Therefore the number of sects, dervish-brothers, street-preachers, and saints in the country is still infinitely large; therefore every Persian is actively religious, even if in the most limited circumstances.

On the caravan paths of Persia, on the roads to the great cities of pilgrimages, Meshed, Kerbela, and so forth, one sees these travellers, merchants and farmers, dervishes and robbers, who wander to distant parts, collecting alms or giving alms. Along the roads there are huge round stones, and on these balls sit the pious ones. When their number has grown large enough, they push the large stone with all their might, move it in the direction of the holy city, work thus three or four hours, and then leave the continuation of their efforts to the following wanderers. This action is pious, for, just as each person is the representative of his family, so the stone is the representative of the earth, the region from which it comes. The stone, too, wants to go to the holy city, and it is good if people help it in this. The holy cities are situated all over the world, even in the lands of unbelievers; in Persia—Meshed, where is the grave of Imam Riza; in Mesopotamia Kerbela, where Hussein died; but Budapest and even Danzig are considered holy. When a pious man has visited a holy city, he is to be honoured all his life for it; especially those who have visited Mecca and bear the title of Hadshi. But Mecca is far away and belongs to the unbelievers, the people of Sunna. Rather one visits Kerbela or Meshed, which secures the title of Meshedi or Kerbeli and great prestige besides. These two are visited most of all; they are situated in Persia., near the large trading centres of the country.

In the great mosque at Ardebil, at the grave of Imam Riza, the founder of the Shiah, rises a golden hand decorated with precious stones. The roof of the mosque is also gilded; one must honour the imam, for what would the world be if there were no Imam Riza? Besides Imam Riza, there are also the great series of twelve imams of the house of Ali who replace the calif in the Shiah. These twelve were members of a mysterious sect, who in their time were the terror of the califate; but little is known of their lives. It is only known that they were holy men. The twelfth disappeared in a mysterious manner when very young, and lives in an unknown place. He is the Imam az Zemam, the Imam of Time; at the end of the world he will return from his secret hiding-place to distinguish the believers from the traitors. But even today, from his hiding-place, he rules over the fate of the Persians. Everything that happens in the country requires his approval, even the constitution which the king of kings once granted the people in a moment of weakness. Before this constitution was given, the Imam az Zemam was to be consulted. How this took place is not known: they say that the shah and the dervish-brothers wrote a list of questions on a paper, threw it into the Sea of Urmia, and then saw the imam in their dreams. The first paragraph of the constitution read "with the express permission of the Imam of Time we grant this constitution to our people".

This happened in 1908, but could occur today just as well. Only religion makes the Shiite a man of deeds, and the way this Shiah reigns over humanity is illustrated by the example of the Egyptian Shiitic Calif Al-Hakim, who cursed the sunlight in his grief at the assassination of the Prophet's grandchild. Upon his command no Egyptian was to see the sunlight. When the sun rose they had to hide in their houses, sleep, and not work. Not until evening was life to begin. The bazaars and government offices were opened in the evening; the farmer, the merchant, and the calif worked at night. It is not strange that this command was given, but it is strange that it was observed. This Al-Hakim who transformed night into day disappeared in a mysterious way, and is now the patron saint of the Syrian Druse-sect and the ideal of all dervishes.

The dancing, weeping, singing dervishes of Persia are not monks in the European sense. "There is no monasticism in Islam," said the Prophet, and every dervish most emphatically opposes the comparison with a monk. No doubt the main difference between a monk and a dervish is the fact that the dervishes are most severely prohibited from being celibate. The dervish must be married in order to be considered full-fledged, since matrimony is a hallowed law of Islam.

The dervishes are organized in official orders for the worship of the master and for the common exploration of the essential nature of Allah. With the Persian dervishes, however, in several instances, Allah and Mohammed have been replaced by Ali, who is honoured as "the forty-times dead and forty-times resurrected".

The wandering dervishes walk through the streets in tattered clothes, wear their hair long, and usually stop at cross roads or in front of any rich passers-by, raise their hands, and loudly recite some mystic formula in order to beg for alms; they are seldom refused. The alms are thrown into a pumpkin shell which always hangs from the dervish's shoulders. This pumpkin shell might be termed the coat of arms of the wandering brotherhood, and plays an important part in Persian lyrics.

In many respects these dervishes remind one of the pupils of the madrasah in Samarkand; in fact, very often they are former students. But merchants, warriors, princes, even foreigners, can be seen in their company. One need not be surprised at being addressed in German, French, or English, by a ragged, long-haired beggar in the street. In the Orient education and wealth are separated. The dervish must be a beggar, even if his order is the chief creditor of the government.

If one asks a dervish who has spent many years in Europe as a diplomat or a merchant for the reasons which led him into the company of the brothers, he will smile condescendingly and omnisciently and reply with the stereotyped formula: "Unfathomable are the ways of Allah!"

The dervishes of Persia are also active in politics. They are inspectors, as it were, installed by God to supervise the activities of the government and play the part of public opinion. Ceaselessly they travel from one city to another, preach of the approaching end of the world in the bazaars, and assert with pride that the best people in the country are to be found in their ranks. And in fact there are practically no great poets, thinkers, or politicians in Persian history who were not dervishes.

Less numerous, but also well organized is the caste of the Saids, the descendants of Mohammed, who alone have the right to wear a green turban (green is the colour of the Prophet). These Saids are not priests in the true sense of the word—the majority of them are merchants, well-to-do tradesmen, and landowners—still as a result of their descent a nimbus of holiness surrounds them. They are considered the spiritual nobility of Persia. Their number grows constantly, for it is not hard to become a Said, that is, to prove in court one's descent from the Prophet.

As distinguished from the dervishes who despise work, the Saids like to become government officials, because they are favoured in this career.

The third spiritual class is composed of the "learned", the "scholars of the scriptures", called mirza, who teach the wisdom of the scriptures to anyone who wishes to know it, in the schools and in the bazaars. Since all knowledge is of godly origin, they are also regarded as servants of God.

The official priests, die mullahs, on the other hand, have less influence than the dervishes, perhaps because they gain earthly benefits from their work and oppose the foundation of sects, which every Persian inwardly greets as a road to the truth.

The leaders of sectarianism, the living mysticism of Persia, are the dervishes, the proud seekers of truth, who for centuries have been inventing the strangest principles of faith. Common to all of them is the fanaticism with which they hate the Christians and the Sunnites. For example, no dervish will eat an apple from a wagon whose wheel or horse has touched a Sunnite. Other Persians do not like to do so either. In the bazaar, if a Sunnite or a Christian has touched one melon of a heap of water-melons with his hand, he is legally bound to purchase the whole stock. No Persian can be expected to eat a water-melon that was lying near one which a Sunnite has touched.

Especially odious are the names of the first Sunnite califs who wrested the throne from Ali. There are some who have these names painted on the soles of their slippers, so that they can step on them constantly and cover them with dirt. No European, I believe, has ever yet hit upon the idea of satisfying his hatred in this manner. The dervish does not carry on discussions, nor does he ever explain his sayings. Let the scholars do that. The dervish only proclaims.

Once a dervish appeared in the meeting of the theological faculty of a well-known Islamic high school, pushed his way into the midst of the professors, and proclaimed: "Ana l'hakk, I am truth", whereupon the whole faculty, horrified, asked for the explanation of this heresy. The dervish refused to explain anything, and was taken before the court of the high clergy, where he refused to take back the sentence.

Some of the clergy wanted to acquit the heretic, since the sentence, "I am truth", can also be interpreted as the affirmation of the unity of all present. Others did not consider themselves fitted to judge the sentence, and explained this on the basis of the saying of Mohammed, "Do not speak of things that you do not understand." A third opinion demanded execution. Upon the command of the sovereign of the country the dervish was executed, but till his death nothing could move him to explain his utterance. By the way, that was the only case in Islam's history of a dervish condemned because of his belief.

The mystical teachings of the dervishes, the Mahdi-cult, the worship of the dervish-masters, are not resented, although they are not always purely Islamic. Towards the sects Eastern rulers were always tolerant, for a sultan once said: "Every error is a step towards the truth."

The main sects are the Ismailians and their branches, the devil-worshippers, the Babists, and the Behaists, the last two of which were forbidden in Persia till recently. The belief in the Mahdi (Messiah) is common to all these sects; the question is contested whether the person of the future saviour will be the fifth, the seventh, or the twelfth of the dynasty of the imams; furthermore, whether he must belong to the holy house of Ali at all. The belief in the house of Ali, thus in the legitimate succession of the rulers, is the main mark of the Islamic sects. In Sunnite Islam, on the contrary, the dignity of leader of the religion is not hereditary in the house of the Prophet, but is transferred in accordance with law to the Islamic sovereign who is most powerful at the time. The calif must be chosen by the scholars of the scriptures, and can be deposed by the same scholars at any time. For this very reason the old califs used to have a successor from their family chosen during their lifetime. The power of the Sunnite calif, in contrast to that of the Shiite imam, who is looked upon as a saint, is limited. Every theologian may repeal a law proclaimed by the calif, for the reason that it is in conflict with the meaning of Islam. A few decades ago the state insurance companies in Turkey were boycotted in this manner, because a few of the learned considered them an objectionable game of chance. The dethronement of the calif was also always undertaken under the supervision, of the clergy, which had to issue a corresponding fatwa.

In Persia, where the Shiah is the official state religion, the priests possessed the same privileges in regard to the shah, though he is no religious ruler like the Turkish-Arabian Sunnite calif. The shah is merely a worldly ruler, and may not interpret the Koran together with the priest, as the calif does, but must blindly accept the interpretations of the mullah.

The supreme court of religion in Persia is the Imam of Time, the twelfth imam of the race of the Prophet, who proclaims the laws from his place of concealment. Therefore till recently the power of the shah was also much less than that of the Sunnite califs.

The origin of this Shiah—which, outside Persia, exists only in India and Azerbaijan, so that it is known only to experts—may be briefly described.

Mohammed left no male descendants after his death. His only daughter, Fatima, was married to his favourite nephew, Ali, who laid claims to the throne of the calif as legitimate heir. According to the Arabian custom, however, a calif was elected, and the election did not go in favour of Ali. Ali became the fourth calif, but he was soon dethroned and stabbed. The dignity of calif then devolved upon the dynasty of the Omayyads.

The son of Ali and Fatima, Hussein, rebelled against the Omayyad calif, Jezid, and after a battle was killed in the desert of Kerbela, in Mesopotamia. His brother Hassan shared the same fate. Ali and Hussein and their descendants—the Alids—now became the upholders of the Shiah. Mohammed, Ali, and Hussein, are the holy trinity, which resembles the Christian one in some respects. Ali was worshipped as the mirror of God, and Hussein is the national saint of all Persia. His death in the desert of Kerbela is the theme of innumerable odes and songs of lamentation, and the day of his death at the end of the month Moharem is a day of atonement resembling no other in the world. This day is devoted to the castigation of the body, in memory of the tortures that the grandson of the Prophet had to suffer. Long processions are organized, in which the believers whip themselves, scratch their faces till they are sore, and finally grasp their swords and make their bodies, and especially the scalp, a bleeding mass.

On the same day passion-plays are also presented, in which the martyrdom at Kerbela is portrayed. Today these passion-plays are not nearly as magnificent as they were only ten years ago, when they were presented at the court of the shah in the presence of the emperor, the government, the clergy, and the diplomatic corps, and were considered the most fanatical plays in the world.

Nevertheless, even now one can see pictures of fantastic horror on Kerbela-day; but it is at the risk of his life that the unbeliever shows himself in the street, and the government that expressly calls the attention of every foreigner to this danger, denies all responsibility for the blood that flows.

As an eyewitness I describe in the following chapter one of these days—the passion-play and the castigation.

CHAPTER 25

SHAH HUSSEIN, WAI HUSSEIN!

The great passion-play on the day of the holy Hussein is prepared carefully. Stands are erected, actors rehearsed, parts distributed. The presentation, which takes place under the open sky in a large arena, lasts several hours and grips the spectator to such an extent that at times the life of the actor who plays the part of the wicked calif, Jezid, is endangered. In former times the part of the calif was always acted by one who was sentenced to death; if he could save himself from the. raging crowd after the end of the performance, he was free from any punishment.

The passion-plays first show how the grim Jezid commands his warriors to get him the head of the youth Hussein; how all, even the criminal servants of the calif, recoil from this deed, until at last one is found who attacks the young Hussein with his troops and drives him into the inhospitable desert, Kerbela. Pursued by enemies, Hussein suffers hunger and thirst with his family. He wants to send his wives away, but they wish to die with the Prophet's grandson. At last the angels come to quench the thirst of the pious ones. The pious nature of the martyrs and the bloodthirstiness of the enemies is shown in many variations.

When the calif's soldiers at last attack Hussein during the night, kill his family, and behead him, the spectators begin to take part in the events on the stage. Stones are thrown at the soldiers, and they are cursed. The last act shows the leader of the troops presenting Hussein's head to the calif on a golden board. The calif is sitting on his throne, surrounded by his retinue, among whom is the Prankish ambassador. The ambassador is represented grotesquely; he wears a fantastic, gold-embroidered dress coat, holds a cross in his hand, and has an indescribably asinine expression. When the chopped-off head of the saint is handed to the calif, he orders presents to be brought which he wishes to lavish upon the murderer. Suddenly the head opens its eyes, looks at the calif, and says: "Allah is the true God, Mohammed is his Prophet, and Ali the true friend of God."

The calif is overcome and disappears howling, with his followers. Only the Prankish ambassador stays, throws away his cross, falls to the ground, and professes Islam. With this, the actual performance ends, but to calm the excited people, dervishes appear and recite pious legends about Hussein.

In these legends they tell that Allah set the head of Hussein in a ring and wears it on his index finger. When the head smiles, people get along well. Nor did Allah forget the blood of Hussein that was spilled on the sand of the desert; he lifted up this blood to himself and made of it the red dawn and the sunset, which did not exist before that. Finally he honoured all people who mourned for Hussein, and bestowed upon them hair with the splendour of the dawn and sunset. Since then there are women and men with reddish hair. Wise men who are not granted this distinction dye their beards with henna, the Oriental hair-dye.

Simultaneously with the passion-plays, processions of martyrs pass along. Men in white garments walk through the streets; their bodies bleed; one wound after another is cut. The old cry: "Shah Hussein, Wai Hussein!" resounds. It is the cry of the pious for the Prophet's grandson. "Shah Hussein, Wai Hussein", the foreigners call this festival. Some pierce their hands, ears, and fleshy parts of their bodies with thin steel needles or daggers, on which heavy weights are hung. All day long these bleeding martyrs stand in one spot, and with heavy chains scourge the few remaining parts of their bodies that are not yet pierced. The heavy weights fastened in the flesh by steel needles hang all over them.

The tricks of the Indian fakirs are insignificant in comparison with the tortures of the pious ones on the day of Hussein. It is amazing that most of them do not perish of their injuries. Strange to say, these wounds heal surprisingly quickly, with the help of a salve that the hakims carry into all houses on the evening of the festival. Nevertheless a number of the martyrs die, and are then sure of a mild judgment before the higher judge, in accordance with the general opinion. They are carried over the bridge of judgment by an angel. This bridge plays a part in the popular Shiah. It is said that man will have to cross it into paradise on the day of judgement; the bridge, however, is suspended above hell and is no broader than a hair and sharp as a dagger. The sinners will plunge into the abyss in a moment. On the great spring festival, the Beiratn, the true believer kills a young sheep as a sacrifice to Allah. The wise men explain that this sheep will await the believer at the great bridge, and on its back the pious man will arrive in paradise safely (for the sheep is innocent and cannot fall down).

The day of Hussein is the most important festival of the Shiah; it is gruesome, bloody, terrible in its effects. Outside Persia, in the Sunnite countries, it was forbidden for a long time, and in Russia it is not allowed either. On the other hand, in Constantinople the Persian ambassador was allowed to organize religious processions with his colony. But in the opinion of the Sunnites the castigation of the body is still a sin that may not be permitted.

Today this custom is dying out, but one still finds Shiitic doctors and merchants, educated in a European manner, who suddenly throw aside their European clothes and run into the street in white garments, and, streaming with blood, shout in ecstasy the magic words: "Shah Hussein, Wai Hussein!"

CHAPTER 26

KINGS, PRINCES, AND ROBBERS

In this book much has been said of robbers and princes; for robbers and princes of all varieties, from caravan-plunderers to legitimate sovereigns, rule the Orient in a manner that is more than strange to the European viewpoint, and is often misunderstood. The Oriental prince is distinguished from the European one mainly by the fact that he is not mentioned in the *Almanach de Gotha*, and today rarely has a coat of arms. All other differences are of an unimportant nature, and mainly determined by local conditions. In Azerbaijan, Turkestan, Persia, Tajikistan, Usbekistan, and Afghanistan, there are princes with a country and subjects, princes with a country and without subjects, princes with subjects and without a country, and finally princes without land and without subjects, who either chase after a rich American woman abroad or spend their youth at home in a debtor's prison. There are robbers who are, so to speak, princes-to-be (sometimes true princes are also among them), who address the king as cousin, marry his daughters, and on occasion are beheaded or promoted to the rank of general. The office of robber can be inherited or attained through personal merits. If robbers kept an ordered household, on the door would be written: "Robber X. Y. Office hours from four to six and after prayers" (for the robbers are very pious). And their mail might have to be addressed: " To Robber G., Garden-house next to the large mosque, Teheran, Persia." Unfortunately, however, the robbers do not carry on an ordered household, but are accustomed to visit the capital merely for a short time, collect the tribute agreed upon, and, should the opportunity arise, dethrone the king. There are princes and robbers of high rank, high aristocracy, who maintain agents among the English and the

Russians, plunder caravans, attack government troops, and blow their noses in ribbons of home and foreign orders. In the capitals live their small imitators, princes without land, but with subjects who must be supported. These princes work mainly as petty blackmailers, hirelings of some high court officials, or are in the employ of rich merchants, earn their money, and share it with their loyal subjects.

Where did all these princes come from? Well, they were simply there from times immemorial, and are much older than the dynasties of the official rulers of the country. In Persia there are princely families whose ancestors made friendly treaties with Alexander the Great, and possess more troops and gold than the king of kings. They know how to use these troops and this money, and see in the shah only a small, distant, local ruler, who actually must be grateful to the princes that, for the sake of form and with a view to foreign countries, they tolerate him at all. Of course, that is true only in the case of princes of the very highest rank. In the battles between the imperial troops and the aristocrats, the former were always defeated. Speaking broadly, the shah had no dependable troops, except for the members of the clan from which he himself came, and which was much weaker in Persia than the clans of several great princes. The power of the shah usually only lasted as long as he

could keep his vassals quiet by clever politics, by cunning, and by occasional murder. But woe to him if he dared to infringe on their rights in any way.

When the election for the first Persian parliament took place, at the distribution of the seats the claims of several princes were not sufficiently taken into consideration. The princes were of the opinion that they alone were entitled to represent their people, at the most in the company of several wise men who could be chosen within the clan. That their subjects were regarded as subjects of the shah, and as such made elections directly for the parliament, no prince could endure. When it turned out that the parliament did not intend to differentiate between the individual clans of Persia, the Prince of Kaschgai rebelled, went to the capital, dispersed the parliament, dictated his terms of peace to the shah, and was thoroughly convinced that he was the sa-viour of his fatherland.

The robbers play a similar part, with the one difference that they also consider themselves "public opinion"; in other respects they can be distinguished from story-book robbers only with great difficulty. They impose tributes on whole provinces, plunder everything that can be plundered, and mock at the diffident attempts of the general govern-ment to take action against them. Usually—unless he was beheaded first—the robber ended as governor of some province, from which he then extorted admirably. If he placed more importance on exteriors, he ended his career with dignity as a high official at the court of His Majesty.

At times, indeed, it is hard to draw the line between the hereditary aristocrats and the professional robbers, since the princes, if they are ambitious, are also partial to the profession of a robber chieftain.

One would assume that in this potpourri of kings, princes, and rob-bers the simple subjects would suffer most. Yet this is not so. During generations the merchants have learned to pay triple taxes to the shah, to the princes, and to the robbers; also they are accustomed to the dan-ger of an occasional robbery. They thrive, nevertheless. And the peas-ant who has the good fortune to live in the territory of an influential aristocrat or robber can lead a more or less secure life, for it is the sacred duty of every potentate in the Orient to take care that his sub-jects are bled only by him, and to that definite limit which just makes their further existence possible. As a rule only those who take part directly in fighting suffer, and they are usually mercenaries or nomads to whom life without occasional plundering seems senseless. The larg-er cities are usually spared and open their doors to the victor of the moment; the merchants who rule in the cities do not wish to have any-thing to do with politics.

Besides the princes, robbers, and lesser scoundrels there is also a court nobility that disposes of enormous riches and is the strangest phenomenon of the Orient. One can easily picture the existence of an Oriental prince or plunderer, but to explain the court nobility to the

169

European is a more difficult task. The high officials and ministers, together with the actual courtiers, form a particular class which possesses large estates in all Persia, but whose members are in the service of the empire or in the personal service of the emperor. Among them are diplomats, the more distinguished eunuchs, governors, and robbers who have "arrived". Pompous titles are bestowed on these people by the shah, which could arise from the fantasy of none but an Oriental. For example, there are nobles who bear the title, "Pillar of Justice", or, "Sword of the Fatherland", or "Protector of the Hidden", and the like.

The number of these titles is infinite, since each can be bestowed only personally and can never be borne by two persons at the same time. They completely replace first names and surnames; the owner is addressed only by the title and the other name is not even entered on the passport. Foreigners usually take the titles for family names and wonder how, for instance, "Pearl of Wisdom" could have originated. When one asks the bearer of a title for his name, he will calmly say: "My name is the Shield of Faith", or some similar surprising phrase.

All this would still be passable if the titles at least would remain constantly with their bearers. But almost every year they change from one courtier to another. For example, when the bearer of the title "Pillar of Justice" dies, a "Sword of the Fatherland" is raised to the rank of "Pillar of Justice"; a "Pearl of Wisdom" may become a "Sword of the Fatherland", and so on. Even without death, however, a transference often takes place, so that one can never know with certainty whether a letter f recommendation addressed to "The Shield of Faith" really does reach the person intended and not some former "Protector of the Hidden". That these titles hardly ever belong to a definite post is just as much a matter of course for the Oriental, as it is incomprehensible to the European that an important person can change his name every few years. To facilitate intercourse with the natives, European embassies have brought out special guides to Eastern titular splendours. These books resemble tables of logarithms, but are always out of date, and no European government can know whether the "Pearl of Wisdom" given as ambassador in London is the same gentleman who was ambassador in Paris a few years before.

How, then, is an Oriental country, with its swarm of princes, robbers, title-bearers, ruled by the autocratic sovereign? The robbers are rogues just as the middle-class officials, and the princes are but slightly different from the robbers. The high officials, to speak mildly, are likewise "high politicians"; the emperor would be swallowed up in the flood of his vassals if the Oriental art of government, anticipating everything, had not put a few expedients of power at his disposal. Moreover, one must not think that the members of this class are in constant feud with the emperor. They form an organic social body, which grants his own rights to each member, and in which all the sharers of the power know how to live in harmonious accord. The power of the emperor is really unlimited in some respects, as long as he respects traditional rights and customs and carries on "wise politics".

The sole ruler—if he is not a miserable "pusher", who then is called a despot—is a friendly gentleman who constantly receives presents from his subjects, courtiers, and officials, contents himself with ruling the harem, and doesn't care a straw for anything else. The inhabitants of the harem are wives and daughters of the king; the latter are often also his wives. In this hen-house sons are born in masses; one hundred, two hundred are no rarity. The older sons receive their provinces, where they rule. If the tribute from the provinces comes punctually, they are good sons; if the tribute does not arrive, they are bad sons and deserve death. In the provinces, besides, there are governors and governors-general. Furthermore, the provinces do not belong to the king at all, but to the individual princes and robbers, who also rule, and indeed more profitably than all the others.

Under these conditions, the harem is an institution of the highest political importance, for there the future governors are produced. Through the inhabitants of the harem, the emperor is related to all the clans, robber-chieftains, and princely families of the country. The princes who are born there are also members of some clan to which they are later sent as administrators. These clans always place great importance on blood-relationship with the governor at the time, about whom they would not need to bother at all otherwise. The prince who belongs half to the province and half to the empire is thus a connecting link between the two, and the harem therefore the most important foundation-stone of the unity of the empire. The correct distribution and the systematic replenishing of the harem with new wives is the well-guarded secret of wise politics, and demands complicated book-keeping which is carefully weighed and managed by the respective eunuchs.

At the heart of the unity of the empire, therefore, are first the emperor who begets the princes, then the wives whose kinsmen have power somewhere, then the princely connecting links, and last the eunuch, who holds everyone and everything in his fat hands". So much for the inner unity of the empire.

But when the country carries on war and must pay tribute to England or Russia, the border provinces pay. The absolute monarch himself does not do it, for there is no state treasury, but only the personal treasury of the ruler. The emperor will not part with his personal treasury, even if the enemy should conquer the whole country. Except for the treasury and the big harem, the emperor owns nothing, his body-guard—which just suffices for the protection of the palace—and the regular army excluded. The soldiers sell fruit on the street corners, and the officers have money-changer's booths on dark corners, from which they do not wish to be separated either. As a result the ruler need not worry about all his border-provinces.

Usually the king is murdered by robbers and by his sons—he never has any brothers. Then another son ascends the throne, who immediately kills all his brothers and begins to beget new princes. The graves of the brothers are touchingly situated in a circle about the future mausoleum.

Thus the Orient was ruled and managed for centuries, and all were satisfied, even the people; everyone possessed an aristocrat who looked after him, except the emperor for whom the eunuchs cared.

A few years ago, when I travelled through Persia, the conditions were still just as I have described them. Since then everything has changed. Achmed-Shah, the last Kajar who begot no children, was dethroned and lives in Paris. Riza-Khan, soldier, chieftain, then Sepah-selar (Minister of War), became ruler. He had ambition and did not want to imitate the old sovereigns. In years of campaigning Riza-Khan removed all the princes of Persia as local rulers; their weapons were taken away; no member of an aristocratic clan may continue to carry weapons.

The few princes who survived had to go to Teheran, where they sit in parliament under the constant supervision of the shah. The bands of robbers were also broken up, and for the first time for centuries the shah is again lord in his country. Now reforms are being promulgated in Persia that should wrest the old country from the dreams in which it has been living since the campaigns of Genghis-Khan. There are no more titles, no aristocrats; the newspaper-reader has taken the place of the story-tellers in the middle of the bazaar-cafe, and the Pearl of Wisdom now calls himself simply by his first and last name.

This change does not mean that Persia has ceased to be a country of legend. The Persians say: "Riza-Khan has two eyes; the one looks into the future, the other into the past." The old Persia of the holy fire, of the heretical Hafiz, and the wise tent-maker can now celebrate a resurrection, for it is not for nothing that the new shah has taken the heretical name "Pehlewi", and christened his son "Sapur" after the name of the great Fire-Emperor. Evidently the reforms do not in all respects signify destruction of the past.

Pious dervishes will continue to travel through the country, preach the end of the world, and mourn for Hussein, the grandson of the Prophet. The believers will continue to call out in ecstasy on the bloody Moharem day "Shah Hussein, Wai Hussein!"

The robber bands, however, the scoundrels, and princes belong to the past in Persia—although a quite recent past. Only in Afghanistan have they remained. There the princes and robbers still tinker about, according to the old models, with them and against them the eunuchs, slaves, bandits, noblemen, spongers, and camel-drivers. They all want to preserve the traditional, comfortable conditions of a true Oriental country. For how long? It will not succeed permanently; the feudal Orient is dying out.

I had the opportunity of becoming acquainted with this feudal East in its prime in Persia during the civil war. In the following chapter the doings of a mighty aristocrat into whose hands we fell may be of interest.

CHAPTER 27

AS A PRISONER AT THE COURT OF DJAFAR-KHAN

It happened at the border of the provinces Mazendaran and Giljan; our caravan had left the territory of a friendly governor only a few days before and was travelling through a region whose political dependence was unknown to us.

A Persian rider in gaily coloured clothes and with a small, black, high hat of sheepskin on his shaved head approached, ordered us to stop, rode up, and said: "I am the messenger of the Khan-Djafar, the ruler of this region. The khan sends you greetings." He paused, then continued good-naturedly: "The Khan-Djafar has reflected about your arrival and thinks it right to have you killed; he sent me to inform you of this decision."

We heard this pleasant news with surprise.

"Why does your khan want to kill us?"

"I do not know."

"When will he kill us?"

"Today he will come here with his soldiers; till then you are to wait."

We dismounted from our camels and began to chat with the messenger about the transitoriness of all earthly things. The messenger, however, proved to be an incurable optimist.

"It is not good to die in the desert," he said. "The khan will come with sabre and guns; he will shoot; you will defend yourselves; blood will flow. And the khan is mightier than the shah; he does whatever he wants."

Soon we noticed that the messenger was taking the greatest pains to convince us of the beauties of life. And when he finally coined the wise sentence: "Of what use is your money, if you are dead", we sat

175

down on the ground and wrote a letter to the khan which was crammed full of praises, and in which we asked the reasons for his grim decision.

The messenger took this letter, promised to deliver it to the khan, and disappeared behind the hills. Soon he returned accompanied by a gentleman of strange appearance, who bowed low and introduced himself as the financial adviser of the khan. Now we were sure of our lives; never yet has a financial adviser in the Orient caused anyone's physical death.

In the endless conversation that began then, we received all sorts of worth-while information about the character of the khan and about conditions in his cosy country. "The khan—the financial adviser explained to us—was deeply insulted by our behaviour. We were crossing his realm without giving him the smallest present. The presents, of course, did not matter to him. But what will be said abroad when it is discovered that even highly esteemed people refuse to give the khan a present? For this reason he wished to kill us; nevertheless, upon the recommendation of his financial adviser, and in view of the fact that enough Moslem blood was already being spilled, he had decided, if ... and so on.

Then we knew that it was a question of toll which the khan was accustomed to levy on every trade-caravan. However, since we were not traders, we had not thought of these payments, and in a conference lasting for hours—which was more tiresome than a bloody combat—we settled the amount of the gift.

After the presents in the form of ordinary banknotes had been handed over, the financial adviser drew from his pocket a rather long letter which he read to us immediately. In this letter, which was written in verse, the khan informed us that, greatly pleased at the arrival of noble travellers, he offered us hospitality, especially since the road onward was blocked for the present, at any rate, by the revolt of the "forest brothers", and he could not permit the high-born strangers to take residence anywhere outside his palace.

There was nothing else to do but to accept the kind offer of the khan with thanks, and to proceed to his palace, led by the financial adviser, who assumed the humblest air immediately after the receipt of the money.

At the court of this khan—whether as prisoners or as free men, I do not know—we spent about ten days, until another present bought us permission to depart.

The khan received us in the court of his palace, presented each of us with a little gold-embroidered hat as a return gift, and, as soon as we had rested, began to complain about his government worries and to question us about the news from distant countries.

Soon we were good friends and became acquainted with all the peculiarities of the court life and Djafar-Khan's art of governing. Djafar-Khan liked peace above all; the first thing that he told me was his philosophy of life. He told me the story of the life of the first Kajar-Shah, who waged war for decades, conquered many countries, mounted the throne of the emperor, sword in hand, was emasculated by his enemies, and finally met death somewhere in the desert. This famous life served as a constant warning to Djafar-Khan. He did not understand why he should starve on campaigns to furnish some future generation of poets with material for bad odes. In accord with this, the life in the palace was arranged. The warlike deeds of the khan were limited to occasional plundering of unprotected caravans (ours was armed), and all the robber-chieftains in the region drew a regular salary from him, for which they were obliged to leave him in peace.

In the morning towards ten o'clock the khan's government affairs, which I was allowed to attend, began. They consisted mainly of the acceptance of bribes from his subjects and courtiers, and in return His Highness granted them a few rights for a more or less brief time. The bribes usually were silver coins, gold wares, hens, eggs, and flour. Everything was accepted. After the ceremony of bribery the khan took exercise. A few fat doves were set free in the court (as in Monte Carlo), and the khan shot them one after another. After every shot some courtier approached and put a few pieces of silver into the outstretched hand of the khan as voluntary congratulatory gift. The khan accepted this, too, with thanks. This game, by the way, was played at all the courts in Persia, formerly even at the court of the emperor; of course, the congratulatory gifts played the main part. Now these times have gone for ever.

After this exercise the khan rested, went into his harem, dined there, and appeared in our rooms in the evening, where he carried on literary studies with me. For Djafar-Khan was a poet who considered the high art of concocting verses the only trait that distinguishes a man from an animal. He usually satvdown next to me and quoted a stanza from Hafiz or Saadi, to which I submitted quietly. Then he began with his poems, which were mostly riddles in verse. I had to solve these riddles, naturally also in verses, with which he could delight himself for hours.

I became court-poet, as it were, and chatted with him for hours about old poets and long-forgotten stanzas. The riddle-problems which the khan gave me were grotesque. For example, he asked in excellent verse: "If a Moslem commits a crime but then changes into a donkey, what should the kadi do?" Whereupon I answered promptly: "Proclaim the punishment and guard the donkey till it becomes human again."

My wisdom touched the kind sovereign, and he went on to ask: "May the man who has changed into a donkey incur debts and be a Moslem?" The answer was: "He can take part in the divine service but may do no business." Thus I gradually became a favourite, and even received an honorary bodyguard of two armed, barefoot fellows, who constantly followed me. The notion of a guard of honour was but slightly developed in Persia. The two did not know whether they should guard or honour me. So they did both. They carried me over the dirty street in their arms and did not let me out of their sight for a moment. When I became tired of this, I tried to run away. But one of the guards roared wildly and grasped me by the shoulder. Angry, I told the khan of the incident, whereupon that mild lyrist inflicted a curious punishment: the man was locked in a cage and condemned not to sleep for a week; in front of the cage that was set up in the city square stood a courtier who had to prick the condemned one with a dagger when he became drowsy. The condemned person himself was happy that the punishment proved to be so mild; for there are worse punishments in Persia; for example, beating on the soles of one's feet. But it is not felt worse than confinement to one's room.

I myself have seen imperial princes receive blows on their feet without feeling any shame, although government officials did this publicly in the market-places. This punishment is also used in the preliminary examination, to "revive the memory of the condemned person", as they say; yet in such cases a substitute may be employed—such people always stand at the entrance to the court and wait for their clientele. Severe punishments are given for theft. The first time the thief's left hand is chopped off, and in cases of repetition first his right leg, then his right hand and his left leg. Apparently this punishment helps, for neither I nor anyone of my acquaintance was ever robbed in Persia. Moreover, I have hardly ever heard of thefts.

Severe punishments are also given for adultery. Nose and ears or one of the two are cut off a man who is caught in a strange harem. Castration, on the other hand, occurs very seldom nowadays. For example, in the territory of Djafar-Khan it was not done at all. The khan, you see, was unconsciously a disciple of Epicurus. We also had occasion to become acquainted with this side of his nature.

The Friday after our arrival he arranged a kind of festival in our honour. The extent of the festivities was modest. We sat in the court and ate muttonband listened to the tones of the native music of the saz. When the meal was finished and we had wiped our hands with the lavash-bread as thin as paper (a kind of napkin which is eaten after use according to custom), the khan assumed a mischievous expression and emitted an indefinable sound. The door into the interior of the palace opened, and on the threshold nine handsome Persian boys with tambourines in their hands and tiny, gold-embroidered Bucharian Tubetei (the size of a skull-cap) on their heads. The boys—they were between eight and ten years of age—bowed before us, then before the khan, and began a Persian dance composed of graceful movements and bows.

The khan, who was visibly enchanted by this court-ballet, reached for a tambourine himself and accompanied the dance with a monotonous song. During the dance each of the boys approached my father in order, danced in front of him a while and bowed, for which, in accordance with the Persian custom, my father stuck a silver coin, which he had first dampened with his tongue, on the boy's forehead. By chance the coin that was stuck on the forehead of one of the boys was twice as large as those of the rest.

After the dance, when the boys had gone, the khan continued to talk a while about Hafiz and religion, bade us good night, and proceeded to his harem. My father and I also went to our rooms, which were connected by a door hung with rugs. Before we had undressed there was a knock at the door of the corridor. At the entrance stood a servant of the khan, armed to the teeth—an immensely tall fellow—with an endless downward curved moustache and an incredibly stupid expression. He led a gaily dressed creature by the hand, tiny in comparison with himself, but in whom I recognized the court-dancer who had received the large coin. "His Highness sends you this blossom of Allah's creation," boomed the servant, as he led the boy into the room. When he was asked why, he answered with a deeply serious official air: "You are guests of the khan, and you gave the boy a coin twice as large as the others. His Highness understands every hint and begs you to have your pleasure with the boy."

Then the hero of the event, the boy himself, took part in the conversation. Blushing deeply, he whispered that it was a great honour for him to do a service to the guests for a night, and that he felt our hesitation to be a serious insult. "They will all laugh at me, if you send me away," the alert rascal asserted. I saved the situation by assuring the servant that, for various reasons which he could not understand, we should not know what to do with the Bitscho (as these boys are called), since our interests lay on another plane.

The servant showed some understanding of our "higher interests", and departed with his pupil. Scarcely had we undressed and thrown ourselves upon the cushions and rugs which served us as beds, when the armed blockhead again appeared on our threshold, this time accompanied by two young girls who looked at us curiously through their veils. Now the servant could no longer be refused. A refusal was also impossibie from the point of view of good manners. The girls stayed with us till our departure.

Nevertheless the khan was hurt by our forgoing the pleasure of delighting ourselves with the youthful charms of his Bitscho. He visited us the next morning and acted as though he were now convinced that he had to do with wild barbarians who could not appreciate his more cultivated feelings. He told me endless stories about the beauties of the Persian past which were entirely in accord with his taste, complained about the corruption of the present youth that was enthusiastic only about the low pleasures ofbexistence, and brought to light a rather comprehensive body of knowledge.

Since, as I have said, I showed appreciation for everything classical except the Bitschos, he soon became reconciled, and even proposed that I should dine with him in his harem. I was careful enough not to enter his harem, for there, from sheer devotion to the treasures of the past, he might possibly have treated me as a Bitscho, too. Outside the harem, where his power was limited by the conventions of hospitality, I could feel safe. When we departed, he gave me a Hafiz manuscript, pulled a long face, and, naturally in verses, made a formal declaration of love, to which I naturally also responded with a declaration of love. But I am sure that his love would not have remained platonic if our caravan had not been protected by armed riders.

Djafar-Khan remained a pleasant memory to me, especially since the rest of our way had nothing to do with the elevated peace of his palace We then entered the territory of the "forest brothers", the Gengehs", the territory of Mirza Kutschuk-Khan, robber and saint.

CHAPTER 28

THE FOREST BROTHERS

We left the dominion of Djafar-Khan in firm hope that we should soon reach Enzeli and consequently the coast of the Caspian Sea, and learn there more details about the situation in Baku. In the meantime our caravan had increased in size, several Russian families who had fled from Turkestan having joined us. The way to Enzeli, however, was not clear, for in all North Persia, as the khan had correctly informed us, the revolt of the forest brothers, the "Gengelis", was raging under the leadership of the preacher and revolutionary, Mirza Kutschuk-Khan. The reason for this revolt is not known. The story goes that years ago some wise dervish who lived a life of asceticism in the desert preached of the end of the world in the marketplace of Teheran. The wise man was hairy as an ape, unwashed, and doubtless corresponded to the portrait of a saint, as the Oriental pictures him. His sermon about the end of the world, however, and the collecting of alms which followed it, would not have stirred anyone, had not the wise man proclaimed something entirely new in his prophecy. With hands widespread he roared: "True believers, soon the time is coming when the sun will rise in the west." With that he gained not only bountiful alms, but also overwhelmed all who were present. For the sun that rises in the west is not only a sure sign of the end of all things but also, according to all sources of wisdom, a sign from above that now no difficulties will be made by heaven in the destruction and extermination of unbelief.

At just that time Enzeli and North Persia were occupied by the English, so that unbelievers who could be destroyed were present in great numbers. The prophecy of the dervish therefore met with response,

182

and the famous forest-brother movement arose, which was joined by all people who wanted to fulfil one more pious duty before the end by killing a few unbelievers. The forest brothers and their fanatical leader, Mirza Kutschuk-Khan, swore to let their hair and nails grow until the last unbeliever had left the holy soil of Iran. Since the revolt lasted several years, it is said that in the end the mere sight of the forest brothers sufficed to move the English "Tommies" to retreat. The central government of Persia remained neutral, since the whole affair took place in the territory of the English occupation and after all was not directed against the interests of the country.

Our caravan, then, on the road from Turkestan to Enzeli, happened into the midst of this sympathetic movement. A few miles beyond the territory of Djafar-Khan came the first signs. Villages were half deserted; here and there one could see human corpses or rusted guns and daggers. The few English troops that met us seemed to be anything but conscious of victory. They asserted that not a single caravan within the territory of occupation was threatened with danger, but the whole region knew the contrary. Moreover we could learn the truth from the natives who met us. Still, for us personally, there was no reason for alarm up to that time. Firstly, we were not unbelievers, after all, and secondly, we possessed a stately guard of Turcomans which had often before driven suspicious-looking gatherings of people out of our path. To the English however, the faith with which we accepted their assurances that peace ruled in the country seemed to be suspicious. In a village which constituted the English headquarters, an English official came to us and ordered us to send our riders home, since there was a decree that no armed natives could be permitted to stay in the country. To our answer that we must have some protection in the centre of the revolting territory the Englishman responded: "The inhabitants of this region are being protected by English troops and require no other protection; if you do not send back your riders, we shall have to arrest you as supporters of anti-English actions."

This solemn assurance that we were under the protection of the English crown made no particular impression on my father. Our Russian travelling-companions, however, seemed not to have lost their faith in European mankind. They begged and implored us not to make difficulties and to do without the foreign guard. "The word of the English garrison has more value than the wild riders," they said; and we had no alternative but to obey the commands of the new authorities, to pay off our guard, send it back, and travel on, relying on the power of the English. Before we continued our journey, my father spoke with the native inhabitants of the village, who told us frankly that on the rest of the stretch there was a bloodthirsty robber behind each stone, who did not see the slightest difference between natives and foreigners. Thereupon we went to the English headquarters with the request that they should at least give us a few soldiers as escort to the next city. The English were honestly indignant that we doubted their word, cursed the Orientals, who, cowardly and cunning, did not want to believe in the power of England, and gave us a certificate which read that "the authorities of the occupation granted the caravan passage".

Only slightly reassured, we continued our journey after some delay. The region exhibited clear traces of a severe battle which must have taken place a short time before; it was devastated and chaotic. We were in a hurry, for we wanted to reach the next city before nightfall, in order to join a troop of government transport. Nevertheless we were surprised by darkness. A few miles outside the city night set in, and we wandered through the desert in the dark where only our camel-driver knew the way.

Suddenly whistles sounded somewhere near, and armed riders appeared out of the darkness, I sat on the humps of the second camel, together with my father, and we saw clearly how the strange riders forced our Chalwadar to give the command to halt. The riders encircled the caravan, and the camels stood crowded together within the circle. They were evidently not real Gengelis; they were ordinary robbers who doubtless were informed of the fact that our caravan was then unarmed. Their leader, a young Persian with flashing eyes, advanced and said: "Unbelievers, step to the side and surrender your property to the true believers." The travellers were searched, and one after the other was led to the side of the road. We, however, did not surrender, nor did the caravan-leaders, who would starve in the next city if deprived of their camels. For us, too, the prospect of arriving in a strange city lacking all our possessions was not at all heartening. The camel-driver began to negotiate with the robbers. "If the Worthy Robber does want to plunder the high gentlemen, why should the poor camel-driver suffer from it." The robber-chieftain gave them audience but would hear nothing from us. Even if we were true believers, it was our fault that we had fallen into such bad company. He suggested to us and the camel-drivers that if we were really good Mohammedans, we should join him and seek riches on the caravan paths. We declined most politely; and were then relieved of our goods. When it came to my turn, the chief asked me whether I would like to become his lover; he would then promise me a particularly rosy future. Luckily it occurred to me to answer that I was already the lover of a wise and holy imam from Meshed, and in the name of God did not want to leave the wise man in the lurch. The authority of the servant of God saved me. At the last moment, when the robber wanted to take his leave with the captured camels, our camel-drivers, who evidently could not bear to be separated from their animals, also joined them. We remained in the desert alone, without guides, and had to seek the next settlement on foot; not until daybreak did we catch sight of the first houses.

Our first visit was to the garrison authorities, who after all were to be blamed for our mishap. For hours we had to wait in the reception-rooms of the English general before he deigned to receive us. Impatiently he listened to our story. His reply was: "The English authorities bear the responsibility for all the property of Europeans residing here, as long as they do not venture into the revolting territory. No one can ask us to be responsible for coloured people or for runaway Russians. Besides, the English army of occupation did not force you to travel, and did not invite you to visit this country at all. You could have stayed quietly where you were. But since you are here the English authorities will take you under the protection of His Majesty the King and, in case you desire it, board you for the present in the prisoners' barracks."

Indignant, we left the general. Our Russian travelling-companions proceeded to the English consul, who did not receive them at all. We, however, abandoned further negotiations, and went to the native quarters which made up nine-tenths of the city here, as everywhere in the Orient, to find possible relatives or friends. Since we had nothing except the clothes on our backs, our situation was somewhat of a catastrophe; nevertheless the first merchant at whose doors we knocked was willing to grant us credit. But it did not come to that, for on the same day we learned from the officer of the mosque that a gentleman was looking for us. He turned out to be my father's brother, who had just arrived from Teheran, learned of our mishap, and immediately hurried to our assistance. We then decided to remain for a few days to procure what was necessary and to notify the Persian government. We wrote to the so-called "Committee of Iron", which possessed the actual power in the country at that time, and we received the most friendly reply, in which it expressed sympathy for us and promised to do everything that was possible for our indemnification.

Since the compensation no longer mattered now that my father's brother had helped us, we did not trouble about it; what could any "Committee of Iron" do towards compensating us? At that time we had more important worries. For we learned—in utter secrecy—that Baku was occupied by German-Turkish troops, that the English troops had fled from Azerbaijan, and that the extreme socialistic party which had been supported by the English had ended just as ingloriously as the Bolshevist in its time. Consequently we had to find our way home as speedily as possible—an extremely dangerous adventure. The English were waging war against the Germans and Turks, and there could be no question of a legitimate trip into hostile country. Yet we hoped to escape the English from Enzeli with the aid of a sailing-boat, just as stealthily as we had formerly turned our backs on the Bolshevists.

Before we rode to Enzeli, however, I had to undergo the most terrible experience of those years.

It was the day before our departure. We—my father, my uncle, and I—were sitting on the veranda of our house when a Persian rider in official uniform entered our court, dismounted, approached us, bowed to my father, and said in Azerbaijanian that he had been sent by the "Committee of Iron". That a Persian official addressed us in Azerbaijanian was an exceptional courtesy, since the officials even in Persian Azerbaijan preferred the Persian language, although the shah, as well as the whole Kajar dynasty, were thoroughbred Azerbaijanians. The official outdid himself in evidences of courtesy, and altogether seemed to be perfectly sympathetic. He had large, honest eyes and wore a kind smile. His whole demeanour spoke of goodness and readiness to assist. "Master," he said, "I am unworthy to kiss the dust from your feet; it is an honour for rne to stand before you, and I owe this honour only to the committee. They beg you to be good enough to excuse them for keeping you waiting for the indemnification till now, but it is the fault of circumstances and fate. The committee did not forget you for a moment, and is happy to be able to fulfil its sacred duty now towards so noble a man as yourself. I bring you the compensation."

The Persian bowed once more, went to his horse, took a leather bag from the saddle, stepped to us, and laid the bag on the table in front of my father. The bag was sealed. "Open it," said my father. The Persian cautiously broke the seal, drew out the cord, enlarged the opening of the bag, and emptied a whole lot of salt on the table. Then he put his slender hand with long red nails into the bag, searched a while and, grinning joyfully, brought something to light. At first I could not perceive what he held; then I shrank back, for on the heap of salt he had placed the head of a man. Blood stuck to its hair, the features were gruesomely distorted, and the wrinkles were salt-encrusted. "That is the head of the villain who caused you discomforts on the way here," explained the messenger pleasantly, too polite to use the word "plunder" in connection with such aristocratic gentlemen. Horrified, we told him to take away the terrible gift, but he would not. It was the compensation, he asserted; it had cost much trouble, and belonged to us exclusively; we might take it with us in the leather bag. It took a long time before we could convince our visitor that we felt entirely compensated by the sight of the head. He nodded, took a scrap of paper from his pocket and scratched a few lines on it which he gave to my father to sign. On the paper was written that we waived claims to the indemnification in favour of the Persian state. The head of the robber was then carried through the streets on a pike and fastened to the wall for all to see; but the English authorities protested against this. We could not search any more for our belongings, since we had expressly renounced the indemnification in favour of the state.

At that time a young man with a fabulous past and a still more fabulous future was at the head of the "Committee of Iron". Then he was probably the most powerful man in Persia. Today he occupies the golden throne which Nadir-Shah once brought from India and is called Riza-Khan-Pehlewi, Shachir-shah-i-Iran.

The day after this gruesome incident we rode to Enzeli, where we almost felt at home. All the emigrants from Azerbaijan were gathered there. We met old friends and relatives, each of whom could relate the most unbelievable adventures. We all felt like castaways who catch sight of the devoutly longed-for haven after many dangers. The strangest rumours about the situation in Baku were being spread; and the only definite news was that the socialists of all degrees had been driven out, that the Germans and Turks were in Baku, and that a national government was ruling the situation. But not until it was confirmed that Fathali-Khan of Choya, a highly esteemed lawyer, had become prime minister, did every doubt disappear and the emigrants rejoice sincerely. For Fathali-Khan was one of ours; he belonged to the class. Now we could actually ride to Baku as victors, on white horses, as it were, destroy all enemies who were still alive, and develop the old glory anew in a better form. So the revolution was over; our restoration could begin. We all thirsted for that.

One's feelings could not be expressed aloud. In Enzeli were the English, in Baku the Germans; consequently everything that was in Baku had to be abused, including the reaction and the new government. So—in spite of the danger of being brought before an English court-martial—we decided to sail across the Caspian Sea once more from east to west, not alone this time, but with about two hundred other owners of oil-land, and their families, Kotschis and a few other people.

Together we bought ourselves a boat which looked suspiciously old, but therefore was not guarded by the English. Among the travellers were four captains, two from my father's ships, so that there was no lack of expert guidance. A few of the Kotschis and their people acted as sailors. During the night all the emigrants boarded the wretched vessel, which was meant for fifty persons at the most. Among our fellow-voyagers was the bride of the Prince Alania, the famous Bolshevist murderer. Only my uncle stayed in Enzeli, to travel back to Samarkand where he lived. Any ordinary steamer makes the trip from Enzeli to Baku in twelve hours; we counted on taking twice that time, but had a supply of water and food for forty-eight hours.

It was pitch-black that night; our ship sailed without light in order to be out of reach of the English, unnoticed, by the morning. The most difficult thing was to board the vessel. The port of Enzeli had no proper harbour, and we had to reach the ship in small boats and climb up loosely hanging rope-ladders. That took some hours.

At last the four captains and the robber-sailors raised the sails, and we began our joyous return home. No one could tell later how many bottles of wine the bloodthirsty home-comers emptied during that night.

CHAPTER 29

SHIPWRECK, SMALLPOX, AND THE BIRTHDAY OF THE CZAR

Our voyage was favoured with the best weather imaginable at first; the sky was cloudless, the sea calm. Most of the people slept on deck; the sole cabin on the ship was prepared for a few women and for me. We crowded on sail, yet attained only a modest speed. That did not disturb us, since we took a long delay into account from the start. We fortunately escaped the only danger that we could anticipate—the English searchlights at Enzeli. After the rich feast we went to bed with the sincere hope of seeing the shore of Azerbaijan soon.

I slept in the cabin together with the women, who were more vengeful than the men, and talked till late in the night about the punishments that in their opinion ought to be inflicted on more than ninety per cent, of the population of Azerbaijan. One could easily become a Bolshevist if one listened to their conversation for any length of time. Terrible tortures were thought out and painted with enthusiasm by tender women's lips; each one discovered fresh means for the final extermination of the enemy. Every malediction ended with the sentence, "Although I am a woman, I would like to witness that." At last I fell asleep, saw in my dreams how the Bolshevists in the world were impaled, heard their moans, and woke up. The moans, however, did not stop. The whole cabin moaned; the tender enemies of the Bolshevists lay on the floor, writhed, called for the captain, and cried. Everything in the cabin was topsy-turvy, and the pale, seasick faces left no doubt as to the cause of the trouble.

Outside a tempest was raging. I left the cabin and looked for my father, who was talking to one of the captains. There I heard that our ship had run into the midst of a notorious northern storm which sweeps over the Caspian Sea every two months and is avoided and feared by seamen. For steamboats this storm is not necessarily dangerous, but for sailboats, especially for such an old, overloaded tub as our vessel, it can be a serious matter.

The four captains, the sailors, and oil-men gathered together on the foredeck and deliberated as to whether we should run for the nearest port while it was still possible. The majority opposed this, arguing that we could not know whether the people in the nearest harbour would not be just as dangerous as the northern storm. The discussion could not be finished. The tempest became worse; the waves rose higher and higher; the wind tore our sails. Suddenly there was a crash. Loud screaming sounded on the deck. The old, rotten mainmast had broken and a man lay crushed beneath it.

Then panic broke out. One mast after another snapped in the gale. At noon we drifted without sails, and only a seaman knows what that means. The women lay unconscious; the Kotschis howled and threatened to kill the four captains. The gusts of wind forced the vessel down almost to the surface of the sea. For the present the helm was still in order. One of the captains steered as well as possible in the circumstances.

So the first day passed. The next day the rudder broke, and, what was even worse, our supply of water was running low. We floated about like the first humans on the first raft. I was convinced that we should sink, and seated myself in a wooden case from which I had thrown out all the contents. In this "lifeboat" I hoped to reach the shore with my father. The panic among the people grew. The supply of water had to be guarded with revolvers. It was meant for the women and the oil-magnates. Three fellow-travellers, a Russian and two former Kotschis, suddenly became criminals in the middle of the stormy sea. They began to rob the people and to assault the maidservants who slept on deck. They were thrown overboard. That was gruesome, but left us entirely unmoved. The ship resembled an insane asylum. Only the captains and the owners of oil-land, who had experienced a great variety of things in their lives, retained their calm. They all stood armed next to the cabin on the foredeck and shouted reassuring words to the crowd. I alone was unarmed. As I have said, I sat in my "lifeboat" and read the only book we happened to have with us, a Russian edition of "Don Quixote de la Mancha".

On the evening of the second day a miracle took place; we spied a regular flotilla in the distance which we were steadily approaching. What kind of fleet it was we did not know. In our condition we no longer feared anyone. We raised the signal of distress and hoped a vessel would hurry to our assistance. Nothing happened, and not until we were quite near did we see people on the strange boats, who regarded us curiously. We noticed three military steamers, which alarmed us somewhat. Up to that time we had never heard of military ships on the Caspian Sea. We began to call for help, signalled that we were without a helm and might collide with them if no assistance were given.

At last the answer came: "Sail carefully, do not collide"–an absurd warning. Were they making fun of us? We tried to cast anchor, without success; one chain-cable tore loose, and before we could put the other in motion we struck one of the vessels. A crash, a shout–and we were torn back by the waves. From the strange vessel came the cry: "Anchor, or we shoot!" In fact, they were levelling the guns at us.

Even today it is inexplicable to us how our captains succeeded in anchoring in the storm in the midst of the strange fleet. Need works miracles. We anchored, stopped, and then noticed that we had sprung a big leak at the collision. The water rushed in dangerously; the Kotschis were organized in haste to man the single-hand pump on board.

It was already dark. The sea and the wind raged. The Kotschis worked on, and my father covered me with a fur. I fell asleep peacefully, "Don Quixote" in my hand.

The next day the storm subsided. In its place came the worry about the leak and the threatening guns of the strange fleet. For the present our time was spent in pumping. We cursed the extraordinary steamers that still brought us no water. Towards ten o'clock our uncertainty ended. A boat was let down from one of the ships and came alongside. Four men, apparently officers, climbed aboard and asked for the captain. They spoke Russian, but did not carry a red Soviet star, so were evidently not Bolshevists, and for the time refused to answer any questions. Their flag was the regular Russian marine flag.

Our four captains appeared, showed their papers, and told them that our ship had been headed for Baku.

"But Baku is occupied by Germans and Turks," said the Russian.

"Thank God," said one of the captains. "That is why we are sailing there."

The faces of the Russians darkened; they looked at us as at suspicious rogues, and murmured something like "deserters".

One of our captains inquired most politely with whom he had to deal, and received the prompt reply: "The High Seas Fleet of His Majesty the Czar."

That sounded fantastic. For two years there had been no Czar; round about ruled Persians, Germans, and Bolshevists, and suddenly the fleet of His Majesty appears upon the high seas. It turned out that the fleet did not recognize the revolution, was fighting against the Bolshevists, and also wanted to have nothing to do with those "Whites" who were not one hundred per cent, monarchists. All this time the fleet had stayed in a tiny military port, but now that the Germans were in Baku, they were sailing, as the officer explained to us, to "fulfil their duty"; that is, to fight against the Germans until the rightful Czar had made rightful peace. It all sounded somewhat crazy. The peace treaty of Brest-Litovsk had long been signed.

Unfortunately, however, the words of the officer were true; the loyal people actually wanted to continue to fight against the Germans; first, because the Czar had not made peace, and also to prove clearly their monarchistic convictions and their rejection of the "Bolshevist disgrace."

According to that, in the eyes of this "High Seas Fleet of His Majesty", we were common criminals who wanted to pass over to the enemy camp during wartime and had been caught in the act. The situation became awkward. That we should receive water or any other sort of help became improbable. On the contrary, they practically sat in judgment over us. Every captain, sailor, and so on had to make his deposition. Then the officers returned to their steamer, and after half an hour announced the verdict. Its purport was: The ship must be sunk with all on board, according to the valid laws of naval warfare.

Again panic broke out among us. The women howled, the Kotschis prepared for battle. The prospect of being sunk by some, stray Russians when we were in sight of safety was indeed appalling. Yet soon the Russians informed us that the execution would be postponed for a day, because on the, day of the passing of the sentence the birthday of the Czar or some grand-duke was being celebrated, and the crew did not want to work. And, in fact, at twelve o'clock the Russians fired a salute in honour of the birthday, and the celebration began. At five o'clock we ascertained by means of a telescope that the whole crew was dead drunk and no longer bothered about the "Azerbaijanian political offenders".

We made the most of that. With great dispatch the helm was repaired, and a sort of sail was patched together. In the night, while the Russians reveled in patriotic reminiscences, we weighed anchor as quietly as possible and got away. Carefully we sailed around the hostile steamers and saw, with no slight surprise, a Russian sailor gaily waving farewell to us. Soon we were out of sight.

The danger of being sunk was past, but not that of death from thirst and starvation. We saw the water rising slowly in the hull of the ship, in spite of the strenuous work of the men at the pumps. Thus the night passed. The next day a third danger appeared, which was not less than the other two. A child on board suddenly showed black spots all over his body and died within a few hours. We had no physician aboard, so we did not know with what sickness we had to deal. After the child several other deck-passengers fell sick. The oil-lords then locked themselves up in the cabins at the stern with their wives, and the captains called the disease black smallpox, although they might just as well have said plague. In the course of two days, that is, till our rescue, eleven fellow-travellers died, and their corpses were thrown overboard. They were mostly Persian servants and their wives who accompanied us. Desperation grew each hour. The last drops of the drinking-water had been distributed among the women and children. The weather became worse. Since the pumps no longer sufficed, a chain of people was formed, armed with pails, who baled the water overboard; nevertheless it continued to rise. The helm and the substitute for sails—our sheets were used—left much to be desired. I spent these worst days of my life sleeping most of the time. I had furnished my "lifeboat" with covers and cushions, lay on its floor so that I could see nothing of the sea or my fellows, and endlessly read my "Don Quixote". When my father came, we spoke about death and wondered whether anyone might possibly remain alive. I did not become seasick; the others were worse off.

The rescue came unexpectedly, as always, and at the last moment, almost as in a cheap novel. On the afternoon of the fifth day we caught sight of a steamer on the horizon which immediately changed its course in answer to our distress signals, and came towards us. The flag was unknown to us, and we were afraid of again falling into the hands of some fantastic government. The only Swede in our company, however, knew something about flags. He gazed at it for a while, took off his hat, made the sign of the cross, and said, relieved: "It is the flag of the German empire." Within an hour we were aboard the Baku steamer which sailed about on the Caspian under the German colours to save refugees who, like us, were looking for their native shore.

On the steamer was a German officer who spoke Turkish, and greeted us in the name of the German army of occupation. When the captain, who knew us well, informed him that there were native politicians, oil-owners, and princes among us, the German saluted us once more and said that he would put all the officers' cabins at our disposal. In fact, he immediately had all the cabins emptied, even his own, and himself slept on the foredeck. The captain made the usual report to the owner of the steamer, who was present; the sailors called us all by our proper titles. Our last worry about the conditions in Baku seemed to have been blown away.

We were the masters again.

From the captain we also learned the details about the situation in Azerbaijan, which sounded satisfactory. The oil-derricks were unharmed, the workmen were loyal to the masters, all enemies seemed to have been destroyed. The whole country was firmly in the hands of the government—the oil-owners. Not even for the women, who again became bloodthirsty after the rescue, was there anything left to be desired. Never in my life, neither before nor after, have I rejoiced so much as on that day, on the steamer not far from the coast of Baku.

The next day we sailed into the port. A guard of honour received us; we saw the old city again, the palaces, the walls. We recognized people who hurried down to kiss our hands, heard the hymn which the guard played, and perceived the barely noticeable, sweet, dearly loved odour of oil which streamed towards us. On shore next to the guard stood the new Prime Minister, Fathali-Khan of Choya, who had heard of our arrival, God knows how, and had rushed to the spot. Next to him a soldier held the Azerbaijanian flag. I never felt much respect for flags and prime ministers, but this time I was touched by the scene. I do not know how it happened. I stood next to my father, who was speaking to the minister, looked at the fresh face, gleaming with ministerial dignity, saw the crescent next to him, and suddenly, completely unexpectedly to myself and all the others, I embraced the man and kissed his full, smiling lips. "Not so stormy," said the prosaic minister. "You will soon have plenty of beautiful girls."

It is glorious to return home after many months of dangerous journeying. As we left the pier and stepped on to the wharf, a division of German soldiers marched by. For the first time I saw German soldiers. They were singing a song which I had never heard, and which I liked very much at the time. The words were: "The birds in the forest sing so very beautifully. At home, in my native land, we shall meet again." I knew enough German to understand them.

At our house they did not yet know of our arrival. Two Turkish soldiers stood guard in front of the door. In the house lived a German officer and a Turkish officer. When they learned that the rightful owner had returned, they hurried to meet us and to assure us that they would move immediately. "Won't you stay with us?" said my father. "There is room enough."

"We have no right to inconvenience you," answered the officer, "but do not worry. An Armenian family lives quite near; they have a nice little house, and we will move there right away."

Thus we entered our native land.

CHAPTER 30

THE TURKISH OCCUPATION

The old oil-city had changed little; but on the way from the shore to the house I noticed the gallows at nearly every street corner. From them hung corpses, and next to each corpse stood a soldier of the army of occupation. A police-officer who met us explained that about two hundred gallows had been erected in the city to maintain the public peace and safety. We were perfectly satisfied with this explanation. My father praised the energy of the army.

Gradually I learned the details about the capture of the city, as well as about the retreat of the English and the entrance of the government troops.

After the overthrow of the communists, a Social-Democratic workers' dictatorship came into power and continued the war against the approaching German-Turkish-Azerbaijanian troops. Since the battle-forces of the dictatorship were not dependable enough, it was decided to invite the English from Persia for the defence of the oil-city. These did not wait for a second invitation. They appeared in orderly columns, fully convinced that their presence alone would suffice to keep the enemy from further attacks. This took place in August, 1918, when no Englishman had any further doubts of victory. But things turned out differently. The troops of the enemy, under the leadership of Nuri-Pasha, besieged Baku, cut off the supply of water, and left it to the besieged to drink the sea-water, which was distilled in the oil-refineries. The water smelled of petroleum, but was bravely swallowed down by the Englishmen. At the same time large workers' meetings were held daily in the city, during which all present solemnly swore to defend their dictatorship to the very last. These meetings were regularly dispersed by the shrapnel of the besieging troops. They shot unerringly, and showed clearly that the Germans and Turks were well informed about events in the besieged city. In fact, every night news was given to the Turks from the roofs of such Mohammedan houses that were high enough for the purpose, and every detail about the position of the troops and the like was communicated.

That happened in our house also, for the women who were living with us did their best to expedite our early return. Fräulein Grete of Königsberg was still among them, and spent the nights—so they told us—on the level roof of our house with her signal lantern. The position of the defenders was really not an easy one. The troops of the workers' dictatorship consisted mainly of Armenians—who, as the reader knows, had reason enough to fear the entrance of the Azerbaijanian troops—and of the English forces, but these considered themselves much too dignified to fight at the front and cared solely for peace inside the city.

One day the Turkish commander asked the English general by letter to leave Baku to its fate and withdraw to Persia. Otherwise, the letter said, the Turkish guns would fire upon the English headquarters in the middle of the city.

The English knew that nothing remained hidden from the enemy, and decided to move their staff into another building two hours before the time fixed by the Turks.

Day dawned; the English moved quietly, ordered breakfast in the new rooms, and disregarded the threats of the Turks. When the clock struck the hour named, a cannon shot was heard, which, to the dismay of the English, hit not their old quarters, but the new ones that had been kept strictly secret.

The Turkish small-calibre guns played havoc with the walls of the building, and the general and the other officers, who were then still awaiting their breakfast, did not know how they would get out alive. Suddenly the cannonade stopped, the telephone rang, and an un- known voice asked politely whether the English general would leave the city at last; otherwise the cannonade would be continued immedi- ately. The English consented. Quickly they packed, gathered the soldiers in the harbour, and confiscated the steamers. In the evening; not a single English soldier was left in the city. I have heard that this good general was later court-martialled for endangering the English prestige.

Henceforth Baku had nothing to depend on but the Armenian troops, which, in their turn, were broken up into several parties, and had but one wish, to escape unnoticed from the besieged town. Nevertheless the task of the besiegers was not easy. Baku is a first-class fortress. The small field-guns could accomplish but little. Besides, they had to be used very carefully in order to spare the oil-fields. Both sides tried to outdo each other in this caution. Although the front was situated close to the oil-derricks and partly included them, not a single derrick was damaged.

Among the Armenian troops—the remains of those troops which in their time celebrated the great massacre under the command of the Reds and slaughtered thirty thousand Mohammedans—the confusion grew from day to day. Someone had spread the news that the plan for the capture of Baku, coming from Hindenburg personally, had just arrived in the Turkish camp in a sealed package. There were even people to be found who swore that they had seen the package with their own eyes. The confusion became panic. The Mohammedans zealously supported the Hindenburg legend, and soon every Armenian soldier was convinced that further defence was a mere waste of time for him. In the meantime the Turks were preparing for a general attack on the city, the plan of which did not originate from Hindenburg, but from the German commander-in-chief in Georgia, Kress von Kressenstein, and the Turkish general, Nuri-Pasha. According to all the laws of strategy, the attack was launched by running fire. However, when the Turks charged and reached the silently threatening Armenian front, it proved to be deserted by all soldiers. The way to the city lay clear. Only a few drunken Armenians were to be found in the trenches. In their condition, however, these could not report anything plausible about the disappearance of the defenders. At first some sort of ruse was suspected; later, when the Turks advanced carefully, they came to the pleasing conclusion that the cannonade had sufficed to drive from their entrenchments the defenders—who were celebrating an Armenian saint on that day. A few patrols that were sent into the city reported that it appeared to be deserted. Thereupon Nuri-Pasha declared Baku captured and congratulated the Azerbaijanian government that was staying in his camp.

Then something happened which is foreign to European warfare. The Azerbaijanian troops which had fought together with the Turks demanded the observance of the age-old Oriental custom that abandons the captured city to plundering. They wanted revenge for the last massacre and to take the victor's reward from the Armenians dwelling in the city, and were able to support their request so emphatically that they convinced the new authorities of their right. The Azerbaijanian government issued the decree customary in such cases which declared the "gold, the lives, and the women of the enemy" the property of the Azerbaijanian soldiers for three days. The Turkish soldiers stayed outside the city during this time. The native troops entered. Only the Turkish auxiliaries, the Kurds, requested of headquarters that they should also be permitted to enjoy the Armenian blood. Their request was granted.

The great vengeance began.

Eyewitnesses of the following three days report that the annals of history could scarcely show a similar massacre. Thorough revenge was taken. As principle the motto was chosen: two Armenians for one Mohammedan; and, what is more, taking into consideration the class-membership of the Armenian victims. For one murdered Mohammedan physician, two Armenian doctors were killed, for one Mohammedan lawyer, two Armenian lawyers, and so on. Systematically all the Armenian houses were stormed and their inhabitants slaughtered. Only those Armenians who had friends among the Mohammedans, and were sheltered by them, could save themselves. The sole difficulty for the Mohammedans was to decide correctly between Armenians and other peoples, especially the Jews, whose facial type is remarkably like the Armenian. Many an Armenian tried to pass for a Jew, and many a Jew was threatened instead of an Armenian. Luckily the farsighted government had decreed that everyone who was attacked and pretended to be a Jew should immediately be examined to determine his Judaism. In contrast to the Jews, the Armenians are not circumcised. This examination saved the lives of thousands of Jews. During the three days only one Jew was killed as an Armenian by mistake. It was much harder for the Jewish girls, who had upon them no proof of their Judaism. The government prohibited the assault of Jewish girls most strictly. To prevent confusion, a few Jewish soldiers who were in the Turkish army acted as experts during these three days, and were easily able to save their countrywomen.

The Turkish Jews, however, were able to recognize only the Azerbaijanian Jewesses. Besides these, there were in Baku Russian Jewesses who also looked like Armenians, but could not be recognized as fellow-believers owing to mutual lack of understanding of the language. At times the first rabbi had to appear. On the spot to settle the race-membership, but usually the testimony of neighbours sufficed, so that not a single Jewish girl was assaulted. In error one Jew was assaulted who wanted to defend his sisters, and tried to put off the soldiers till the arrival of the rabbi. The three days were free only in respect to Armenians, the conquerors took thorough revenge for the thirty thousand Mohammedans.

Again blood flowed in the streets of the oil-city, this time Armenian blood. Men and women were killed mercilessly. The victors pillaged the Armenian houses completely. A few cut open the bodies of their victims, smashed their skulls and laid themselves on the corpses, howling in the fever of victory, literally bathing in blood. They tore the bodies into shreds, bit through the throats of enemies, drank their blood, became intoxicated with the riches of the enemies, and celebrated the great revenge. Several hundred Armenians were not put to death immediately, but were taken to the large city square and there guarded by soldiers. Every Mohammedan—child, woman, or old man—might come and kill as many Armenians as was required by the precepts of mortal vengeance. The Armenians stood chained and were given up to the avenger on demand, together with a dagger. Some dipped their clothes into the blood to show it at home as proof of their vengeance. No one was spared, not even children. It is hard to say how many people lost their lives in those days. The experts state that there were about sixty thousand; in this, the number of raped women is not taken into consideration. At the end of the second day the pasha granted his officers permission to take part in the plundering also. Everyone considered it his duty to commit murder in the streets; even imperial princes were no exception. Bloody shreds of Armenian flesh became the token of those three days.

These three days, with which the Russian rule in the oil-land ended, were surely the most horrible that the Caucasus has ever seen. It was as though under one chapter of history a bloody line was drawn at last, which would put an end for ever to the Russian sovereignty.

Not only did the streets and alleys of the city become the stage of gruesome scenes, but the sea, the green, dark Caspian Sea, became the grave of many thousands of Armenians. Before and at the entrance of the Azerbaijanians, the hordes of fleeing Armenians streamed to the harbour. One ship after another, filled with wealthy refugees, left the shore.

Even the small boats and sailboats struggled out upon the open sea, and in a short time the port seemed desolate. The small, packed skiffs were sunk by a rising gale. From the decks of the overfilled steamers many people were hurled into the water. What the avengers in the city could not accomplish the sea completed.

Only the oil-derricks were again spared, although there, too, engineers lost their lives. Nevertheless no derrick caught fire; the new authorities, who were thirsting for oil, took good enough care of that. This did not prevent the extinction of the inhabitants of the Armenian poor district, Armenikend, not far from the derricks.

When the third day was drawing to an end the government announced by cannon-shots that peace and order had again taken command.

Not all obeyed the cannon-shots. After three days of murder it was hard to bring men to their senses. Then the government, escorted by the Turks, entered the city and erected gallows at every street-corner.

Everyone who disturbed the peace after the cannon-shot, robbed, murdered, or was caught at theft, was promptly hanged. Next to each gallows stood an officer, and a handful of soldiers, with a rope ready. That inspired exceptional respect in the population. Hundreds were hanged at the order of the stern authorities, and swung on the gallows for days; each bore a sign on his body with the description of his misdeed: "hanged for theft of a pound of nuts", or something similar.

No punishment other than death was inflicted. That was effective. Before the conquest, Baku was swarming with criminals of all kinds; five days after the capture, the city was a model of honesty, security, and order.

After the restoration of order the new government also began to take interest again in the welfare of the inhabitants, and what it did first was to try to lower the enormous prices of provisions. That was done in the following manner: all food-dealers were gathered together and the highest legal prices read to them. It was announced that whoever asked more would be hanged. Then something important was added which, as I heard later, the German coercive measures neglected. "In case the provisions disappear from the markets entirely, which is the customary result of such decrees, every fifth food-dealer will be automatically condemned to the gallows." This addition, as one can imagine, was unusually effectual. Feverishly the dealers attended to the importation of provisions, and occasionally even sold them below the cost-price. They were taught community feeling as easily as play. The half-starved city that had seen only camel-meat and nuts during the siege again breathed freely. But the gallows remained for months. In the opinion of the army of occupation these should not be empty, since that could possibly be taken for weakness and might harm the authority of the government.

Nevertheless, after a few days there were no more criminals, and so either innocent people had to hang or the gallows must come down. Both were undesirable; therefore recourse was had to a peculiar remedy which originated in the brain of a native physician.

They simply took the corpses of the people who died in the government hospitals or anywhere else without leaving relatives worth mentioning, carried them to the gallows during the night, and hung them up. In the morning the population could see the newly punished criminals, and the state authority was stabilized anew. Luckily this happened in the cold season, and a corpse kept for several days, at any rate. God knows what expedient would have been used in the summertime. I soon knew the truth about the origin of the hanged, and therefore was doubly amused at the impression that they made on the population.

At home everything remained in the best of order. The German girl, accompanied by our good wishes, travelled to Germany. During the massacre a special watch stood in front of our house to correct possible confusions as soon as they arose. The large house again lived according to its traditional customs. The women, children, and servants who dwelt with us did indeed look somewhat starved, but they had remained healthy. My father also asserted that the number of children had grown.

I believed him, but personally could never determine how many people, actually lived in our house.

When the news of our arrival spread, our Kotschis appeared immediately, for they had much to report, and declared their allegiance to us anew. Then the official visits began. One of the first who appeared was the Turkish pasha, the conqueror of Baku. He was surrounded by a circle of German officers who outdid each other in felicitations and friendliness. I acted as interpreter between them and my father. The Turkish general told us that he was continuing to send steamers out daily to help the refugees who might still be afloat and in trouble as we were.

After the official visits the balls that everyone gave in everyone else's honour began. After long months of flight and hardships people now tried to recover their losses. The German officers set the fashion. The whole place was dumbfounded when it was seen that they actually paid with real money for everything that they took or consumed in stores.

According to the general view it was not proper for a conqueror to pay for something that belonged to him, but they could not be convinced. It even lessened the German authority among the people. One literally had to force the customary presents on the Germans. Every officer looked embarrassed when he was handed a silver box or a golden dagger. Never before had one seen such strange conquerors in the Orient.

Much more numerous than the German officers were the Turkish ones, who naturally were more comprehensible to us. Some of them stayed in Baku for good and married the daughters of the owners of oil-land, and each time this gave rise to endless festivities. When departing from these festivals, again and again the gallows with the corpses at every street-corner could be seen, recalling the danger that had been overcome, the bloody battles, and the rule of the Reds which was now past.

A week after our arrival our oil-fields were in order again. Never before had the workmen accomplished as much as at that time. The black gold again streamed from the depths as in the olden times when it was still sacred; when, like the eternal flames, it was consecrated to the peaceful Ahura-mazda, the good god.

CHAPTER 31

THE ENGLISH

The German-Turkish occupation lasted only a few months. After the collapse of the German Western front and the Turkish-English armistice, the allies evacuated Azerbaijan. The Azerbaijanian front was Eastern battleground. There the Germans and Turks remained victors till the end; in September, 1918, the English troops still retreated before them. It was intended to undertake a campaign to Turkestan, when the news of the armistice arrived. Among the troops which had just celebrated a glorious victory, this news caused consternation; for us, the Azerbaijanian's politicians, it might mean ruin in certain circumstances.

After all, the same Azerbaijanian politicians who had driven the English from Baku, supported by the Germans and Turks, now were to welcome back the vanquished English general who had retreated to Persia. The liberators of the oil-land were celebrated with guard of honour and festal send-off. Two hours later the first transport-steamer of the English army of occupation appeared on the horizon. The same guard that had escorted the last German officers was then drawn up on the pier to receive the "new masters". Of course, the whole cabinet also gathered at the shore. The English arrived; the general, who, to our surprise, was not the one who had recently been driven away, landed, looked at the Azerbaijanian flag for a while, and asked without greeting anyone: "What kind of rag is that?"

"The Azerbaijanian national flag, Your Excellency," answered the Minister of Foreign Affairs.

"Curious," muttered the general. Then he stood there silently for a time and suddenly gave the command to sing the English national anthem. This was done, and the general, satisfied, moved into the palace assigned to Tiim. Thus the English occupation began. It lasted several months, during which the English acted as though they were doing us a favour by sojourning in the richest oil-land of Asia. If anything displeased them, they prohibited the government from doing it with the argument that it violated the principles of civilization. Such a prohibition, which the English never expressed otherwise than orally, always ended with the following sentence: "We ask that you follow our advice, since otherwise we should have to leave your country to its own fate and withdraw to England." That sounded kind, but was only slightly convincing. The English did not take the least trouble to adapt themselves to the customs of the country. They lived as in England; which often led to unpleasant consequences.

English officers—just as the German and Turkish officers—received free admission into the famous club of the oil-lords. One day four went there, ordered a supper, and after they had dined they put their lower extremities on the table. In Azerbaijan this custom is unknown, but there is a proverb there: Seat a pig at the table; it will put its legs on the table. The officiating member of the club, Prince Ali, approached them and requested the Englishmen to take their legs off the table. The officers did not consider him worthy of an answer, and continued to chat as though nothing had happened. The prince repeated his request, whereupon one of the officers took his pipe from his mouth and said something that sounded like "go to the devil". The prince then beckoned to several waiters, who threw the upholders of the British culture out of the club as gently as ever they could. A few owners helped them, and an Englishman lost his sabre.

The next day all the newspapers contained paragraphs: "English officers thrashed by oil-owners." The English general raged, appeared before the president of the oil-council, threatened to shut the club and to shoot the implicated oil-lords. Strange to say, he dropped both intentions when it was explained to him that the oil-club was a closed society and could exclude every non-owner or objectionable guest.

That was also the custom in England, he said, and confiscated the

papers that described the episode. The officers involved were transferred to England.

The Englishmen made use of the months they spent in Azerbaijan
to become acquainted with the Christian families, that is, Russians,
Armenians, and Georgians. Among the Christians the Englishmen were
very popular, as saviours from the Turkish yoke, and there were numerous marriages between the Christian girls and English officers. At every
wedding all the officers of the garrison appeared, celebrated till dawn,
and congratulated the young couple.

At last the day came when, in accord with a resolution of the English
parliament, the English were to give up their care for the civilization of
Azerbaijan and return to their native country. For the corps of officers a
train of parlour-cars was reserved, the last two of which were set aside
for the young wives. Their husbands were to travel together with the
unmarried officers in the front cars. On the day of departure all the relatives of the women gathered on the platform. With tears and parting
wishes the women, boarded the last two cars and their husbands the
first. The general made a farewell speech. A whistle blew; the train
began to move. The train began its journey to Europe, but without the
last two cars, which remained standing on the tracks, because they had
not been attached to the train. The poor wives stayed where they were,
ridiculed by all, and did not know what to do for shame and anger.
Only one single officer returned later to call for his wife. The others
were not heard of again. For them the little colonial adventure was
ended with the departure from the city.

Thus the English occupation ended, and for the first time in many
years Azerbaijan again became absolutely independent. Russia was in
the throes of civil war, and was not dangerous. Friendly treaties were
made with all the neighbouring states, with Georgia, Armenia, Daghestan, and Persia. The oil government, supported by the parliament,
maintained peace and order on the fields, in the deserts, and among
the nomad clans.

For the oil-lords, who now came into power, this time was the best
of their lives, as it was for me, too. The peaceful life of the old East was

to begin anew, undisturbed by speeches of parliament, resolutions of the government, and other European inventions. The parliament was guarded by our Kotschis, who searched every representative and took away his weapons for the duration of the session—to avoid disagreeable incidents.

The wise General Taghi-Sade—who in his time had come into conflict with the Prince Bebutoff—set forth his programme in a long speech in the parliament; the main point was the following sentence, which was received with loud applause: "Our poor people need three things: whip, penitentiary, and teachers."

According to these principles government would be to the satisfaction of the ruling class. In fact, they did rule thus, till the Soviet star emerged again in the north and made the oil-lords, princes, ministers, and members of parliament taste the bloody whip. Until that time there were no more exciting events in the country. Sometimes still in dark alleys revolver-shots would crack. Now and then a few suspicious people might disappear; and from time to time the oil-lords, ministers, and members of parliament gave ceremonious receptions at which the diplomatic corps appeared in full numbers, and the papal nuncio wished the republic good luck.

How these happy and glorious times came to a conclusion may now be related.

PART III

THE FLIGHT

CHAPTER 32

THE OVERTHROW

One day we gave a reception that lasted till late in the evening. Two gentlemen, the Minister of Commerce, Ali-Bey, and the military governor of Baku, Murad-Girei-Tlechas, stayed longer than the rest, sat in the salon with my father, and chatted about the last meeting of the parliament, and about the disturbances that had arisen in Armenia—close to the border of Azerbaijan. Nothing was pending in the parliament except a motion for granting a rather large sum to combat field-rats, a question which did not arouse the slightest interest in anyone. Matters stood much worse in regard to the disturbances in Armenia; it was feared that they might mean crossing the Azerbaijan border. The government sent all the troops at its disposal to the border of Armenia in order to be able to assist at the critical moment. This alarmed my father. The north of Azerbaijan, as well as the capital, remained unprotected, which appeared especially dangerous because manoeuvres of troops were announced at the Russian border. The military governor, to whom my father communicated his doubts, only smiled and said: "As long as I sit here and drink coffee, you may feel assured that no Russian will enter the country."

In fact, just a few days before, a treaty of friendship had been made with the Russians, which made a sudden attack apparently impossible. Soon after the governor and the minister took their leave. The minister proceeded to the parliament, and the governor entered his car. From the balcony I could still see the night-patrol which was just passing greet the governor and call out the customary "long live". When he arrived at home and left the car, several armed men approached him and declared that he was arrested. "At whose command?" he asked. "By order of the Cheka of the Socialist Soviet Republic of Azerbaijan," was the answer.

During this night the unexpected overthrow occurred; from Jalama, from the Russian-Azerbaijanian border came trains filled with Russian soldiers. They surrounded the city quietly, and their leaders, sailors as well as several Azerbaijanian convicts, sent a delegation to the parliament that was just assembled with the demand to surrender since a defence would be useless. One can easily imagine what happened that night in the parliament, completely taken by surprise. The Minister of War, General Mechmander, declared that resistance was out of the question. The parliament was forced to accept the conditions of the communists. A deed of capitulation was quickly drawn up, in which the communists expressly bound themselves not to persecute a single minister, member of parliament, or oil-magnate in any way but to grant them free withdrawal from the country. How the Russians kept their promise can be seen by the fact that within one month after the overthrow of Baku not a single minister was still alive, and of the members of parliament and the oil-magnates only those were not in the prison of the Cheka who could not be replaced as oil-experts. Thus the Red revolution took place, costing more lives than the last two massacres together.

My father and I knew of the events that night, and next morning we were awakened by a servant who informed us that the Bolshevists had taken the city. Through the window I saw the entrance of the Red troops, saw the brutal faces, tattered figures, wicked Bolshevik grimaces, and envious, hungry Russian eyes which coveted the riches of the oil-city.

The same day the work of the Cheka began. The governor and thirteen leading politicians were condemned to death. The communist government arrested everyone who could not prove indisputably his "decent" convictions or his indispensability to the oil industry. The murder of the general and the thirteen took place in a ceremonious manner—later on murder became more prosaic. Escorted by soldiers armed to the teeth and armoured cars, they were led through the streets, as was said, to "awaken disgust with the capitalist bandits in the workmen, and in the rest fear of the Cheka".

The imposing procession passed our house; I stood in front of the door and looked at the condemned. The general recognized me, waved his hand, and pointed to his neck as a sign that now no doubt his head would be cut off. I waved likewise. Later I found out that the fourteen who were condemned to death had secreted iron rods from somewhere, and with these primitive weapons had knocked down a number of the soldiers who were to execute the sentence. The general was said to have sold his life most dearly. One of the people who finally succeeded in killing the condemned, later told me horrible details about this event. The fourteen were literally beaten to pieces.

Thus the Bolshevik rule began; or, if you wish, the "free Socialist Republic" of Azerbaijan.

That, however, was only a modest beginning; not until a few weeks later was the true face of the conqueror unmasked.

Every day hundreds were arrested—Kotschis, bankers, nobles, teachers, students, journalists were thrown into the prisons of the Cheka. At the head of the Cheka was a Russian sailor who could now make use of his marine experiences. In small ships the prisoners were taken put to sea where the Cheka was officially located on the small rock-island, Nargen. In reality the prisoners were shot on the ship near the island and thrown overboard with a weight. Even the Azerbaijanian Soviet government often did not know which of the prisoners had already been disposed of. Thousands lost their lives in this way. With its systematic cruelty and its despotic power the work of the Cheka reminded me of what I had read about the Holy Inquisition. People disappeared without trace, and even their nearest relatives did not dare to inquire into their fate. But whoever did try was promised a meeting with the prisoner in Nargen; he was put on board a ship and likewise remained missing for ever; that is, was thrown overboard near the island.

That was even worse than a massacre. The Orient knows massacres, bloody days, bestial cruelty, which breaks like an explosion, so to speak, soon giving way to the inherent phlegm of the population, but methodical extermination of whole masses of population is entirely unknown. That, however, was the idea of the Cheka, the systematic extermination of the "class of owners". The communists called that time "the great days of the terror". No one was sure of his life. It was not necessary to commit a crime. The suspicion that some member of the family cherished disloyal thoughts was enough to carry him off with all his relatives to Nargen—provided that he was not essential for the oil industry.

The age of the suspected person made no difference. In the opinion of the Cheka everyone between fifteen and eighty years was mature enough to be condemned to death. The famous General Taghi-Sade, who was a hundred and one years old, was sentenced to death. The class-conscious workmen who heard of this surrounded the palace and blocked the way for the Cheka, who at first wanted to shoot at the workmen with machine-guns; but at the last moment the general's pardon arrived from Moscow. The aged man was plundered and banished.

A few days after the conquest and the subsequent taking-over of the oil-wells by the government, members of the Cheka came to our house and explained to my father that, as an "old bandit, bloodsucker, and criminal", he was sentenced to death. However, the execution of the sentence would be postponed for an indefinite time if he declared himself willing to guide the oil industry, and especially the oil transport to Russia "honestly", of course under the supervision of several communists, until experienced successors had arisen from the ranks of the proletariat. In the event of satisfactory performance of his duty the prospect of a possible pardon was held out to him.

My father consented and was summoned to the board of directors of the governmental oil industry, where he was designated daily as a "suspicious but temporarily irreplaceable bandit". He worked, and the communist directors approved his crazy actions. Whoever objected to this hair-raising nonsense was declared guilty of sabotage. The industry went to ruin gradually in this way. Of course the "bloodsuckers" were at fault.

Besides the terror, the stimulation of the revolutionary spirit was not neglected. For example, one day a regular "act of faith" was

arranged in front of our house. The wax figures of the "bloodsuckers"
and their international aiders and abettors—Wilson, Clemenceau, and
Lloyd George—were thrown on to a huge pyre and burned solemnly
during the singing of the Internationale. The figures of the accomplices
in dress-suit and monocle reminded me very much of the "Prankish
ambassador" in the Persian passion-plays. The celebration was even
filmed and shown in all Azerbaijan. Many years later the film came to
Berlin, where I could watch it at my leisure. The Berlin critique spoke of
excellent pictures at that time.

The symbolic burning of wax figures did not suffice. The awakened
Russian proletariat demanded something tangible, and so the famous
"week of plundering" was thought out, which put everything that pre-
ceded into the shade. The week was prepared for thoroughly, and
important general instructions were issued. These began with the establishment of the fact that, as a result of the brutal capitalistic management, the revolutionary proletariat lacked many things necessary for the
household and other purposes—clothes, money, furniture, and the like—
which were plentiful in the houses of the bandits and their employees.
Therefore the proletariat was given the right to take anything that they
liked from all the houses during one week. The non-proletariat population had to keep quiet and watch calmly. All opposition was to be punished by death as revolt against the power of the state.

It is impossible for a European to imagine this communistic week of
plunder. For days the dregs of the Russian workmen marched through
the city. Most of the Russians and Mohammedans made no use of the
right to plunder. However, there was all the more plundering on the part
of the scum. They went into a house, searched it, and simply took along
everything portable. Only what the inhabitants wore on their bodies
was left behind—the suit and underwear. Everything else—dishes, furniture, food, laundry, samovar, gold, money, and so on—was carried off. Of
course, many conflicts took place, and the soldiers had to take a hand to
lead the wailing housewives off to the Cheka for "revolt against the
power of the state". The more quick-witted proletarians even invaded
the holy of holies of the Mohammedan houses—the harem. The Moham-

medan women were undressed, searched, and their covers and veils taken. Conditions were worst for the poor Mohammedan families, whose entire property consisted of cheap silk covers, which seemed expensive to the plunderers. On these covers the whole family sleeps; they are a symbol, as it were, of domesticity and female honour. Now they were stolen "for the purposes of the world-revolution".

To the owners of oil-land, this week of plunder seemed like play. People who had lost millions after the taking over of the oil industry by the government and confiscation of the banks, and who were in daily danger of being shot, had small interest in cooking utensils and other dishes. The middle class came off worst, for they were deprived of their last property, and, when all is considered, had nearer been substantially richer than a good worker. Many men killed themselves as dishonoured because their harems had been invaded. In the homes of the middle class a harem is the room that the woman of the house, usually only one, occupies with her children. At the end of the week the middle class could no longer be distinguished from the rabble. The homes of the owners were also plundered, but they were not so badly affected, for they had found an opportunity to hide the most necessary things in time.

I was also robbed; I led the people through my room and called their attention to one thing and another that they might be able to use. They thanked me in surprise and helped themselves. When they were gone, our house looked rather empty. Except for a few old chairs and beds that had formerly stood in the cellar, only my library, for which, in spite of my repeated indications, the worthy plunderers had not shown the slightest interest, had been left behind. That hurt me not a little. My father and I were indifferent to this wholesale thieving. We knew that either the Bolshevists would be chased away and we could then establish ourselves again, or we should be shot one fine day. Perhaps, too, we might be able to get away. We could do without our furniture, in any event.

After the plunder new folk-amusements were thought out for the proletariat. First the inhabitants who did not work had to sweep the streets under the supervision of the working ones and take the dust-bins out of the city, by virtue of the manifesto: "The proletariat cannot stand any dirt!"

Then we were driven out of our house within twenty-four minutes. On the form that was made out for twenty-four hours, as usual, in place of the crossed-out "hours" stood the laconic word "minutes". This expulsion was a trifle for most of us after the week of plunder. After all, one had nothing left to take.

Some communist organization moved into my father's house. We shifted our residence to our former offices, where we were allowed to occupy only one room.

Thus the first weeks of the communist rule passed. My father and I were soon sick of it, and decided to flee to Georgia, where there were no communists yet.

The undertaking was difficult. My father was carefully guarded, especially when he went out with me. They knew that he would not leave without me. So we decided to escape separately and at rather long intervals, and to hide somewhere in the country for a while, to meet later at the border of Georgia on a set day. I, who was not so well known, was to ride to Gandja—a city in the interior of Azerbaijan—with the consent of the government, officially to take a rest in the country and return later. Since we had many friends in Gandja and communism had not penetrated so deeply there, my father hoped that I should easily find the way from there to the border. His own scheme was to take a tour of inspection to the oil-fields a few months after my departure, and then to evade the guard with the help of a few friends. In the beginning our plan met with no difficulties. I was given permission by the government to leave the city—without permission I was not allowed to travel—and entered a cattle-truck of the train for Gandja; I chose this because the communists and soldiers travelled in the. passenger-compartments and I could no longer stand the sight of them. With me were the Azer-baijanian peasants, a few of whom knew me, and tried to make the trip as pleasant as possible. They cursed all communists, so that I almost felt as though I were among owners of oil-land. On the way we stopped often and for long, because the locomotives needed repairs again and again. The Russian conductors were drunk. Several times the soldiers ransacked the cars in the search for "Whites", cursed the "stupid natives", and threatened with the Cheka.

I sat at the entrance of the wagon, looked at the deserts, fields, and mountains, saw caravans on their way, heard the peasants sing monotonous songs, and joined in the singing.

At that moment the land of Zarathustra seemed as though still untouched by the Reds; it was spring.

When the oil-desert ended, fruit trees, the villages, and gardens of the territory free from oil appeared. Sometimes I got out of the train at stations, broke fruit from the trees, and shared it with the peasants.

Thus my farewell trip through Azerbaijan began.

CHAPTER 33

IN GANDJA

Gandja is the old capital of Azerbaijan; a hundred years ago it was still an independent principality whose khan waged war against Russia. The Russian general and Georgian prince, Ziziani, captured the city and destroyed it together with all its inhabitants. Since then it has been desolate, has lost its Oriental character; is no longer a city, but only a row of buildings. Only the bazaar and the small market-place, where once a famous poet was impaled by the khan betause of a libellous poem, are still reminiscent of the Orient. As in many Oriental cities, in Gandja the railroad station is some little distance away. At the station I had to report to the police, and after countless questions was given permission to proceed. Officially Gandja is situated on a river of the same name. This river, however, does not exist, although a bridge leads over a deep river-bed, where one can sometimes discover a small stream in the springtime. This river-bed plays a great part in the life of the city; it separates the Armenian quarter from the Mohammedan. If the inhabitants of one section threaten the others, machine-guns are set up on the bridge, and peace and order are restored. When I arrived at Gandja the place was already very much Bolshevized; everywhere one could see red flags, Russian soldiers, and military notices which I knew by heart from Baku. Only in the Mohammedan quarter did one forget the new rulers. Into that part communism did not force its way so quickly. In the bazaars and in the shops people publicly and loudly cursed the "liberators" of the East.

Something was brewing in the city. In the Mohammedan section peasants were seen streaming in from the villages and camping in the market-place. The merchant with whom I lived, an old friend of our family, consulted with strange visitors every day and asked me not to leave the city rashly—he winked significantly—since my flight to Georgia might not even become necessary. Upon hearing these hints, I became curious and pestered him with questions, until he told me that the Mohammedans, supported by a few Russian officers, were planning a revolt against the Bolshevists. The leader of the revolt, he said, was Prince Mansur, a relative of the Persian Shah, who had been living in the city secretly for some time. After a successful uprising they hoped to get help from the English in Georgia, and then to drive the Bolshevists from the whole country in a general revolution. I was enthusiastic about the plan, for neither I nor anyone else guessed how many troops the Russians had at their disposal, and how easily hundreds of thousands of Bolshevik soldiers could flood the country.

I forgot the object of my journey and decided to devote myself to the liberation of the fatherland. The merchant introduced me to the conspirators, and these led me to Prince Mansur, who accepted my cooperation in the revolt. We made bloody schemes, and already saw the moment at hand when we would besiege the oil-city.

Larger and larger became the number of followers, firmer and firmer the conviction that only a small *coup d'état* was needed to regain freedom. In the end we worked almost publicly at the plot. Only the exceptional folly of the new authorities explained the fact that they had not noticed our plan before.

At last the long-desired day arrived. Beyond the city our cavalry was collected, and waited for the sign that the leaders of the Russian, battle-forces were taken by surprise and destroyed. This is the age-old strategy of the Oriental *coups d'états*. At that time we knew no other. Our strategy succeeded. The Russian officers killed the Soviet leaders. We galloped into the city. The Bolshevik soldiers, whose number was not especially large, and who suspected nothing of the revolt till the last, were killed even before they could reach for their weapons. In a few hours we were masters, and free Azerbaijan again had a foothold on its first piece of land.

I was among the first who rode into the place, and later guarded the bridge. However, with that, my military career ended. I transferred to politics, spoke in the mosques all day, and thereupon took possession of the broadcasting station, where I vainly exerted myself, together with a few friends, to send a wireless "to all". Immediately after the revolution the first government measures were taken. The Russian "Whites" who had allied themselves with us, in accordance with the tradition of their country, suggested a pogrom against the Jews. This suggestion, however, we curtly rejected, although the Russians had already had notices printed with the inscription: "Beat the Jews, save Azerbaijan!"

This was absolutely senseless, for in all Gandja there was only one Jew, who, moreover, led the modest life of a pedlar. I confiscated the notices, destroyed them, and declared to the Russians that they must not forget they were in cultivated Azerbaijan and not in wild Russia, whereupon the Russians suggested a pogrom against the Armenians. This was also rejected, since we had already taken revenge in the massacre of Baku and now wanted to spill no blood needlessly. It was not easy to move the Russians to continue to work sensibly. We dispatched messengers to all the surrounding villages to spread the news of the liberation.

With Oriental calm—after all the demonstrations were finished—we began to equip ourselves for a campaign against Baku. Our army consisted of several hundred horsemen and badly armed peasants. Nevertheless, the capture of the capital seemed not impossible to us. But before we could start the campaign we found out that a Bolshevik army of twenty thousand strong was nearing Gandja. The city and the whole province had been surrounded by the Russians in a gigantic circle, and had been cut off from the rest of the country. Every hour the circle became smaller, and we remained ignorant of what happened outside it. Not until later did we learn that similar revolts had broken out everywhere, but thanks to the Red system of surrounding, they were kept isolated from one another and were suppressed. There were rebellions in almost every city. The whole land was aflame, and yet everything ended in a massacre throughout Azerbaijan, with which the Cheka celebrated their victory.

223

A few days after the revolt, Gandja was thus surrounded; in a few hours the Russians occupied the Armenian section of the city and approached the bridge, which we defended with machine-guns. The capture of the bridge was paid for dearly by the Russians; more than a thousand men fell in the attack. New attackers always charged forward over the fallen; the number of the defenders dwindled away noticeably. Nevertheless, we would have defended ourselves till the very last cartridge, had not the Russians attacked also from the rear, from the Mohammedan side.

Finally our guns were silenced. The work of the Cheka began. How they worked is illustrated by the fact that in one month practically nothing of the Mohammedan section was left. Without exception all the inhabitants of the city were arrested and brought before the revolutionary tribunal. The court procedure was as simple as one can imagine. Name, profession, and age were quickly demanded, the answers noted down, and in ninety cases out of a hundred the sentence "Shoot!" was executed on the spot.

It was organized mass murder, which one cannot even soften by calling it "terror". Before the revolt, Gandja had forty thousand inhabitants; after the hasty court proceedings it was a dead city, with the exception of the Armenian quarter, where the courts dealt less severely. After this mass murder, the Bolshevists issued a proclamation which said that the revolutionary people of Gandja had suppressed the revolt of the beys and the khans with an iron hand. That not much of the revolutionary people itself was left as a consequence of the "suppression" was not mentioned, but let it be noted here for future historians. The conflict ended, I hid for a few days in my merchant's cellar. When he was arrested, I left my hiding-place, went out into the street, and asked of the first passing soldier how I could reach the building of the Cheka. Somewhat surprised, he gave me this information. Arrived at the Cheka, I asked to be admitted to the presiding officer of the court. He was sitting at the table, busy with papers. "Comrade, please make out a permit for me to leave the city," I said in Russian, and approached him ingenuously.

He looked at me wildly, pushed his papers aside, and asked who I was.

"Young communist from Astrakhan, son of a workman. I was in Gandja on behalf of the Communist Youth Organization, was attacked by enemies of the proletariat, and want to return home to re-enter the ranks of the fighting workers," I answered absolutely calmly. My Russian was entirely without accent. According to my age I could not be a "White" officer either. "Papers?" demanded the officer of the Cheka. "Have destroyed them in accordance with the general instructions of the party congress after the 'White' revolt."

The man examined me curiously, considered a little, and asked: "What did Comrade Lenin say about the right of self-government of the peoples?"

"Self-government till independence!" I answered.

"What does communism lead to, economically speaking?"

"From the domain of temporary economical anarchy to that of systematic production," I answered fluently, according to the ABC of the communists of Bucharin, which I had already learned by heart at the time of the first Bolshevist invasion.

The examination had been passed. The communist smirked with satisfaction, and made out the desired paper for me, with which I proceeded to the station. There I showed it to the station-Cheka who, however, did not agree to its contents at all.

"The Cheka of Gandja may merely give permits to leave the city, for the trip on the railroad, the approval of the railroad-Cheka is required," a sinister bureaucrat shouted at me. The station, you see, was outside the city limits. When I wanted to leave the station to look for the new Cheka, the official did not give me back my paper. I looked suspicious to him, he explained, and must either stay myself or leave my papers behind. I chose the latter, hastily left the territory of the station-Cheka, and went hours out of my way not to come into the territory of the Gandja-Cheka. A person has good luck only once. The second time I might be recognized.

I was in a very bad mood. I was all alone, knew nothing about the position of the villages which I had to pass according to the agreement with my father; moreover, I had to wait for my father ten weeks at the border of Georgia, near the town of Naftlug. Ahead of me was a broad road that led into the unknown. I decided to travel on foot, in the hope that one of the villages would appear, and walked the whole day without meeting anyone.

Towards evening I began to pass gardens along the road. At the edge trees had been planted. Suddenly I noticed a movement behind a bush. The barrel of a gun flashed, and a voice spoke: "There goes some boy." There was nothing striking in the sentence except the language in which it was spoken. It was the German language, and, what is more, with a Swabian accent. I put up my hands as a sign that I had no evil intentions, approached the bush, and asked in German : "Who are you?"

"Defence-guard of the district of Helenendorf," was the German answer. Then followed the friendly invitation: "Come nearer, have no fear!"

CHAPTER 34

GERMANY IN AZERBAIJAN

The colony of Helenendorf is one of the strangest things in Azerbaijan. A few miles from Gandja, in the midst of a territory that is known even in Azerbaijan because of its wild seclusion, one comes upon a piece of Germany that can in no way be distinguished from Germany itself. The village, that is almost a metropolis for Azerbaijanian conditions, has several thousand inhabitants, who have built up for themselves regular two and three-storey villas with slanting roofs, and in the centre of the village-square have built a gigantic red brick church.

In the village live thoroughbred Swabians whose ancestors emigrated from their native land more than a hundred years ago, strayed to Azerbaijan—of all places!—and there created a model German town among Aisors and Kipta, Ossetians, Chani nomads, and robbers, paying no attention to the ceaseless clan feuds round about.

In spite of the pure Azerbaijanian influences that have surrounded them for a hundred years, these Swabians have not lost a single one of the characteristics they brought along, and have taken over practically nothing from the natives. Most of them do not understand a single word of the language of the country. Not all of them can speak good "High German," for their mother-tongue is Swabian. They need no other languages, since they come in contact with almost no one. The people of Helenendorf take good care to preserve their German characteristics. They often send members to Germany, and make sure that they are in no way behind a rich German village. For years they have had a school in which teachers, brought from abroad, instruct in "High German"; they have employed German physicians, and their pastors must be educated German theologians. In my time the pastor of Hele-nendorf was a real Baltic baron for whom the community had enor-mous respect. The whole village attended church for his Sunday ser-vice, and sang psalms with enthusiasm. Most of the colonists were fairly well off, owning extensive estates which they cultivated them-selves; vineyards being their chief source of income. Their neighbours, the Mohammedans, have no vineyards, therefore the colony has a monopoly in this field. Their wine and their cognac are famed through-out the whole Caucasus, which makes it possible for the Swabians, in their villas built and furnished in German manner, to lead a life for which all Azerbaijan might envy them.

The nomads tell legends about these colonists, which is easily understood, when one compares the life in the nomads' yourtas or in the tiny clay huts of the native villages with the "Sunday afternoon con-cert with coffee and dance", customary in Helenendorf.

On their very rare visits to Helenendorf the Azerbaijanian peasants felt as though they were among more aristocratic people than those of the richest palaces of the oil-princes. Only one thing have the Germans taken over from the Azerbaijanians, and that not voluntarily—the colour of hair and skin which among them becomes darker from gener-ation to generation. Today one comes across people in Helenendorf, who by their appearance might be taken for Azerbaijanians. This is all the more strange since no intermarriage has ever taken place as far as can be traced. The German colonists, who want to have nothing to do with the "coloured" natives, will soon be "coloured" themselves. Every-one who knows the life of the German colonists will confirm the fact that no "race-shame" is at the bottom of this. Mixture between natives and colonists is highly improbable; it is most likely that the climate influences the hue of the skin. But it is remarkable that blond children are found among the new generation of the Aisors who live near Hele-nendorf. For a German would never degrade himself by contact with an Aisor woman. Changes and transformation of peoples must then be possible in other ways than that of blood-mixture. It is noticed wher-ever Europeans live next to the Orientals for several generations. I know Russian families who have been settled in China for generations, and whose youngest children born in China showed a marked Mongolian type, and yet, except for the cheek-bones, slit-eyes, and short noses, resemble their parents unmistakably. Nevertheless, all this has nothing to do with a mixture of blood and obliteration of race-characteristics. In Helenendorf it took a hundred years for the children to become darker. Of course the mothers see hardly any other faces than those of colonists.

As I have said, the colonists lead a very secluded life. They do not show the slightest interest in political events and worry about only the one question: to whom they must pay their taxes this time—punctually, as always. The payment of taxes was the only contact between them and the government of the day. But if the Swabians did not think very much of their government and their neighbours, these showed all the more interest in the rich colony, and it was by no means always of a harmless nature. In periods of general disturbance the nomads had no more sincere desire than to plunder completely the German colony.

And during the overthrows in Gandja some regular division of troops could easily have taken the road to Helenendorf. There, besides other treasures, spacious cellars stored with wine and cognac lured them. Against all these disagreeable matters the Germans founded a defence force, well armed, which blocked all entrances to the colony, but preserved strict neutrality. If, for once, there were no troubles and the government was able to hold the nomads in check, this guard was dissolved. Often enough the various fighting parties have tried to win the colonists to their side, but always in vain. The Swabians protected their village, left politics to the natives, waited for the end of the uproar, and calmly inquired to whom they must pay taxes in the future.

It was the members of the company of guards who had stopped me on the highway. They led me into the village, where I found shelter with one of the colonists and gradually recovered from the excitements of the revolt. At that time—that is, just after the suppression of the uprising—the official communist authorities bothered very little about the peaceful village. So I could feel safer there, only a few hours' distance from Gandja, than anywhere else in the whole country. For weeks I now led a holiday life, I drank the colonists' wine, went to church, and paid court to the German girls. The colonists knew very well from where I came and where I wanted to go; so they asked me no questions and treated me like a summer visitor who wanted to rest a few weeks in their town. Only a few made a request—quite accidentally during conversation—in case I should ever reach Georgia. Georgia, that was occupied by the English, was a closed paradise for all of us. They asked me then to deliver one message or another to their relatives in the German colonies near Tiflis.

No doubt I owed the good treatment on the part of the colonists to my knowledge of the German language, which proved very useful, though certainly they smiled at my High German and at my inability to express even the most trivial thing in Swabian. I was not the only refugee who sought protection in Helenendorf. Not all met with the same welcome; one had to appear trustworthy to be welcomed. One point in my favour was that some of the colonists knew my father.

Among the few besides myself who enjoyed the protection of the colony, there was a well-known Armenian oil-magnate who arrived direct from Baku one day with a truck and samovar—all the worldly goods that he had left; his house was near mine. He went to church every day and prayed reverently that he might be destined to leave Azerbaijan alive. I soon made friends with him, and we racked our brains as to how we could most easily reach the border. It turned out that the Armenian was the fortunate possessor of a paper in which was written in black and white that the bearer was commissioned to buy up fish-nets, all over the country and abroad, where-ever he thought it necessary. This sufficed to convince the communists in the country, who were not too alert, of the harmlessness of my friend. The railway officials were cleverer. Nevertheless, he did not dare to travel alone, because if not by communists as an oil-magnate, he might be killed by the Mohammedans as an Armenian.

So we decided to travel together. I was to protect him from the Mohammedans, and he would protect me from the Armenians whose villages we had to pass through, and who were never averse from murdering a non-Armenian occasionally. To deceive the communists he prepared a certificate showing that I had to accompany him everywhere as his secretary and expert on fish-nets. For a time, however, the departure was not to be considered, for through the whole country the communists were in search of the beys, khans, and oil-sharks. (My father was still waiting "peacefully" in Baku. He was no shark, but an expert with bandit tendencies.)

Every village was surrounded by the communists and had to deliver up its bey and khan, together with all weapons. Villages which refused to do that were razed to the ground by the Russian artillery; the inhabitants were shot. Some villages had no khan or bey, and yet were commanded, with threats of the cannonade, to "deliver up the aristocrat". The poor fellows had no alternative but to choose a rather fine-looking peasant from their midst, who sacrificed himself for the general welfare, was delivered up as a "bloodsucker", and was shot by the Russians. On the other hand, many villages which actually did possess a khan refused to give up their lord and were consequently destroyed. The result was that—in order to save their people from the very worst—many provincial noblemen left their hiding-places and reported to the Cheka, naming the villages from which they came. They were shot immediately. We knew exactly what was going on in the country and therefore wanted to wait until the conquerors had calmed down a little, before we continued our flight.

So we stayed in Helenendorf for the time. My Armenian friend prayed in church, and I perfected my German and observed the attempts of the government to Bolshevize the colony. First came agitators, then soldiers who pitched their tents inside the colony.

Lastly appeared a Latvian police-spy commissioned to influence the people "in spirit", and he was the indirect cause of my departure. The Latvian arranged "social evenings" where one began by dancing. In the course of the evening stray actors sang Bolshevist songs. At the close the Latvian mounted the stage and made a speech, whereupon all had to rise and sing the Internationale, or at least listen to it respectfully.

These affairs took place every week, and I wondered at the patience of the colonists, for I was much less patient. When I attended one of these gatherings for the first time and listened to the speech, I remained in my seat during the Internationale. For this I was arrested by two soldiers on the very same evening and led to the Latvian.

"Why did you remain seated during the Internationale?" he asked.

"I was so deeply stirred by your speech that I could not get up," I said.

"Don't talk nonsense! Who are you, anyhow? What are you doing in the colony?"

"A young communist from Baku. I am travelling on behalf of the Association for the Promotion of Fishery to buy up nets."

The Latvian looked at me idiotically, for an Association for the Promotion of Fishery was doubtless the most stupid thing one could invent during the civil war in the midst of the revolts. Yet even this did not seem impossible to him. He asked for my name and the address of the Association. I answered the first thing that happened to occur to me, whereupon he promised to inform the Association of my disloyal conduct, to make inquiries about me in any event, and ordered me not to leave the colony till he received information about me from Baku.

I promised, then went straight to my Armenian friend and wakened him. It was late at night. We left the hospitable Swabians the same night, in our truck, not forgetting the samovar.

We showed our fishery certificates to the soldiers who met us, and pointed to the truck that we wanted to fill with nets. They believed us and raised no difficulties. In the next village the truck fell to pieces. We bought horses and entrusted our fate to the credulity of the village communists and the loyalty of the country population to their lords.

CHAPTER 35

ACROSS AZERBAIJAN

We rode through the country of the holy fire, avoided the larger villages occupied by the Russians, visited the most god-forsaken regions, the smallest clans, the wildest canyons and lost settlements in the centre of the untouched land of Zarathustra, that had remained unchanged for thousands of years. Nothing reminded us of oil or of people who thirst for oil. We rode through fields that were not oil-fields and through orchards that formed whole provinces. In half-dilapidated clay huts that stood among their gardens, lived people who often did not know that there was somewhere along the Caspian Sea a dark, sticky fluid because of which people fought for the country.

They would scarcely believe that the Russians again ruled in the country and were no longer true Russians, that they had murdered their Czar and now, having lost their master, plundered foreign countries and cities. When we rode into some mountain settlement in the evening, the elders of the village would gather together; the mullah would make a speech in which he greeted the noble guests and asked whether we desired women, gold, or sheep. They had nothing else, but these belonged to us because we were apparently lords. When we refused women, gold, and sheep, the people gratefully kissed our hands, killed a sheep, and made a feast in honour of the guests who did not rob anything. At the feast they sang songs about the old khans, about the nightingale that died for love of the rose, played the saz—a kind of violin with three strings that is held like a cello—and danced the wild knife-dance which all the peoples of the Caucasus want to imitate. Yet it is inimitable, because it can be danced only among the snow-covered mountains, on Persian rugs, with the saz and thrusts of knives, and in front of a beautiful woman. A dancer who holds six daggers in his mouth and four in his hands throughout this performance reminds one of the holy Hussein.

Often the dance ends with deep wounds from which the dancer suffers, but which only increase the enthusiasm of the spectators. This dance is not always meant for spectators; it may be performed—like the snake-dance—for a certain person whom one loves and whose love is desired.

The man, stiff with daggers, circles round the woman, executes battle-gestures to drive away her enemies—in this case the wounds are a sign of the courage of the lover—and tries to embrace her. The woman always withdraws and sets him tasks which he must fulfil. Now she throws a handkerchief on the ground which the man must pick up with his teeth—without interrupting the rhythm of the dance. Now he must lay the dagger flat on the ground and invite the woman to step on it as a sign of the power she has over him. Now she throws small coins into the air, which he must catch without losing any of his daggers.

This is the dance of the man. The woman dances differently. For her, too, the dance is a means of conquering, yet her dance is born in the desert. It is slow, has but few steps, and is not limited to the feet but expresses itself through the whole body. The belly, the hips, the thighs dance; the hands speak, but the feet remain without special expression. The power of the Oriental woman is not in them. The rug on which the woman dances is very small. She does not leave it; you see, the dance is meant for a man in the desert, and where the rug ends, there is burning sand. And the man who sits close before her on another rug loves her body, but not the lightning-quick bounds in which he himself is a master.

Consequently a truly Oriental dance with all its symbolism, and sensuality is possible only in private. It is not meant for the public, but for the most intimate circle of friends. Therefore it is absurd to endeavour to present it on a European stage. Orientals who dance before hundreds in Europe on the dance floor are really making fun of their audience.

The same is true of the song that is always a love-song, no matter what its subject. Its guttural sounds, which no European ear can endure, are not music, but resonant sensuality which manifests itself in the squawking, howling, nasal noises. It is useless to judge this outburst of wild sensuality according to the laws of harmony, although it is also subject to strict rules. In the East sensuality has different standards. A European who does not know them and so cannot understand them will seem a barbarian to the simplest shepherd in the remotest spot of the East.

Dance and songs accompanied us on our flight through the land of fire. In the villages, on the mountains, in the gardens and deserts, we heard constantly the same sounds, saw the same gestures, which have probably been familiar there since the first man wooed the first woman. In the regions which have no oil and which know no Kotschis, no Cheka, and no sharks, there are no other themes but love, battle, and blood.

The people who sing their songs among gardens and mountains can drive many a scientist mad, especially if he is an anthropologist and attempts cranial measurement in the interior of Azerbaijan. I do not know whether this has as yet happened, but if it has there was surely a sensation in the academies. The shape of the skull in the people of this country corresponds to none of the usual proportions. The head of the peasant is shaped arbitrarily and does not conform to the characteristics of his race, but to his parents' sense of beauty, or rather to the current fashion. When a child is born his head is treated in a manner similar to that used until a short time ago for the feet of the wealthy Chinese woman. It is put in a definite form that determines its growth and gives it the desired appearance. Usually the skull is drawn out lengthwise so that it looks like a pumpkin. If one meets a Caucasian with the top of his skull lengthened towards the back, it is proof that the owner is a son of a peasant from a certain region of Azerbaijan. I do not know how this custom arose; as far as I know, it is otherwise found only among the Indian tribes of South America. One might suppose that this process would affect the mentality of the people in some way, but strange to say, this does not appear to happen. The owners of the reshaped skulls are not at all mentally impaired; as far as their intelligence is concerned, they are absolutely equal to their environment. I know people of this type who have even studied at European universities. The shaped skull satisfies the artistic taste of the peasants, and its possessors are very proud of the peculiarity. However, it is harder to satisfy their warlike sense than their aesthetic taste.

In various villages yearly fights are arranged to which the "Pehlewans", the knights, assemble from the whole country. They form two parties, and, armed with sticks, carry out a regular gladiatorial battle on the field, before numerous spectators who make bets. Most of the participants return home streaming with blood. Formerly such mass tourneys—which are called war games—were organized in Baku also, but later they were prohibited by the sensitive owners of oil, because they "aroused evil instincts".

Now these games are no longer needed to satisfy war desires. The Pehlewans had enough to do in real fighting, and the dwellers in the mountain villages soon thought more of seeking hiding-places than skirmishes. But that also is taken care of in Azerbaijan. Almost every mountain village has a high stone tower near its fields. Those towers are centuries old and did great services for the peasants in former times. When one bey fought with another or robbers attacked the country, the peasant left his hut, which he could always easily build again, took wife, child, and cattle, and moved with the whole village into the tower, which had room enough for all. This meant that the peasants did not want to have anything to do with the conflict, but trusted themselves to the protection of Allah. The fighting beys knew very well that their future taxpayers, who wanted to be spared, were hidden in the towers, and craftily contented themselves with the destruction of the clay huts.

Robbers were not able to capture these solidly built, angular towers. Often for months the peasants occupied their Noah's ark and awaited the return of quietness. The village towers were respected by all as an extra-territorial sanctuary, because they were the people's only place of refuge.

No aristocrat, no matter how grim, dared to touch these village sanctuaries; that was reserved for the Bolshevists. When the population of a few villages withdrew to their towers after the revolts, the Russians ordered that all towers in the country should be estroyed as remnants of feudalism. They said that a peasant had nothing to fear in the workers' republic. Towers were demolished that would have proved valuable monuments for archaeology. The people saw themselves despoiled of their last and oldest traditional protection.

The life in the deserts and mountain settlements is not so monotonous and dull as one might think. Time has taught people to create amusements for themselves. They exist in the country to excess. Of course an Azerbaijanian amusement will never appear as such to a European. Besides the dance, the battles of the Pehlewans, and riding feats, which are among the boldest in the world, there also are the cow-races, for example, in which I took part myself. For these people the cow as a racehorse takes the place of all the theatres and motion-pictures of Europe. To the non-Oriental nothing seems more absurd than this performance.

The greatest joy of the peasant, even of the most ignorant, is in poetry, the beautiful literature which is more loved in the desert among the very wildest nomads than in all the literary salons of the world.

The poetic art that lives in the desert is not always pure art. There are verses that are an absolutely practical necessity for the nomad. And the ability to write verses is an indispensable function of each and every nomad chieftain. The leader of a clan and his generals and vassals are usually illiterate. Since the territory of a clan normally includes enormous stretches of sand, and the nomad army is widely scattered and far distant from headquarters, the ruler must communicate with his troops through messengers. All these are illiterate, therefore the command of a prince cannot be written, but must be transmitted orally. The messenger learns the order by heart, repeats it a few times for the ruler, and proceeds to the recipient, and as his words are in verse form, the messenger can neither forget his commission entirely nor misstate it all too arbitrarily. With the very complicated Oriental rhyme-technique and metre the change of a verse would cause considerable difficulty. One can also recall a forgotten word more easily through the known rhyme or the prescribed measure than in prose. In this case poetry is not only art, but also a diplomatic institution which makes possible a faultless news-service between the people. However, the command in verse form may never be short, imperious, nor simple; it must also show literary value, that is, be adorned with endless courtesies, metaphors, allegories, jests, and quotations from older poems. So a ruler is bound also by the laws of literary courtesy. These poetic commands are cited with pleasure outside official intercourse, too, and a sovereign who writes good poems enjoys much more prestige than a brave but literarily insignificant hero.

Therefore it is no wonder if the Eastern wisdom of governing prescribed, above all, poetic talent for the sovereign. These poems, so important for the state, can be found not only in Azerbaijan, but wherever there are nomads: in Turkestan, Arabia, North Africa, and so on. In addition to these, there is also a pure literature, *l'art pour l'art*, which, as I have said, is treated as an exquisite, noble queen throughout the Orient by everyone from the mightiest shah to the poorest beggar. The most brutal Azerbaijanian robber, the most ignorant peasant near Gandja, loves the art of poetry with a devotion that is reserved for only the secluded aesthete and literate in Europe.

In every village that we visited in our flight, in every settlement, we met literary epicures who recited the last fruits of their own or of a strange muse immediately after the first salutation, and asked for literary news. The poets who travel from village to village, from town to town in Azerbaijan—by the way, in Persia, too—are received and treated as princes everywhere. People overwhelm them with presents and signs of friendliness, listen to their poems, and are particularly pleased if the poet starts upon the works of old masters after he has exhausted his own productions. The national poet who wanders through the country in Azerbaijan or in Persia is a schooled master who has studied the high art at some Oriental academy in Samarkand or in Tabriz.

The poetry taught at Eastern universities is a comprehensive science. It can also be learned outside the universities in the associations of poets or at their historic meeting-places in Gandja or Shemakka or elsewhere in Azerbaijan. It demands of the student, in addition to the talent, a diligence and perseverance which would suffice for the attainment of several learned degrees in Europe. Besides the customary history of literature, the poet must learn rhyme-technique, metrics, the science of plagiarism, improvisation, and study in dozens of other fields of knowledge, but above all he must have skill in the metaphor, which is the alpha and omega of all Eastern poetry. It has been counted in the works of great masters that they have from a hundred to a hundred and twenty figures of speech in a hundred lines. There are figures of speech of first and second rank, and others which mean the study of a particular science to understand them. A poet must know how to make, upon the command of the master, poems with a double or triple meaning. He must make verses that are obscene or pious according as one reads them in Persian or Arabic, strophes that contain a strictly limited vocabulary: for example, that consist only of geographic expressions. And he must know how to perform several other feats that would completely disconcert a European poet.

I have read poems that offered one meaning when read from left to right, another from top to bottom, and a third from bottom to top, and they delighted the Azerbaijanian shepherd in the same way as the Persian Shah. There are poets who have sworn never to use certain letters, and others who find their pleasure in forming the most surprising metaphors from uncommon conceptions. There are dictionaries in which all possible metaphors and rhymes are noted next to each concept. Finally, the poet must understand the secret writing of poetry, a highly complicated art, which conceals certain ideas behind certain numbers, verses behind conceptions, and behind the verses a secret meaning comprehensible only to the initiated. No one except the educated poet can decipher the secret writing of the author. For this reason, too, poets were always kept at the princely courts of Azerbaijan, who travelled through the country in the event of the outbreak of war and took care of the news-service. The writing of a poet may fall without danger into the hands of the enemy, for one must be a mathematician, literary historian, poet, calligrapher, theologian, and alchemist, to penetrate its meaning.

I will repeat here one of the simplest examples of this code, purposely choosing the easiest example that I know, and one at which the expert would laugh. The more complicated ones, however, cannot be reproduced. If one wants to inform the sultan of the name of a rival, one writes the metrically faultless verse: "If you are admitted into the Kaaba of the society, then build the pillars of the Hadsch and say thanks to God." At first the non-specialist does not notice at all that there is a riddle involved; yet the whole verse is only a metrical attachment to the words "the building of the pillars of the Hadsch". These conceal the riddle. The rest has a more or less clear meaning, and does not need to be specially interpreted. It means: "If after long wooing / after difficult pilgrimage / you are heard by your beloved / arrive in the Kaaba of the assembly with her / then give thanks to God." These words already contain the indication that the sultan will have to deal with difficulties in his courtship. The other incomprehensible sentence, however, contains the name of the rival. For the "pillars of the Hadsch" (pilgrimage) are the consonants of which the word Hadsch consists. These letters are called Ha and Dschim. To build the pillars means the same as to pronounce them, that is, to say "Hadschim". The thanks, however, which one must say at the same time, are the word "hamd". If one connects this word with the Hadschim, one obtains "Hadschimhamd". Since the letters "o" and "e" are not written, this means Hadschi Mohammed, and so is a proper name.

You will perceive that it is not easy to be a poet in Azerbaijan. As I have said, my example is extremely primitive. Not last among the tasks of the poet is the ability of setting and guessing riddles in verses, as well as making parodies. Composing and solving riddles is part of the mental education of every high-class Oriental.

Before an apprentice becomes a poet, he must pass a special examination before a high board, during which many sorts of questions are asked, to test his scientific preparation and literary talent. The problems given are often quite grotesque. For example:

"In a sonnet, with what would you compare the hips of your beloved? And with what the hips of your wife?" and the like.

The graduate poet enjoys the greatest respect everywhere, and, in contrast to other scholars, is allowed to make money with his knowledge. He usually does that most successfully. The majority of wandering or domiciled poets acquire considerable riches, for there is no one in the Orient who would refuse a poet a fee. Even the poorest peasant will pay for a good poem with a fat sheep or a donkey. What I have said is true, not only of Azerbaijan, but of the whole Islamic Orient.

In Azerbaijan there is another literary custom that has long since disappeared in other countries, and that I was able to observe during my flight. People continued to cultivate it in spite of revolutions and uprisings. I mean the poetry contests that were formerly customary at all princes' courts, and even today delight the heart of the Azerbaijanian peasant. When they take place, not only all the inhabitants of the village, but all lovers of literature in the province assemble. These contests are open to every poet and take place in an open square. The poets sing their verses out loud, or ask those present to set a theme. Then they improvise immediately. The mightiest aristocrat contends with the tattered beggar. He congratulates the other if he is defeated, bows before the master, and kisses his hand. The poet-master is garlanded with flowers and rides through the province in a flower-covered carriage.

I have witnessed only one poetry contest, and that one became a sensation. It was won by a sixteen-year-old, nameless beggar-girl, who sang her love-songs dedicated to the moon, and with these carried off the victory. Nevertheless, she renounced all honours, because, as she said, she was in love with the moon and composed poems and lived for it alone. In fact, she lived only on the banks of rivers, and every evening she regarded the image of her beloved in the water. She never wore a veil although she was extraordinarily beautiful. Later, I have heard, she was drowned one moonlit night in the Arakan River.

Such incidents are still possible only in the most remote regions of the land of Zarathustra, and nowhere else, not even in the Orient. Of course it is difficult to become acquainted with the country as I saw it.

The stranger sees only dull, long-headed peasants, who speak an incomprehensible language, look wild and dangerous, and wear rags. The stranger is never admitted to the poets' festivals, but will probably become ill with malaria. And even assuming that he could see a poets' gathering, he will see only a society of wild village-dwellers, whom he does not understand and who obviously do not want to understand him.

Therefore I do not advise anyone to visit the unknown Azerbaijan for the sake of its poetry. He will see and hear nothing of it.

And yet it is a wonderful people that dwells there in the mountains and deserts, with artificially-shaped skulls, with the horned head-dress of Alexander the Great, with towers that no aristocrat attacks, with cow-races and dagger-dances, with love-songs and poets' contests, and finally with sixteen-year-old, unveiled girls who fall in love with the moon and marry its earthly image in the water.

Has all that become lost today? I do not know! The Socialist Soviet Republic, Azerbaijan, has freed the people, awakened them, put them in the Cheka, and Russianized them. For how long?

CHAPTER 36

AMONG THE DEVIL-WORSHIPPERS

Our journey was accomplished as we had expected. In the Mohammedan villages whose inhabitants scrutinized my travelling-companion suspiciously, I made a speech in which I vouched for my friend and introduced him as a thoroughly dependable man. In the Armenian villages we changed roles, and I, in my turn, was introduced as a friend and "safe". Generally just a few words sufficed to dispel the original suspicion.

Since other nations than Armenians and Mohammedans, and these indeed in various degrees, were unknown to us in that region, we hoped to reach the border at the right time undisturbed. But it turned out that even we did not know the land of Zarathustra well enough. I was surprised when told at one village, although it was not inhabited by Armenians, that no guide could be provided to the next village because it was inhabited by people who were believed to be capable of anything.

The Armenian oil-magnate, who advised particular caution, and had suspicions of danger everywhere, immediately became worried and inquired what religion, race, inclinations, and customs, were prevalent in the village. After hesitation the peasants reported that its dwellers were Jezids, that the Jezids were devil-worshippers, and as such certainly dangerous. However, since every cult, even devil-worship, seemed an advantage to us after the Bolshevist terror, we decided to continue our journey bravely and to pay the suspicious community a visit. The Jezids received us in a friendly manner, spoke to us in Azerbaijanian and displayed nothing devilish in their nature. However, the lack of any visible place of prayer and of the priest showed that there was something

243

queer here. We remained several days, and gradually learned from the village elder the details about their curious cult.

The majority of the Jezids live in Turkey, near Ankara, where is the grave of the founder of this religion, the Sheik Adli. But this religion has nothing in common with the Black Mass or the European Satanism—as far as I could determine. The Azerbaijanian devil-worshippers are peaceful and shy people who fear the sunlight, but are not prejudiced against the gods of other religions. The devil is simply closer to them. They worship him in the form of a golden peacock.

According to the views of the Jezids, God is a vague and distant being that can perform only good, in itself, and therefore does not need to be worshipped. The devil, on the contrary, is in the immediate vicinity of man, rules over his fate, and must be appeased and prayed to—since he pursues only evil. It is not known which is the more powerful, God or the devil, and therefore, since one can depend on the goodness of God, one must take pains to win the favour of the devil, who hates God, but otherwise is accommodating and honest. This is the official view of the Jezids, who may no doubt be regarded as a last branch of the fire-worshippers.

Their neighbours, indeed, do not trust their mild view of life, and accuse the Jezids of every crime, every deed of cruelty that they can possibly imagine. For example, the Persians maintain that the Jezids are all descended from the Calif Jezid, the murderer of Hussein, and on that account alone are damned. The Turks say that the Jezids know only love of men, that they reproduce in an unnatural way, and the like.

The Jezids have a definite ritual which is said to be rather uncanny, but contains nothing criminal. Every year in August they gather at the grave of the wise Sheik Adli, and there execute the famous dance around the golden peacock. The dance starts at sunset and lasts all night. The dancers hold torches in their hands and are fantastically dressed in white gowns; during the performance they sing songs of praise to the devil. In the middle of the circle which the dancers form, stands the golden peacock, the symbol of the "Jescht", the evil spirit. At its side, in a circle, sit the musicians who accompany the dance with hellish music. Quite close to the peacock—which is enthroned on the grave of the sheik—stands the ruler of the Jezids, the recognized representative of the devil on earth.

Since the Eastern governments are very tolerant and support every faith, the "representative of the devil on earth" was also officially recognized and treated as a sort of high dignitary. For a time he is even said to have drawn a salary from the government that conformed to his position. These Azerbaijanian devil-worshippers, who annually send their representatives to the devil-dance, are very pious and mock at the naiveté of their neighbours who will not believe in the power of the devil. In private life they show a diffident nature. The only thing that is striking about them is their aversion to sunlight. They do not like the sun, hide from it, and whenever it is possible do not leave their houses until the coming of darkness. Their village, by the way, was the only one in which neither my travelling-companion nor I had to recommend one another.

Our trip through Azerbaijan lasted one month in all. We arrived unhindered at the border river which separates Azerbaijan from Georgia. Not a single time did we come into contact with the new authorities, which can be explained only by the fact that the peasants always guided us to a village as yet untouched by Bolshevists. The Russians seemed to be rather inactive in the country on the whole, probably because they had but little interest in the Azerbaijan that began beyond the oil-fields, and were satisfied when there were no revolts and they were left in peace in the cities. Only after the revolts did Red riders travel through the country and leave bloody traces behind them everywhere.

They did not meet us. We were very careful, since our fishery-papers were suspicious enough, after all. Arrived at the border, my companion had no more heartfelt desire than to swim across the river with the greatest speed and to leave the Bolshevist paradise. Only because of a feeling of comradeship did he journey along the river with me to look for the place where I was to meet my father. However, we remained some distance away from the actual river because the Bolshevist border-guard was certainly more dangerous than the devil-worshippers and the cow-racers in the interior. There we met with a mishap, the only one during our trip. Some peasants who were acquainted with the Bolshevists because of the proximity of the border district and the guard, suspected us of being at least the representatives of the Cheka or some Soviet. In spite of our Azerbaijanian and Armenian protestations that we were genuine oil-magnates, we were locked up and searched. In this way they found our fishery-papers, and then someone who could read had to be hunted up. He read them through and confirmed the fact that we were thoroughgoing Bolshevists.

The situation became threatening. The peasants scratched their heads, argued, and finally informed us that we were condemned to the following punishment: We must be undressed and tied to a tree; empty boxes would be tied to our bellies with their openings just touching the belly. The hungry mice who would be in the wooden boxes should eat up our bowels if they wanted to. Then it would soon be disclosed whether we were Bolshevists or not. My companion almost fainted.

The position became more and more critical. Shortly before we were led off, however, the elder of the village appeared and said that a high-born and noble bey from Baku had arrived, and since he knew every-one in Baku, wanted to examine us. I now hoped that the stranger would know either me or my companion—if not both of us. But what happened I could not have imagined in my wildest dreams.

The door opened, and a noble stranger entered accompanied by the peasants. At first I did not believe my eyes. In national costume, armed with daggers and several other murderous weapons, with a fur hat and Azerbaijanian mantilla—as we had never yet seen him—there stood before me . . . my own father.

That was the best luck I ever had.

Three days later all three of us were in Georgia on the border estate of the Prince Dschakeli, our old friend. How it all happened, the mad adventures that my father experienced in his flight from Baku, as well as the circumstances of our crossing the river, I cannot describe here. A friend of mine who fled in a similar manner through a different border village has told the details elsewhere. As a result, that border village no longer exists today, nor do most of the inhabitants of that border region.

They had to walk the path to the Cheka "because of support of the enemies of the people".

So I shall rather remain silent.

CHAPTER 37

THE LAND OF THE HOLY GEORGE

We were most heartily received on the estate of the Prince Dschakeli. My father stayed there for a rest and sent me alone to the capital of Georgia–to Tiflis–where, after my wild flight, I was to become acquainted with the life of this city, which is considered the paradise of the East.

Unfortunately I arrived in Tiflis as a prisoner, as an unmasked, highly suspicious Bolshevist. On the way, in the train, my person appeared most questionable to a Georgian officer. He demanded papers of me which I did not possess, and information that I could not give. His supposition that I had travelled to Georgia as a Bolshevist agitator seemed so grotesque to me this time that I did not even try to refute it, but just let myself be arrested and thus made my entrance into Tiflis as a dangerous revolutionary.

Before my arrival the officer had telegraphed to the Minister of the Interior, announcing his success as a criminologist, and asking for reinforcements. His three soldiers did not seem sufficient guard for so dangerous a man as myself. As he said, he had to take into account the possibility that at the station I might be freed by irresponsible gangs or attempt flight on my own account.

Consequently a whole company of Georgian troops awaited me at the station. In their midst I entered the capital–instilling fear in all the people. I was led through the main street, and for the first time in my life saw the most beautiful city of the Caucasus, though unfortunately my view was obstructed by the escort.

On the street-corner I suddenly caught sight of an elderly Georgian gentleman from Baku whom I knew. He looked at the procession curiously. I waved to him and shouted in Azerbaijanian: "Scarcely have I escaped the Russians when your Minister of the Interior arrests me."

The gentleman recognized my situation, waved back to me in a friendly manner, and raised his hand in front of the troop. Thereupon the company stood still as one man. The officer stepped forward and said: "I beg to report that I am commissioned to bring a dangerous political offender whose real name is as yet unknown to the department for political criminals."

The gentleman smiled and motioned with his hand once more. Thereupon the officer stepped back and roared at his soldiers: "Fall back!" He took one deep breath, waited a second, as though he hoped to awake from a dream, and then shouted in a very military voice: "The prisoner is to be released!"

I shook hands with the kind friend whose name I can no longer recollect, and said: "A thousand thanks for correcting the stupidity of your Minister of the Interior. I don't like to spend the night with bedbugs. By the way," I continued, suddenly taken aback, "how is it that you can countermand an order of your idiotic Ministry of the Interior?"

"A trifle," my acquaintance assured me. "I can do that at any time, for you must know I am Minister of the Interior here."

I spent the night in the house of the friendly old gentleman and moved to the hotel the next day. There I immediately found dozens of Azerbaijanian emigrants, and gradually began to recuperate from Bolshevism. I wandered through the streets of Tiflis, drank Georgian wine from huge drinking-horns, and visited the famous sulphur baths, of which it is said that they can make a man of a eunuch. A hundred and fifty years ago this quality of the baths became fateful for the whole country. Aga-Mohammed-Khan, the Shah of Persia, who was a eunuch himself, conquered Georgia, devastated Tiflis, seized all the women, and began to bathe in the sulphur baths. Since this did not help—because, as the Georgians claim, the shah was an unbeliever—he devastated the country once more, killed all the men, and withdrew to his native land. Shah Feth-Ali, famed as a mighty warrior and wise man, was the only shah who had no harem. His brother begot the princes for him, and indeed very successfully, for Aga-Mohammed-Khan left three hundred nephews who were regarded as sons of the emperor.

Georgia or Gurdschistan, the land of the holy George, is the country of eternal spring. The Georgians are Christians; the origin of their race is unknown even today. Their art and culture, to which Byzantium and other Christian countries owe very much, originated in pre-Christian antiquity. Georgia now looks back upon a culture of three thousand years.

The holy Nina, who converted George to Christianity, founded churches and monasteries in the warlike country. The monks and priests who inhabited them remained leaders of the army at the same time, fought against the unbelievers, against the Georgian princes, conquered, and were conquered, until the great Queen Tamara came, the most splendid queen in the Orient, unified Georgia, and erected an enormous iron wall in the canyon of Daryal, through which the stream of hostile nomads invaded the country every year. Besides the holy Nina, Tamara is the greatest national heroine of Georgia, and even today is still extolled and praised in song throughput the whole Caucasus.

At the end of the dark canyon of Daryal near Tiflis stands the castle, Mzcht, from which Tamara ruled over her lands and her men. In this castle she received her generals, priests, knights, princes, merchants, and peasants. Everyone might be admitted to her presence; even more, everyone might become her lover. It sufficed to step before the queen and to express one's wish out loud. No one was ever refused. Each Georgian had the right to sleep with the queen.

The queen had read the "Arabian Nights". She knew how the grim Sultan Shahriar had his newly married wives executed at sunrise. She considered herself called to avenge these women. Therefore the eunuch appeared every morning arid beheaded her happy lover, even if he was the bravest general. In this way her diplomatic wisdom also avoided much unnecessary jealousy among her subjects. The beheaded corpses were thrown into the Aragwa River. Even today this generous art of love of Tamara inspires Georgian, Persian, Russian, Indian, and Armenian poets to songs in praise of the noble queen. The poets had another personal reason to sing in praise of Tamara. For only one man was not surrendered to the sword of the eunuch, but rather to the jealousy of the subjects. He was the knight Schato-Rustaweli, the greatest poet of Georgia, who immortalized his queen when he wrote his famous epic for her, "The Man in the Tiger Skin". From the poet and the queen originate a famous race of princes, who for the sake of rank denied this illegitimate descent, and about ten years ago, when it was disclosed by Georgian Socialists, removed to Paris.

A thousand anecdotes are current about the wise queen and the lovesick poet. Even today these two are still considered the spiritual leaders of Georgia, Rustaweli and Tamara are figures of antiquity. But Georgia also has modern shrines of saints. At Tiflis on a romantic mountain is situated the monastery of the holy David. To this monastery the Georgian girls make pilgrimages on Sundays, remain standing there near the damp cemetery wall and look at each other shyly. At last they pluck up courage, bend down to the earth, lift up little granite stones, and bravely press them against the wall. If the stone remains sticking to the wall it means that the girl will marry a brave and warlike man during the very same year. Round about in the bushes the young men lie in wait, ascertain who will marry during the year and follow the girls that pleased them to their homes to become acquainted with them and court them.

The cemetery wall and the tomb about which this custom grew up do not harbour the mortal remains of some Georgian hero. At the monastery of the holy David a Russian is buried, indeed a rather prominent Russian, His Excellency, Privy Councillor Gribojedoff, Minister in Persia of His Majesty the Czar. Gribojedoff, one of the greatest Russian poets, became diplomat, ambassador, and minister only by chance. During the Russian-Persian war he was a young attaché at the Russian general headquarters. The Persians were defeated and begged for immediate peace. Now, since the Russian commander-in-chief had no suitable Russian diplomat at hand, the attaché Gribojedoff was entrusted with carrying on the peace negotiations. He succeeded in putting through splendid peace conditions with the Persians. The general sent him as courier to Petersburg to Nicholas I with the message of peace.

In one pocket Gribojedoff had his peace treaty, in another his resignation that he wanted to hand in at the same time, so that he might now devote himself completely to literature. The Czar would hear nothing of Gribojedoff s withdrawal, did not want to leave him to literature, but named him—then scarcely thirty-seven years old—privy councillor, minister, and ambassador to the court at Teheran.

Gribojedoff had to yield. In the capital of Georgia, on the way to Persia, he married the fifteen-year-old princess, Nina Tschawtschawadse and took her to Teheran. The marriage lasted only a few months. The Persians hated Gribojedoff, who wrote better poems than the shah, and of whom it was said that on the basis of his peace treaty he wanted to abduct the women from the imperial harem.

A plot was concocted against him. Supported by eunuchs and priests, the mob stormed the building of the embassy, killed all the inhabitants, and, last, the poet-ambassador himself. Only the Princess Tschawtschawadse, who happened to be staying in the summer residence, remained alive. She brought her husband's corpse to Tiflis, and entombed it in the monastery of the holy David. As martyr, poet, and lover, Gribojedoff quickly became a national hero in all Caucasia, and his grave became a place of pilgrimage for the young girls who looked for brave and warlike husbands.

These Georgian girls, who often are veiled like the Mohammedans, are the most beautiful women in the world. Some remote regions, as, for example, Abchasia or Mingrelia, are positively notorious for them. The story is told that an old sultan forbade his subjects to visit these countries because the subjects, fascinated by the beauty of the women, never returned home. Another sultan who attached less importance to morality became a beggar because he squandered his treasures for the sake of the Georgian women, whom he had abducted by crafty eunuchs. Here the tradition is wrong. Probably this sultan was ruined by the eunuchs, because for centuries the girls of Georgia were sold by their Abchasian fathers for ridiculous prices all over the world. Between

Morocco and China there was hardly a single harem with no Abchasian woman, and no slave-dealer who did not constantly have them in stock. From Morocco to China, in Algiers, Egypt, Syria, Turkey, and Persia, one found sultans who were half or three-quarters Georgians and preferred the Abchasian girls, the countrywomen of their mothers.

Moreover, the beauty of these girls has a proper explanation in the legends of their people. The Abchasians are descended from a mighty hero of antiquity who lay chained upon a rock for centuries. Daily his liver was torn by an eagle. This hero was freed by a favourite of God. He killed the eagle, remained in the mountains, and married there. From him the people of the Abchasians are descended, and with them the most beautiful girls in the world. For a small price, besides the girls, the rock on which this Prometheus pined in chains is shown to curious tourists.

In the same measure as the girls are beautiful, the men are brave. If there is chivalry left anywhere today, with defiance of death, honouring of women, spilling of blood, revenge, and songs, it is in Abchasia, the Georgian province inhabited by the descendants of Prometheus.

The dying chivalry of Europe and Asia has withdrawn today to the mountains of Georgia. There it is rooted deeply in the people. Together with the Riviera-like landscape, the glorious mountains, rivers, and valleys, palms, castles, girls, and poets, it would make the life there that of a garden of Eden, if there were no politics. The life of a Georgian was a dream of paradise before politics broke in. The people are the kindest, gayest, friendliest, and most hospitable in the world. Only in Georgia can one become fully acquainted with the pleasures of existence. Only there can one find wine that makes one fiery without drunkenness. Only there can one find girls that bring nothing but good fortune and battles that have no fatal consequences. The Georgian dances, sings, and loves, empties the gigantic drinking-horns, draws his dagger from its sheath now and then, rushes through the mountains on his horse, composes songs, tells jokes in such a matter-of-course manner that it makes every other mode of living seem wrong. It is a glorious fate to be a Georgian, to live in Georgia. The whole world ought to become Georgia.

I spent many months in Tiflis; at first alone, then with my father, who came from the border and showed me the country. I would have stayed there till today if there had been no politics. Georgia was a democratic republic which boasted of being the first in the world to have realized the principles of the second International. The representatives of this International, Kautsky, Vanderville, and Macdonald, came to Georgia, drank Georgian wine, admired the Georgian people, and felicitated the Georgian government. When they rode away, the days of the republic were numbered.

Soviet Russia declared war on Georgia. The foreign ambassadors condoled with the government and packed their things. The princes and peasants drew their daggers from their sheaths. But the war was hopeless. The Russians had hundreds of thousands of troops, the Georgians only thousands. From the mountains and out of the valleys came the knights in medieval armour. Finally tens of thousands came together but not hundreds of thousands.

So it happened that we, too—my father and I—packed our bags one day and rode to Adjaristan, to Batum, where the huge ocean liners dock which connect the East with the West.

It was very easy to travel to Batum. Here there were railroad trains and sleepers. The city, Batum, however, received us with a sinister face. Dead silence reigned in the streets. We rode to the steam-ship office. "When does the next steamer leave for Constantinople?"

"There are no steamers to Constantinople."

"And to Trebizond?"

"There are no steamers to Trebizond. There are no steamers at all."

"Why not?"

The man stared at us. "Don't you know that the plague is raging in the city? No steamer may come in, none go out. Hundreds are dying every day."

৯৯

CHAPTER 38

FAREWELL TO THE EAST

The Indian plague is not much worse than an Oriental massacre; but Europe pays more attention to it. No one was allowed to leave the city of Batum; no steamer was permitted to enter the harbour. We were not afraid of the plague for according to general knowledge only the lowest classes of the people fall sick of this disease. Nevertheless, we did not leave the few streets that were still spared by the plague. Every two hours we touched our left arm-pits, for there the first signs of the plague appear.

Other preventive measures than this self-examination did not exist as far as we knew. The plague begins with the formation of a boil under the arm, which reaches the size of a man's fist within a few hours and is extremely painful. Then the fever sets in. The body becomes black and swells. Within twenty-four hours death comes. Not more than one hour after death, decay starts.

There is no remedy for the plague. One can burn down a house that is infested by the plague and isolate its inhabitants. However, since one cannot surrender half a city to flames, Batum contented itself with simple disinfection and the isolation of the infected streets.

So the plague-smitten section of the city was cut off from us, but we ourselves, as half-infected, were cut off from the rest of the world.

Since the plague breaks out almost annually in Azerbaijan and Turkestan, we were accustomed to it and did not worry about its outcome. We knew that it exterminated one or two thousand nomad clans every summer and then disappeared as quickly as it broke out. But in Batum—which is almost Europe—it caused a veritable panic. At that time many refugees from Russia were living in Batum. These became hysterical at the mere mention of the word plague, just as many other foreigners—that is, not Orientals—who imagined themselves to be doomed to death.

The plague troubled us mainly because it hindered our departure. At the same time the Bolshevists were drawing nearer. We became more restless every day. Europe, which had experienced a kind of plague in the form of the Spanish flu, locked its doors to us. It required the most enormous efforts on the part of the European colony to ease these locks a little.

At last, after inoculation against the plague and presentation of all medical certificates imaginable, the inhabitants of the non-infected section were given permission to leave. Hundreds now streamed to the city physicians to submit to inoculation. My father and I were not among them; we were opponents of it. It is certainly not without danger, causes pain, and does not guard against the pestilence at all. Besides, inoculation seemed superfluous to us, for we knew that we should not be infected by the disease; it had passed us by too often.

So we contented ourselves with explaining this to the doctor, and instead of the usual fee paying him ten times that sum. For that we received our inoculation certificates. There was nothing left to stop our departure. The situation at the Georgian-Russian front was hopeless; the conquest of Tiflis might happen any day.

At last we boarded the ship, a big Italian steamer that was to take us to Constantinople. It was equipped with bars, orchestras, and staterooms *de luxe*. For the last time I saw the palm gardens of the Adjaristan capital; the beautiful girls who sat under the palm trees and painted their lips in European fashion; the Adjaristan saloons in which the descendants of Prometheus can empty dozens of cups without becoming drunk; and the mighty, blue mountains.

In fair weather, when one stands at the seashore, one can see a small white cloud far back at the horizon. This cloud does not move. It is there eternally. Now rosy, now snow-white. That is the snew-capped peak of the Elbrus.

There, near the Elbrus, the last knights—the carefree Georgians— were now fighting with the advancing enemy.

Here in Batum, in the meantime, one fought with the foreign consuls who would not visé the passports, with the steamship companies which had not enough steamers, with the friend who advised against an overhasty departure.

Here, as there, in the mountains as in Batum, the battles were hopeless from the very start for one of the two sides. The bravest knight cannot gain ground against a hundred thousand muzhiks. No consul can withstand certain temptations. The Reds entered Tiflis. Their Cossacks stood before the gates of Batum. We moved into the three-room apartment and stood before the huge doors of the great dining-room, where dinner was soon served.

A whistle; the gang-plank is raised. The Italian consul waves his hand. Azerbaijan, Georgia, Adjaristan, the blue mountains sink into, the darkness in the dark-red glow of the evening sun.

At the table we meet acquaintances, the Armenian friend who fled from Helenendorf with me, an Azerbaijanian who had become a Dutch consul somewhere, and a host of fleeing politicians, princes, magnates, and Bolshevist-haters, which we also were, after all. At the table speeches are made; high politics come in contact with upright finance. A general instructs us about the strategic significance of the Caucasus, and the waiter announces that after the departure from Georgian waters all prices are to be understood in gold.

On the next day the Anatolian coast emerges in the distance. We stop at Trebizond. That is still Asia, the domain of the revolting Mustafa-Kemal, who is fighting against England. The captain warns us: "You had better stay on board." We do not stay.

Ruschti-Pasha, who lived with us in Baku, calls for us and shows us an agreeable ceremony. An extraordinary procession is marching over the market-place. The heralds in front, then a donkey. On the donkey rides a dignified gentleman backwards, facing the tail. His face and long beard are smeared with sour milk. Behind the donkey follow the cheering people.

"The man is a Bolshevist," the pasha instructs us. "He was caught and is being led through the city for the general edification. Afterwards they will take him to the shore, put him in a boat, give him provisions for three days, and command him to ride to Russia. We do not kill the Bolshevists. They are our allies!"

We shake hands with the pasha and leave the territory of Anatolia. Two days more and we are at the Golden Horn. Mosques, palaces, noise, and the High Gate. The army of occupation of the Allies receives us in the form of the Commission Interallied, consisting of one Englishman, Frenchman, Italian, American, Greek, and Turk. The commission is strict but just. That is why the passengers of the third class must transfer to a special boat and are taken to quarantine. In the second class a dozen doctors are raving with the list of diseases preventing admission in their hands. Next to them work the political police with a similar list.

In the first-class saloon there is merely a grey-haired university professor who shakes hands with each traveller. After him the members of the commission do likewise. Upon leaving, every passenger of this class receives a medical certificate with the stamp of the professor and a political one with that of the commission. The handshake of the professor showed that our state of health was free from plague, typhoid, and cholera, and that of the commission expressly confirmed our political integrity.

I did not know that, I thought that the gentlemen had simply come on behalf of their governments to congratulate the noble foreigners on their rescue.

"Look how polite people are in Europe," I said to my father. "They drove us out of our home, out of our house, and here the representatives of the leading powers and of science receive us."

"Yes, yes," my father answered me, "we are still far behind Europe."

We left the steamer, rode to an international Grand Hotel, and on the way saw posters in the European style: "The biggest Revue in the world at the Petits Chants today."

"Ten thousand Christians killed in Anatolia," the newsboy shouted at the same moment. For the first time we bought a French newspaper. At that moment Europe began for me.

The old East was dead.

"The Orient of the Imagination"

by *Tom Reiss*

"Essad Bey" was just 24, in 1929, when *Blood and Oil in the Orient*, his first book, was published with the promise blazoned on the cover: "More thrilling than any adventure novel, more instructive than any travel guide, as colorful as only life itself can be." Essad Bey's books took readers into a somehow reassuringly strange world of the mysterious orient at the darkest moment of the twentieth century. At a time when the borderlands of Europe and Asia were squeezed between two totalizing ideologies—Nazism on one hand and Soviet Communism on the other—his world promised that there were hills and valleys that could never be conquered.

By the time he died, twelve years later, in 1942, at age 36, Essad Bey, who always maintained he was "the son of a Muslim aristocratic father and a revolutionary mother," had published at least fourteen more books—not counting two novels he wrote under the name 'Kurban Said'—as well as unpublished manuscripts, hundreds of articles and letters written to a fascist salon hostess, his powerful protector, with whom he maintained an "intellectual love affair" that contains novels and worlds within worlds in its pages—letters ala Scheherazade, written to save himself from deportation to the Nazi camps. For, in fact, 'Essad Bey' was an invented person, the creation of a Jewish refugee named Lev Nussimbaum, who outwitted the Nazis by transforming himself into a Muslim desert adventurer and becoming a bestselling author in Nazi Germany. But what, if anything, was factual when it came to Essad Bey?

Born to a wealthy Jewish family in 1905 probably in Baku, Azerbaijan, the southernmost city in the Russian empire, Lev escaped the Bolsheviks by fleeing to Germany in 1920. (Raised by a Baltic German nurse, he was later most comfortable writing in German.) In Berlin he adopted the name Essad Bey and converted to Islam at the Ottoman embassy in the last year of that old empire's existence. By age 25, he was an internationally famous author of sprawling historical romances filled with tall tales of his own personal heroism. Even as Goebbels was systematically purging Jewish writers from German publishing, Lev managed to publish 16 books, most of them international bestsellers and one an enduring fiction masterpiece—*Ali and Nino*—all by the age of 32.

As a 26-year-old Lev tackled biographies of Mohammed and Stalin simultaneously, and both were in bookstores before he was 27. They were international bestsellers and warmly received not only for their colorful writing style but for their insights into these two world-historical figures. The biography of Mohammed is the only one of Lev's books that has always remained in print in one language or another, and the original New York Times review of it sums up the idiosyncratic nature of his work:

> "The texture of this fine book is as a Persian carpet. There is material underfoot. But it is magic to the eye. We walk firmly on what we are bound to believe, we look at what transcends belief, and the question is how we can rend the credible from the incredible without tearing asunder the whole design."

His books are readable seventy years after they were written, in no small part because Lev narrated even the driest analysis of oil-pricing mechanisms as though it were a Caucasian folk tale. In his books and his articles, as in his self-image, what Lev cared about was intellectual and emotional truths of the human heart and existential condition, amorphous things that could not be captured with the sharp angles of a scientist's or academic's tools. He would write in his deathbed memoir:

> "It is apparently difficult, particularly difficult for a 'literary man,' to 'photograph' instead of rendering. The temptations of literature are enormous. In the memory, perspective shifts. Involuntarily, the writer begins to prefer the truth of atmosphere to the simple truth of facts."

But Lev's chief ongoing invention was always himself. With status of "Orient expert" of *Die Literarische Welt* (before he left the journal, at 28, Lev had published 144 articles in it, even more than his colleague

Walter Benjamin), he fashioned himself as a Weimar media star—a professional "Man of the Caucasus." Though he received much attention in America, it was always German readers who mattered most to him. Yet almost as soon as *Blood and Oil* appeared, a few politically driven German reviewers took it upon themselves not merely to warn the public away from the book but, in a sense, to "out" the author. Lev, who by then was appearing on the Berlin café scene dressed in his "native" costume—sometimes a Caucasian warlord's fur hat and caftan, sometimes a turban with a gemstone set in the center—was perceived as a kind of ethnic cross-dresser, as well as something far more devious. Many Jewish journalists and scholars were writing books on the Middle East at the time, often out of a deep and sympathetic knowledge of the Muslim world, but they did not tramp around Berlin dressed in turbans, speak of their filial ties to warrior chieftains and call themselves by fancy Turkish names.

The following review of *Blood and Oil*, from the influential right-wing journal *Der Nahe Osten* is typical:

> "This book is one of the most miserable publications of recent years. . . . The author, who introduces himself as 'Mohammad Essad-Bey' and pretends to be the son of a Tartar oil magnate from Baku, has turned out to be a Jewish dissident named Leo (Lob) Nussimbaum, born in Kiev in 1905, son of a Jew named Abraham Nussimbaum from Tiflis. When one compares the accounts in the book, according to which the author was threatening Russian ministers at the age of ten, and in which the author pretends to be a relative of the Emir of Bukhara and an expert on Muslim customs, one gets a clear idea of the whole grotesquerie. . . . The Muslims will presumably firmly reject their alleged fellow believer 'Mohammad Essad-Bey.' (Essad=in Arabic asad, esed=lion=Lob=Leo?)"

The scandal had only a positive effect on book sales and it made Lev—or rather, Essad—famous, but when it came to the accusations about his identity, the critics did have a point: while never publicly deviating from his story that his father was a Muslim lord, Essad was sharing an apartment in Berlin with his father, who made no secret about being a Jewish businessman named Abraham Nussimbaum. "The many peoples that I have visited, the many events that I have seen, have made me into a complete cosmopolitan," he wrote in a 1931 newspaper. In 1931 in Germany this was tantamount to admitting one was a Jew, but Lev did not seem concerned.

Some prominent Muslim refugees at the time did reject him, misreading the humor in his work as an attack on Islam or Muslim independence movements in general, when Lev's writing was anything but anti-Muslim. The leading point man in the Islamic faction of the assault on Lev was an Azeri nationalist living in Constantinople named Hilal Munschi. Munschi summed up the attacks on Essad Bey's character in a series of pamphlets he published in German and Turkish.

When I visited Baku in 2000, specifically to interview the various Azeri "partisans" of the Kurban Said debate, I was actually handed copies of Munschi's ancient attacks on Lev's character and "background," in Azeri, as though they were contemporary news reports. I was shocked by the vehemence of the language—until I realized that I was reading attack literature from the early 1930's, resurrected seventy years later as "evidence." "You see! You see!" shouted one prominent Azeri professor, waving his finger in the air, "it is all the proof we need! Right there in Munschi's article, he exposed the swindler for what he was!" My article on Lev in *The New Yorker*, which had appeared in 1999, apparently sparked a renewed debate, as prominent Azeris had to deal with the suggestion that *Ali and Nino*, their "national novel" had been written by a Jew named Nussimbaum. Luckily, since my book *The Orientalist* has appeared around the world, many younger Azeris have embraced the multicultural truth of their greatest novelist: that he was very much a cosmopolitan, and that if he was not a pure-bred Azeri, he was a quintessential Bakuvian, epitomizing that city's unique mix of modernity and tradition, Jew and Muslim, West and East.

While certain Muslim refugees and the right-wing press attacked Lev's inauthentic "Orientalist" writings, some on the pro-communist Left went after him for his unflattering depictions of the Soviets and the Revolution. *Vorwärts!* the leading left publication, simply dismissed his books *Stalin* and *OGPU*, saying that Essad Bey did not have "the necessary dialectical-materialist schooling" to understand events in Russia. Attacks from the right and left made him a controversial figure in Germany, and Lev's general response—to smile enigmatically and keep on writing more books—seemed to have the effect of keeping everyone guessing: What were his real politics? What was his racial background? What were the true motives of the "story swindler"? With his eclectic subject matter, odd clothes, sarcasm and purposely Caucasian-accented German, Lev simply didn't fall into any of the generally accepted categories of the day. The venom spat out at him became so potently inchoate that a Prague paper would eventually accuse him of pursuing "purely Bolshevist rather than Islamic interests," while in Warsaw he was denounced as "a Marxist werewolf." This accusation that the author of some of the most scathing exposes of Bolshevik terror was himself a "Marxist werewolf" suggest the extent to which Lev's mysterious persona had perplexed everyone. "Who is this Essad Bey?" Trotsky wrote in a letter in 1932, underlining the sentence. It was a question many people wanted answered, but was it even clear that Lev knew the answer himself?

Lev preempted "unfriendly" and humorless critics in the lighthearted introduction to his second book, *Twelve Secrets of the Caucasus*, announcing that he was "aware from personal observation, that there are such things as hospitals and secondary schools for girls in the Caucasus." Indeed, coming from Baku, where many such innovations were first introduced to the Muslim world, he was more than aware of it. Readers of his articles would know that he held ambiguous views about Western "progress" in the East, not because he wished to insult the Orient but because he felt an overriding nostalgia and loss at the disappearing traditions he witnessed in the modernizing Baku of his youth.

"But things which would be in place in an encyclopedia will not be found here in a book which has no wish to be confused with the heavy artillery of scholarship."

Twelve Secrets of the Caucasus is "a kind of curiosity shop of world history in its loyal preservation of all that is no more, all that is outlived and forgotten." As a leading exposer of the Communist onslaught in the Caucasus, Essad was keenly aware that modern innovations could bring just as much destruction, but in his works on the Muslim Orient, he chose a comic-romantic tone. This tone was invariably misunderstood by Muslim expatriates as glibness about their situation, but his later personal correspondence, as well as a close reading of the books themselves, reveals that it was anything but glib. Lev's attachment to the "Orient"–his view of himself as an "Oriental"–was perhaps more real than his understanding of himself as a European or as a Jew. Of course, he was all of these things.

Lev's Orient was a different one from that of his detractors. One of the most striking chapters in *Twelve Secrets* describes a place Essad calls the "political Switzerland of the Caucasus," the Valley of the Khevsurs, or Khevsuria: "There a man could at last be safe." One stubborn American reviewer tried in vain to pinpoint Khevsuria on a map, regretting that better ones had not been provided in the book, but he did not realize that the answers were not to be found in his geography. Lev provided further guidance:

"Khevsuria is quite near Tiflis, and yet the land is free, independent, and no policeman dares to follow his victim there. A gigantic wall of rock surrounds Khevsuria and separates it from the rest of the world. . . . From the cliff wall down into the void there hangs a long rope. Whoever has the courage can catch hold of the rope and let himself down to the Khevsurs. The police never follow. . . . Through it the first immigrants must have entered the land. Only the refugee dares use the rope, to be accepted if he is so inclined into the society of the Khevsurs and protected for ever from all dangers.

This is the Orient Lev Nussimbaum is from: a mountainous realm insulated from political and ethnic conflict, a refuge where no secret policeman can follow, and where anyone with the courage to climb down a rope into the abyss is accepted—in short, the Orient of the Imagination.

Tom Reiss writes about international politics and culture for *The New Yorker* magazine. He has written for *The New York Times, The Wall Street Journal*, the *Financial Times*, and other publications. His work often focuses on how individual lives are affected by history, and is known for its rich juxtapositions of cultures and time periods that bring forgotten people and places to life. He was born in New York City, to an American father and a French mother, and he grew up in Texas and Massachusetts, where he graduated from Harvard College. A 1998 travel magazine assignment in Baku, Azerbaijan, led him to discover the unsolved mystery of Kurban Said, and to write *The Orientalist.*

For more information on Tom Reiss, Essad Bey and *The Orientalist* please also check

www.theorientalist.info

Printed in the United Kingdom
by Lightning Source UK Ltd.
135910UK00001B/206/P